Form and Flow

Urban and Industrial Environments

Series editor: Robert Gottlieb, Henry R. Luce Professor of Urban and Environmental Policy, Occidental College

For a complete list of books published in this series, please see the back of the book.

Form and Flow

The Spatial Politics of Urban Resilience and Climate Justice

Kian Goh

The MIT Press
Cambridge, Massachusetts
London, England

© 2021 Massachusetts Institute of Technology

All rights reserved. No part of this book may be reproduced in any form by any electronic or mechanical means (including photocopying, recording, or information storage and retrieval) without permission in writing from the publisher.

The MIT Press would like to thank the anonymous peer reviewers who provided comments on drafts of this book. The generous work of academic experts is essential for establishing the authority and quality of our publications. We acknowledge with gratitude the contributions of these otherwise uncredited readers.

This book was set in Stone Serif by Westchester Publishing Services. Printed and bound in the United States of America.

Library of Congress Cataloging-in-Publication Data

Names: Goh, Kian, author.
Title: Form and flow : the spatial politics of urban resilience and climate justice / Kian Goh.
Description: Cambridge, Massachusetts : The MIT Press, [2021] | Series: Urban and industrial environments | Includes bibliographical references and index.
Identifiers: LCCN 2021000488 | ISBN 9780262543057 (paperback)
Subjects: LCSH: Urban ecology (Sociology)—Government policy—Case studies. | Climatic changes—Government policy—Case studies. | Urban policy—Environmental aspects—Case studies. | Local government and environmental policy—Case studies. | Climatic changes—Political aspects—Case studies.
Classification: LCC HT241 .G64 2021 | DDC 307.76—dc23
LC record available at https://lccn.loc.gov/2021000488

10 9 8 7 6 5 4 3 2 1

For the youth of Red Hook, Brooklyn, and the children in the kampungs of Bukit Duri, Kampung Pulo, and Muara Baru

Contents

Acknowledgments   ix
List of Figures, Tables, and Appendices   xiii

    Introduction: Climate Justice and Urban Futures   1
1 **Disparate Yet Interconnected Cities**   23
2 **Nature of Contestation**   49
3 **Nature of Flows**   89
4 **Plans and Counterplans**   115
5 **A Political Ecology of Design**   149
    Epilogue   183

Appendices   187–200
Notes   201
Selected Bibliography   237
Index   261

Acknowledgments

This book is a product of a love affair with the continually revealing ecologies and politics of the Southeast Asian cities I grew up in and the turn-of-the-millennium Brooklyn I called home, an intertwined wanderlust and awe for newness in thinking and designing the urban, and a habit of following compelling stories to new places.

Four scholars, especially, have guided my ways of thinking and understanding. I am indebted to them. I am especially grateful to Lawrence Vale. His openness to, indeed, passion for, ideas and experiences has guided me through the sometimes chaotic terrain of research life, except for that time when he let me guide him, and members of his family, along slippery riverbanks and hair-raising traffic medians in Jakarta. I have leaned on Larry's unique ability to see across points of view, to search out and make sense of the connections, and to pinpoint the interesting stories. Gabriella Carolini inspired a real appreciation for scholarship. She demonstrated, through her advice and her own research, the value of careful, probing analysis, especially when conducting interdisciplinary research. Neil Brenner opened my mind the first time I saw him speak, and inspired critical investigations that I very much continue today. I thank him for his ease and trust, unparalleled combination of intellectual acuity and generosity, and comradeship. And Ananya Roy models every day what it means to be a critical scholar and an accomplice to social movements for justice. She challenges me, not to find my voice—which she knows I have—but to make sure it is present.

I enjoy a wonderful academic home in the Department of Urban Planning at UCLA Luskin School of Public Affairs, in Los Angeles, with enthusiastic and supportive colleagues, students, and staff. I am delighted to develop and finish this book here. In particular, I thank Anastasia Loukaitou-Sideris,

Vinit Mukhija, and Dana Cuff, all of whom were instrumental in me finding this home here; I also thank Liz Koslov, who shares with me writing sessions and deep discussions on academic and life's work; Mike Manville, who from the first fall moving into our adjacent offices has been a trusted friend and generous colleague; and Mike Lens, Paavo Monkkonen, and Amada Armenta, for constant support and encouragement.

So many people were crucial in helping me see and understand during my fieldwork in multiple sites and cities across three countries (five, counting peripheral excursions) in three continents over the eight years between my first wanderings in Jakarta and the completion of this book.

My deepest gratitude to Dian Tri Irawaty, Elisa Sutanudjaja, and Marco Kusumawijaya at the Rujak Center for Urban Studies in Jakarta; Jill Eisenhard at the Red Hook Initiative in Brooklyn; and Damaris Reyes at Good Old Lower East Side in Lower Manhattan. This book owes its heart to you.

I thank all those who shared what they know with me in New York, Jakarta, Rotterdam, The Hague, Houten, Utrecht, Washington, DC, Bangkok, and Singapore. I am especially thankful to those whose privileged viewpoints and knowledge, often over multiple interviews, contributed to pivotal points of understanding during the research. In addition to Dian, Elisa, Marco, Jill, and Damaris, they include Nancy Kete, Henk Ovink, Amy Chester, Sandyawan Sumardi, Edi Saidi, Gugun Muhammad, Rita Padawangi, Oswar Mungkasa, Ivo van der Linden, Arend van Woerden, Florian Boer, Kees Bons, Peter Letitre, John Jacobs, and Arnoud Molenaar. And to Barry Beagen, Ivana Lee, Ariel Shepherd, John Taylor, Yantri Dewi, and AbdouMaliq Simone, who opened my eyes to Jakarta.

I will be forever grateful for the deep intellectual camaraderie of friends and colleagues. So many I met as a student in the Department of Urban Studies and Planning at MIT continue to be wonderful interlocutors and confidants. Especially Lily Baum Pollans, Eric Chu, Linda Shi, Alpen Sheth, Alexis Schulman, Lyndsey Rolheiser, Lili Knorr, Leah Stokes, Zachary Lamb, and Hannah Teicher, who each offered invaluable feedback on this research. I'm fortunate to continue building a scholarly network of friendship and comradeship. This includes Hillary Angelo, Sai Balakrishnan, Hiba Bou Akar, and Delia Duong Ba Wendel, who show how sustained academic collectivity works, and, among so many more, Juno Parreñas, Noah Tamarkin, Bettina Stoetzer, Ju Hui Judy Han, Jennifer Chun, Nina Flores, Amy

Acknowledgments

Ritterbusch, and Hannah Appel, who embody that special circumstance when critical scholars are your friends too.

I am privileged to have studied for my PhD at MIT DUSP. My thanks to all the faculty who have advised and guided me, in addition to Larry and Gabriella, Eran Ben-Joseph, Phil Thompson, Balakrishnan Rajagopal, Bish Sanyal, Anne Spirn, Lawrence Susskind, Brent Ryan, Amy Glasmeier, Xav Briggs, Miho Mazereeuw, Jim Wescoat, Dayna Cunningham, Miloon Kothari, Diane Davis, and Annette Kim. And, in remembrance of JoAnn Carmin and Judy Layzer, who each pushed against my sometimes less exacting nature and made me a better researcher and writer; and in remembrance of Tunney Lee, whose generosity and cheer belied his central role in the story of spatial planning and social justice in Cambridge-Boston and beyond.

The research in this book was funded in part by a Faculty Career Development Award from the UCLA Office of Equity, Diversity and Inclusion; a Northeastern University Tier 1 grant; the Center for International Studies, the Aga Khan Program for Islamic Architecture, the William Emerson Travel Fund, and the Harold Horowitz Research Fund, all at MIT; and by the US-Indonesia Society. Thank you immensely. I also thank the UCLA Council on Research; the Harvard Program on the Study of Capitalism, the MIT Program on Environmental Governance and Sustainability, and the Lloyd and Nadine Rodwin Fellowship at MIT, which helped fund research that contributed to the intellectual foundations of this book.

Thank you to Beth Clevenger, Robert Gottlieb, Anthony Zannino, and the team at the MIT Press, who took a firm interest in this book early, and showed trust and belief in the work through the process, even during some extraordinary times in global affairs. Thanks also to the anonymous reviewers who commented incisively on drafts of this book.

To my dearest Aya, who witnessed and supported the final writing of this book during a work-from-home order in the midst of a global pandemic. Our adventures, in so many ways, have only just begun. But already you've shown me so much what it means to be in love and struggle. To us, for new experiences and cares. And to our little one, at time of writing still waiting to enter the world.

Finally, to my parents, without whom all of this would simply not be, and my brothers.

An earlier, more concise version of chapter 3 was published as "Flows in Formation: The Global-Urban Networks of Climate Change Adaptation," *Urban Studies* 57, no. 11 (2020). Earlier development of the concept of insurgent urban landscapes was a part of "Urban Waterscapes: The Hydro-Politics of Flooding in a Sinking City," *International Journal of Urban and Regional Research* 43, no. 2 (2019). Parts of chapter 4 were published in "Terrains of Contestation: The Politics of Designing Urban Adaptation" in *Perspecta 50: Urban Divides: The Yale Architectural Journal* (2017).

Sources of Reprinted Materials

Excerpt from Lyn Hejinian, *My Life* (Los Angeles: Sun & Moon Press, 1987), used with the permission of the author.

Excerpt from Theresa Hak Kyung Cha, *Dictee* (Berkeley: University of California Press, 2001), by permission of the Berkeley Art Museum.

Excerpt from Alfonsina Storni, "Running Water," in *Poetry* 26, no. 3 (June 1925): 117.

Excerpt from Emily Dickinson, "Declaiming waters none may dread" J 1595/F 1638, in *The Poems of Emily Dickinson: Reading Edition,* edited by Ralph W. Franklin (Cambridge, Mass.: The Belknap Press of Harvard University Press). Copyright © 1998, 1999 by the President and Fellows of Harvard College. Copyright © 1951, 1955 by the President and Fellows of Harvard College. Copyright © renewed 1979, 1983 by the President and Fellows of Harvard College. Copyright © 1914, 1918, 1919, 1924, 1929, 1930, 1932, 1935, 1937, 1942 by Martha Dickinson Bianchi. Copyright © 1952, 1957, 1958, 1963, 1965 by Mary L. Hampson.

Excerpt from Annie Finch, "Landing Under Water, I See Roots," in *Calendars* (Dorset, VT: Tupelo Press, 2003), by permission of the author and Tupelo Press.

Excerpt from Lucille Clifton, "water sign woman" in *How to Carry Water: Selected Poems of Lucille Clifton* (Rochester, NY: BOA Editions, Limited, 2020). Copyright © 1991 by Lucille Clifton. Reprinted with the permission of The Permissions Company, LLC on behalf of BOA Editions, Ltd., boaeditions.org.

List of Figures, Tables, and Appendices

Figures

0.1 Diagram of the book structure   21

1.1 Sites: New York, Jakarta, Rotterdam   24

1.2 The Hudson River Park with new condominium towers, June 2010   26

1.3 Lower Manhattan in darkness after a blackout caused by an explosion at a Con Edison power plant, November 1, 2012   28

1.4 Red Hook Initiative as storm recovery center and soup kitchen, the Sunday after Hurricane Sandy, November 4, 2012   30

1.5 Looking south from Medan Merdeka, July 2013   33

1.6 Ruins in Kota, January 2013   34

1.7 Ciliwung River at Kampung Pulo, Central Jakarta, July 2013   35

1.8 Rendering of Jakarta National Capital Integrated Coastal Development (NCICD) Giant Sea Wall masterplan, October 2014   36

1.9 Watersquare Benthemplein, Rotterdam, June 2014   38

1.10 Floating pavilion, Rijnhaven, Rotterdam, June 2014   42

1.11 Sites, strategies, and networks: urban regions and interconnections among primary plans, led or supported by state or city, and alternative visions or "counterplans"   43

2.1 Houses destroyed by fire in Breezy Point, Queens, November 7, 2012   51

2.2 Red Hook waterfront warehouses, with Lower Manhattan skyline in the distance, May 2014   53

2.3 Map of Red Hook, Brooklyn, and Lower East Side, Manhattan, including Hurricane Sandy surge impact, and location of Red Hook Initiative and Good Old Lower East Side   54

2.4 Temporary boilers at the Red Hook Houses, Red Hook, Brooklyn, in May 2014   55

2.5 Rob Smith, an alum of the RHI Digital Stewards program, inspects networking equipment, November 2018   59

2.6 The FDR Drive along the East River, with Rutgers and La Guardia Houses behind the first row of buildings, and Vladeck Houses and the East River Park in the distance, August 2014   60

2.7 Volunteers for Chinatown / Lower East Side community organization CAAAV Organizing Asian Communities distribute supplies, November 2012   61

2.8 Rebuild By Design finalist teams and sites   63

2.9 Kampung Bukit Duri, Jakarta, July 2013   67

2.10 Kampung Pulo during a flood, Jakarta, July 2013   68

2.11 Taman Jokowi, July 2014   69

2.12 Map of Jakarta showing kampungs in relation to city landmarks and the proposed National Capital Integrated Coastal Development (NCICD) Giant Sea Wall masterplan   71

2.13 Organizers from Urban Poor Consortium (UPC) and Muara Baru residents, July 2013   72

2.14 Ciliwung Merdeka with designers, researchers, and Bukit Duri residents, July 2013   73

2.15 Ciliwung River at Jatinegara, Central Jakarta, during a flood on July 22, 2013. Kampung Pulo is on the left of the river, Bukit Duri is on the right.   74

2.16 Jakarta Coastal Defense Strategy (JCDS) diagram. Bold dark lines show proposed sea walls   76

2.17 NCICD Giant Sea Wall plan. Thin light lines show the proposed sea walls along a "winged" form and retention lakes between the outer walls and coastline   77

2.18 Looking out over the Jakarta Bay, with the towers of Pantai Mutiara, an earlier gated development on reclaimed land, on the left, May 2017   80

List of Figures, Tables, and Appendices — xv

3.1 Map of Dutch Delta Works   93

3.2 Maeslant storm surge barrier, Nieuwe Waterweg, Rotterdam, September 2014   94

3.3 Room for the River project in Nijmegen showing "floodable" island and ancillary channel, July 2016   95

3.4 At the Deltas in Times of Climate Change conference, (left to right) Victor Coenen (Witteveen+Bos), Purba Robert Sianipar (Coordinating Ministry for Economic Affairs, Indonesia), Ad Sannen (Royal Haskoning), and Sutanto Soehodho (deputy governor, DKI Jakarta) discuss the NCICD masterplan, Rotterdam, September 2014   103

3.5 Diagram of global-urban networks   106

3.6 Diagram of conceptual interfaces, relationships, and formations   111

4.1 Great Garuda sketch by Gijs van den Boomen, August 2013   121

4.2 On the edge of Waduk Pluit, July 2013   125

4.3 Participatory design concept by Urban Poor Consortium for a new kampung typology at Muara Baru, exhibited at the *Jakarta Vertical Kampung* exhibition at the Dutch embassy in Jakarta, July 2013   127

4.4 Ciliwung Merdeka's design for a "humanitarian vertical kampung," exhibited at the *Jakarta Vertical Kampung* exhibition at the Dutch embassy in Jakarta, July 2013   128

4.5 Strenkali upgrading project in progress in Surabaya, July 2014   129

4.6 Rendering of the "Big U" proposal at the south tip of Manhattan by BIG team, 2014   132

4.7 Aerial rendering of "Living with the Bay" proposal by Interboro team, 2014   133

4.8 Concept drawing of "New Meadowlands" proposal by MIT+CAU+ZUS+URBANISTEN team, 2014   134

4.9 Rendering of "Resist, Delay, Store, Discharge" proposal for Hoboken by OMA Team, 2014   135

4.10 Aerial rendering of "Hunts Point Lifelines," South Bronx, proposal by PennDesign / OLIN team, 2014   136

4.11 Rendering of "Living Breakwaters" proposal by SCAPE team, 2014   137

4.12 Red Hook Initiative, designed by SUPER-INTERESTING!, March 2010   145

4.13 Red Hook Initiative during Sandy recovery, November 2012   146

5.1 New embankment and access road along the Ciliwung River, at Bukit Duri and Kampung Pulo, Jakarta, May 2017   150

5.2 Temporary flood protection measures, Red Hook waterfront, Brooklyn, February 2019   152

5.3 Henk Ovink at the Deltas in Times of Climate Change II conference, Rotterdam, September 2014   154

5.4 Diagram of counternetwork in and beyond Jakarta   165

5.5 A sociospatial typology of coastal urban adaptation strategies   169

5.6 Extended scales and levels of urban ecologies, connected to local social relationships and global networks   179

Tables

3.1 Table of actors in Rebuild By Design and Jakarta NCICD Masterplan   90

3.2 Timeline of relevant events in Rotterdam   99

5.1 Theory, findings, and implications   160

5.2 Synthesis of plans, counterplans, and connections   163

Appendices

1 Methodological Excursions   187
2 List of Interviews Conducted by Author   193
3 List of Planning and Design Documents Analyzed   197

Introduction: Climate Justice and Urban Futures

It is hard to turn away from moving water.
—Lyn Hejinian, *My Life*

On October 29, 2012, Hurricane Sandy hit the New York City region. The storm killed forty-three people in the city, and caused an estimated $19 billion in economic damage. Beyond the sheer death toll and financial losses, Sandy cemented in municipal and popular imagination the vulnerability of the metropolitan region to the rising threats of disasters related to climate change. Images of a darkened lower Manhattan, rows of houses destroyed by fire in the Rockaways, cars floating in underground parking lots turned into pools, physical devastation rarely seen in post-9/11, twenty-first-century New York, tuned public attention to the issue, and galvanized city leaders, climate scientists, and urban planners, designers, and engineers.

In January 2013, just weeks later and halfway around the world, massive floods once again inundated Jakarta, Indonesia, claiming at least thirty lives and displacing tens of thousands. The floods, caused by heavy rains but exacerbated by a breached flood canal, captivated a global audience as prominent landmarks such as the Hotel Indonesia roundabout were submerged. The event called attention to the predicament of the city, considered one of the most vulnerable to climate change, with its failing infrastructure compounded by acute social and environmental inequities. The city's frequent and severe floods are predicted to worsen to catastrophic conditions in the coming decades.

New York City and Jakarta are distinct cities, with vastly different social systems and built environments. And the events here might be considered isolated—linked only by timing and the encumbrances of too much water too fast. But in specific ways they occurred not only in parallel but also in relation to each other. The disasters prompted eye-opening responses in both cities, high-profile and ambitious plans launching each toward what could be a significantly different urban future. The events and responses also exposed persistent social and spatial striation in both cities, longtime patterns of marginalization that were accentuated in the wake of the disasters and at risk of being entrenched and exacerbated in the future plans. In both cities, community groups on the ground mobilized in response to the perceived injustices and oversights of the prominent plans.

These cities were caught up in a set of intersecting moments: transformative environmental and political change on global and local scales, and shifting ideas about the present and future of cities. This book explores how interconnections among these cities and another distinct, somewhat unlikely city, Rotterdam in the Netherlands, also confronting social and environmental challenges linked to broader changes, reveal the emerging dynamics of global and urban environmental struggles. On the one hand, the emergence of a new wave of large-scale urban interventions around climate change. These interventions are driven by environmental urgency, urban development pressures, and global networks of expertise, and mobilized toward new modes of capital accumulation in the face of environmental catastrophe. On the other hand, the rise of social movements organized in response to historical injustices and present-day challenges. These movements often harness for themselves the tools and strategies of professionalized planning and design and the power of networks, questioning, resisting, and proposing alternate visions.

New York, Jakarta, and Rotterdam, as individual cities and in their interrelationships, are exemplary of these new globally constituted and locally contested configurations of urban responses to environmental threats. But they represent an increasingly general condition: the interconnected social, spatial, and environmental conflicts and motivations that now affect cities in every part of the world.

Scholarship on urban climate change responses has not taken adequate account of these emerging, disparate, interconnected contexts. It has tended to reinforce divisions between the spatial and social aspects of cities, drawing a line between designed and engineered physical solutions, on the one hand, and government policies or community-based measures, on the other.

It has tended to assume urban phenomena to be contained and cohesive, relying on conceptualizations of the city as a static, bounded territory, neglecting connections across regional and global networks, and broader processes of urbanization. And while attuned to the unequal impacts of climate change, it has not necessarily followed the emerging cross-scalar and historically determined geographies of unequal climate impacts and formations of climate justice movements.

This book is posed in elaboration of and counterpoint to these discourses. Exploring what I call a *political ecology of design*—the intertwined, envisioned, and contested social and spatial politics of urban climate change responses—I examine environmental plans in New York, Jakarta, and Rotterdam through the lenses of urban design and socioecological spatial politics. Looking, at one level, at high-profile initiatives, including Rebuild By Design in New York, the Giant Sea Wall masterplan in Jakarta, and Rotterdam Climate Proof, I also search out alternate narratives—the "counterplans"—including community resiliency initiatives in Brooklyn and Manhattan, and grassroots design activism in the informal kampungs of Jakarta. I ask: *In the face of climate change and uneven social and spatial urban development, how are contesting visions of urban futures produced and how do they attain power?*

This question deals in an interrelated manner with politics, environment, space, and design. To address it, I probe a set of topics that can be more directly disentangled. First is the contestation around environmental issues in cities. I explore the processes of urban socioecological marginalization, particularly in the context of climate change impacts and responses. I show how poor urban residents are historically and spatially marginalized in environmentally risky sites that are now both threatened by climate change and sought after for high-value urban development. Second is the development of globally interconnected urban environmental planning. I explore the new global and urban networks of professional consultants, public and private agencies, and transnational institutions that are reconstituting the ways in which large-scale urban environmental plans are conceived and implemented. I show how they develop new funding and organizational structures, employing powerful narratives of experience and expertise. Third is the production and legitimization of urban environmental visions. I explore the sociopolitics of designing urban environments and chart the multifaceted ways in which the design of urban resilience is understood, invoked, and harnessed through formal and informal processes.

Through this crosscutting analysis, I show how intertwined global and local political-economic and climate-environmental changes constrain struggles over urban futures. I argue that these changes have set up the conditions for new organizations of large-scale urban environmental planmaking globally, and as well the resistance to those plans. New York, Jakarta, and Rotterdam, ostensibly disparate but interconnected, represent an exemplary formation of how this new wave of planmaking is organized globally and refracted in response to local conditions. It is critical to recognize these emerging formations. They present implications for global environmental management as well as for the urban governance of all cities. They affect the efficacy with which we approach global climate action as a collective, planetary pursuit, and the prospect for justice and equity in cities, increasingly the sites of climate change response strategies.

In this book I highlight as well my own experiences as an architect and urban designer. Having worked professionally on design projects related to social and environmental resilience, I now, as a researcher, investigate the spatial politics of urban responses to climate change. In the book I foreground the close relationships with community activists I developed in practice and through fieldwork and the global fluency and access to international consultants and government officials born of professional and academic privilege.

Climate Change and the Future of Cities

From the Eastern Seaboard of the United States to coastal regions in Southeast Asia, the impacts of climate change challenge how we live and work in and around cities. Storm surges and flooding from sea-level rise threaten health and disrupt livelihoods in low-lying coastal areas; extreme weather events including hurricanes and wildfires disrupt infrastructure networks and critical services; severe and prolonged heatwaves lead to mortality and morbidity, particularly for vulnerable urban populations; and warming, drought, and variability and extremes in precipitation cause food insecurity, particularly for poorer people.[1] In response, urban governments are proposing ambitious plans to protect against and adapt to climate impacts. These involve extensive reconfigurations of built and "natural" environments, and massive economic resources. They promise both safety from ecological threats and the perpetuation of economic growth. Yet they often involve intractable social questions, including how, who, and what to protect on sites that are home to already marginalized urban residents.

Responses to climate change are typically discussed as matters of *mitigation*, that is, reducing the production of greenhouse gas (GHG) emissions, and *adaptation*, changing the ways and the places we live in response to projected impacts. The notion of adaptation—or, in a term that is increasingly popular, *resilience*—has taken on greater prominence among scientists and policymakers as global efforts at mitigation appear inadequate. A report by the Intergovernmental Panel on Climate Change (IPCC) in 2018 highlighted the necessary levels of adaptation and mitigation associated with keeping global warming within 1.5°C above preindustrial levels (warming likely to happen within the next one to three decades).[2] But the proliferation of adaptation initiatives brings up important concerns about life in our cities and on our planet. The focus on adaptation risks precluding mitigation efforts—actions necessary to cut emissions and halt irreversible change. Cities' plans for mitigation and adaptation also raise foundational issues of equity. Activists worldwide have rallied around the notion of *climate justice*, asserting that already marginalized and vulnerable populations are most at risk from climate change impacts, and that climate change responses threaten to reinforce or, alternately, have the potential to alleviate such injustice.

Climate change is a confounding problem. It challenges our ways of knowing, our understanding of ourselves and the world we live in. It relies on systems of knowledge that are scientific, often constituted on a global scale. Yet it impacts communities on the ground in uneven ways. According to Sheila Jasanoff, scholar of science and technology, "Climate change . . . tends to separate the epistemic from the normative, divorcing is from ought . . . it detaches global fact from local value."[3] Climate change takes place on spatial and temporal scales beyond the scope of normal understanding. Indeed, for historian Dipesh Chakrabarty, it forces us to reconsider deeply held distinctions between human and natural history: "The geologic now of the Anthropocene has become entangled with the now of human history."[4] And climate change necessarily dwells in uncertainty, where decisions with long-term consequences have to be made on the basis of incomplete information, present-day costs needed to forestall the probability of future threats.[5]

The nature of the problem of climate change disrupts foundational ideas of urban planning—about the place of the city on the planet, the place of nature in society, and the place of history in considerations of the future. Planning is generally thought of as an endeavor to envision a better future society and to consider ways to achieve it—to get there from here.[6] But climate change denies planning its traditional core modes and methods. Three central issues emerge in probing climate change and the future of cities. First, these are global-scale problems, with global and local impacts, involving a complex array of entities and interconnections. Nation-states take part in international, multilateral climate negotiations, primarily the UN Framework Convention on Climate Change (UNFCCC), and receive input from a global scientific body, the IPCC. At the same time, local-level governments learn, share, and influence through networks such as C40 Cities, ICLEI Local Governments for Sustainability, and 100 Resilient Cities, and react to and inform national-level constraints and dictates in a system of "multilevel governance."[7] In addition, governmental agencies such the US Agency for International Development (USAID), nongovernmental groups and philanthropic organizations such as the Rockefeller Foundation, lending institutions like the World Bank, and environmental advocacy groups all play their roles at each of these scales and levels. What are the effective and appropriate scales and levels of planning and action?

Second, initiatives in economic development and environment, classically seen to be at odds, are now clearly intertwined. The stated embrace of environmental issues by institutions such as the World Bank,[8] concerned about the impact of climate change on economic development, is paralleled by an increase in the marketization of environmental initiatives, what critics have termed and debated as the "neoliberalization of nature."[9] Initiatives to rethink climate change approaches, particularly in times of economic distress—such as the Green New Deal, conceived at the time of the financial crisis of 2008 and given new life after the 2018 US midterm elections and global climate activisms in 2019—focus on measures to address at once failings in market systems and ecosystems. In the long term, economic and ecological outcomes are interdependent. This has further repercussions on urban governance and issues of justice. We now routinely hear terms like "urban vulnerability" employed in discussions of economic competitiveness. Infrastructure built to secure and protect centers of economic activity and flows of resources in the face of climate change impacts are often unevenly and selectively implemented, deepening inequities in cities and resulting in "ecological enclaves."[10]

Third, the scopes and scales of globalized urbanization entangle and complicate urban climate change responses. On one level, we see what might be called the "metropolitanization" of climate change.[11] Cities, as such, popularly understood as large, dense, physical agglomerations of people and things, activities and services, are viewed as a large part of the problem and a necessary part of the solution.[12] They are understood to have specific vulnerabilities as centers of population density and political and economic activity,[13] and as centers of concentrated mass and form of the built environment.[14] They are characterized as sites of large GHG emissions and of opportunities to implement low-carbon strategies. Based on these premises, city managers and urban researchers rush to find ways to "climate proof"[15] or "future proof"[16] cities. These actions attempt to address the multiscalar and multilevel problems of climate change with the control of specific urban conditions.

But, on another level, urbanization needs to be understood as a historically specific and dependent *spatial process*, and not solely as the conditions of particular places. These urban processes involve the cross scalar and continually contested social, spatial, and ecological outcomes of political-economic systems and sociocultural conflicts.[17] First, they are intensely spatialized. Researchers such as Neil Brenner and Christian Schmid have challenged conventional ideas about urbanization, particularly the distinction of urban and rural. They and others assert that increasingly potent processes of globalized capitalism in the late twentieth and early twenty-first centuries are transforming not just large, dense agglomerations but so-called hinterlands as well, including agricultural regions and sparsely inhabited zones. Large-scale reorganizations of territories and circulations of labor and material—such as forest clearing and fires in the Amazon and oil pipelines through remote regions in North America and Siberia—are directly linked to the processes of capital accumulation and spatial development in places we generally see as "cities."[18] Such planetary-scale processes imply that it is necessary to think beyond the accepted dichotomy of urban and nonurban in understanding emerging social, spatial, and environmental problems. Second, they are deeply dependent on time and place. Researchers including Ananya Roy have explained how historical differences of place and power, such as colonial and postcolonial relationships in cities of the Global South, as well as subject positions and embodiments outside those considered the norm or the typical, demand different understandings and concepts of the urban. They show social and spatial patterns that do not conform to universal ideas about urban growth and inequality, and demand a more multivalent, historical, and power-informed account of urban processes and places.[19] This is particularly important given the ways in which unequal relationships of the past contribute to unjust environmental conditions of the present.

Such relational, expanded views of urban and global processes complicate easy notions of what constitutes a "sustainable" urban place in the face of climate change. They implicate ideas about global and urban socioeconomic development, about relationships between society and nature, and about the politics of envisioning urban space. They force those of us invested in understanding urban change and environmental change to think about broader interconnections and landscapes of change—what sociologist Henri Lefebvre termed an "urban fabric" in his reflections on planetary-scale processes of urbanization[20]—as well as more positional, embodied, historically specific trajectories of global and local power relationships. In the following two sections, I explain my approach to these multivalent problems. In the first, I situate the dynamics of urban resilience and resistance, laying out the ways in which ideas about climate change futures underlie contestation and movement building. In the second, I propose a set of three conceptual lenses to see and understand the issues delineated here, on urban nature and society, on scales and levels of urban interventions, and on designing urban futures.

From Resilience to Climate Justice

To see the urban fabric in climate change more precisely, we need to understand better emerging struggles over places and environments. Two dynamics around climate change responses situate these struggles well. The first is the tensions between the promotion of and resistance to "bouncing back" to prevailing conditions, and the second, the rise of new movements for justice that cross historical moments and local to global scales.

Against Resilience
"Stop calling me resilient," states a sign stapled to a post in New Orleans, "Because every time you say, 'Oh, they're resilient,' that means you can do something else to me."[21]

"Resilience" has emerged as a primary theme in global discussions on urban climate change policy, preparedness, and planning.[22] The concept is typically formulated as the ability of a system, entity, group, or individual to withstand shocks and stresses, to recovery quickly from disasters, and to maintain essential functions.[23] Formulations of resilience appear across fora and documents by global and national development and disaster management agencies.[24] In one example, the 100 Resilient Cities initiative, launched by the Rockefeller Foundation in 2013 (and formally ended in 2019),[25] forged partnerships with prominent global philanthropic, finance, design, and technology security organizations,[26] linking aspects of urban development, the built environment, and various manners of security. The concept of resilience—from its initial psychological and ecological inceptions to, now, its ascription to people and places responding to social and environmental threats—aligns well with the idea of adaptation. Indeed, it seems desirable for cities—people, institutions, systems—to "survive, adapt, and grow" and to "bounce back."[27]

But, *bounce back to what?* The means and modes of urban development that got us into this quandary in the first place? "Resilience" begs to be made accountable. Concepts around environmental actions are often vague and easily coopted. Invocations of "sustainability," for example, have been criticized for lacking specificity. They are easily "greenwashed"—that is, overstated in their environmental claims or made to mask deeper harmful practices. Parallel critiques are emerging around resilience. Is the particular characteristic of resiliency—bouncing back—necessarily positive or progressive, when the status quo is unjust or ecologically unsustainable?[28] Or, is resilience becoming an ideology of development-as-usual, perpetuating unjust systems in the face of emerging crises?[29]

Criticisms of resilience join a swell of concerns around justice in climate change responses. The responsibility for, vulnerability to, and action around climate change are unequally distributed around the world. Historical and ongoing global inequality exacerbates the problem. Poorer people in less industrialized countries are least responsible for historic and present-day GHG emissions but are often the first to suffer the consequences of impacts such as rising sea levels, drought, and stronger storms. Witness the continuing calls by small island nations facing imminent existential threats for much stronger global climate action. Poorer countries and peoples are also less well prepared to assert their interests in negotiations, resulting in cascading levels of inequalities in facing and preparing for changing climates.[30]

Simply taking action is often not the just course. Cities are attempting to institutionalize or experiment with the control and management of climate change across multiple levels of urban governance.[31] But such urban climate change responses are invariably intertwined with systemic and entrenched modes of urban development, patterns of marginalization, and structures of governance. These lead to new modes of urban planning and development centered on regulating carbon and building resilient infrastructure but tuned to old objectives of social control and economic growth, what researchers have called "climate urbanism" and "urban ecological security."[32] These new modes of planning and development often end up protecting and maintaining systemic inequalities. For example, the development of protective infrastructure or control of land use in response to climate threats can result in the eviction and displacement of marginalized residents living in low-lying riverbanks and coastal areas or on steep hillsides. Alongside, the selective planning and enforcement of infrastructure development or regulations can exclude or further harm poor communities, such as when protective infrastructure for wealthier enclaves causes ecological damage to surrounding areas.[33] These actions compound the impacts of climate change on already marginalized groups, who suffer from emerging environmental threats *and* the plans through which cities hope to evade such threats.

In these contexts, dominating notions of resilience—bouncing back or recovering to status quo conditions—codify inequities into urban governance systems and solidify their emplacement in the built environment. And yet, for many groups who have struggled against social and environmental threats exacerbated by climate change, resilience continues to be a powerful notion for how individuals and communities take on and overcome systemic challenges. Take, for example, the work of organizations such as the Red Hook Initiative (RHI) and Good Old Lower East Side (GOLES) in New York, explored in this book. This is especially critical in light of the continued absence or discriminatory actions of the state. How do ground-up organizations for resilience among marginalized communities develop into more broadly just urban institutions and practices? Such a question takes on pitched significance at the present moment. The dynamics and urgencies of climate change bring different notes and arcs to the notion of disparate environmental outcomes. They have broached new justice movements, and alongside, new challenges for critical considerations of urban futures.[34]

For Climate Justice

On September 20, 2019, hundreds of thousands of people across all continents came out in protest for the Global Climate Strike. Led and voiced largely by youth climate activists, the protest was embodied in particular by Swedish teenager Greta Thunberg, whose solo school strike, begun a year before, reached a climax that fall with a voyage across the Atlantic Ocean on a zero-emissions sailing yacht to give a speech at the UN Climate Action Summit in New York City. A resounding call during the climate strike was for *climate justice*.

Demands for climate justice are at once familiar and resoundingly new. Marginalized communities—often poor communities of color in North American and European countries, and poor and working-class communities in most countries—have suffered disproportionately from exposure to environmental harms. Toxic waste sites and polluting industries tend to be located in areas home to marginalized communities because of the intersection of market forces, economic inequality, uneven regulations, and systemic racism—a point made stridently by Robert Bullard in his book *Dumping in Dixie*.[35] Protests, advocacy, and research around this issue have given rise to vigorous environmental justice (EJ) activism movements and scholarship. "Classic" EJ research and activism were largely focused on specific localities, groups, and harms, with more critical scholarship pointing to the systemic processes underlying the formation of injustice.[36] More recent scholarship has attempted to globalize EJ, highlighting the transnational nature of inequities and fights for recognition by indigenous groups and farmers around the world,[37] and the potential injustice of environmental actions, such as "green gentrification," when efforts to clean up hazardous postindustrial sites led to rapidly rising rents and other living costs, driving out poorer residents.[38]

Climate change continues to disrupt foundational notions of environmental injustice. While EJ research and activism tended to be place-based and community-specific, climate change dislocates the notion of site and scale, attributing the source of harms to broader, indeed global systems, while impacts remain locally felt and unevenly borne. While EJ concerns have generally been bound to the repercussions of particular industrial processes and periods, with specific actions and time periods to remediate the harm, climate change presents both fairly short-term and immediate grave threats (such as to low-lying island nations and eroding delta regions) and the most systemic, serious, and long-term impacts and necessary transformative societal responses (such as changes in political economic systems and substantial procedures of decarbonization) measured in many decades and in abstract scientific parlance.

The rising global climate justice movement builds on and refers to EJ concepts and movements. But it is fueled and given form as well by a different set of events and efforts. It emerged in conjunction with a set of global, cross-boundary pro-poor people's movements, often highly critical of capitalism, particularly the systems supporting transnational fossil fuel economies.[39] The calls for climate justice coalesced as a global movement leading up to COP15 in Copenhagen in 2009.[40] It was further propelled by the Occupy Wall Street and antiausterity protests of the early 2010s. More recently, we have witnessed the surge of a global youth climate movement, epitomized by the school strike for climate actions (also known as Fridays For Future) mobilized after Thunberg's solo protest in the fall of 2018, and in the activism of the Sunrise Movement in the United States, particularly around the 2018 midterm elections and after.

The movement for climate justice is born of historical global inequities and disparate vulnerabilities. It builds on notions such as "ecological debt"—the assertion that historical and current exploitative and exchange relationships between richer countries of the Global North and poorer countries of the South perpetuate unequal environmental burdens[41]—and calls for a "just transition" to a postcarbon economy.[42] It is transnational, and manifest in local and extralocal organizing and movement building. It tends to be highly critical of market-based solutions and technological fixes.[43] And it is conceptualized as transformative, in that the movement calls for systemic change in the political-economic structures that have led to our climate urgencies, particularly the fossil-fueled industrialized systems that contribute to unequal global power relationships and continue to devastate natural systems.

The climate justice movement has important implications for urban space, climate change, and justice because of its structures of formation and modes of organizing. It is shaped through multiscalar and multilevel institutional frameworks and networks, through the actions of widely dispersed institutions, activist groups, and sites. Its emergence, on an international scale, relied on global movements (often against globalization), often through and in response to global institutions (such as the transnational environmental organizations and actions around multilateral conferences). At its core the movement gains strength and legitimacy from community- and place-based struggles and organizing, including concerns for the lives and livelihoods of fishers and farmers, and the rights of indigenous groups. Key proponents of climate justice, such as the members of the International Climate Justice Network and of the Climate Justice Alliance include longstanding environmental justice advocates and labor rights and racial justice organizers focused on place and community-based work. As Elizabeth Yeampierre, co-chair of the Climate Justice Alliance and executive director of UPROSE in Brooklyn, New York, stressed during a conference on climate change and managed retreat in 2019, climate justice is at the intersection of racial injustice and climate change. She asserted her commitment to the rights and agency of the marginalized communities she represents, who have faced racial injustice and environmental problems, now heightened because of new climate threats.[44]

Climate justice thus reframes and recalibrates concerns of environment, location, and position to the causes and impacts of climate change as well as to the institutional frameworks within which climate change discourses are taking place. This reflexivity of spatial and temporal scales and of positionality poses critical lessons and challenges for thinking about urban futures and climate change.[45]

Just Urban Spatial Climate Politics

The problems of climate change in and around cities, propositions for and resistances to a globalizing urban resilience, the calls for climate justice ringing from local to global—these dynamics compel urban climate change researchers to take seriously critical and interrelated concerns. Urban climate change responses have to be understood within the full sociospatial topographies in which they operate. That is, researchers must be attuned to the various spatial scales across which and sociopolitical and institutional interconnections through which these responses are articulated. They need to frame their ways of seeing and understanding around the ways in which historically determined social relationships condition unjust environmental outcomes across spatial scales and temporal periods. The following three conceptual lenses offer an approach toward a scalarly reflexive and historically informed view of urban spatial climate politics.[46] Together, they focus the analyses throughout this book.

Nature of Contestation: The Socioecological Relationships of Urban Marginalization

Urban centers have always been sites of contestation, in which unequal power relationships and systemic oppressions play out spatially and over time. Often, this contestation involves, in an interrelated way, social and environmental factors. Environmental initiatives in cities have often been presented in an uneasy, and contradictory, relationship with urban development. Witness, for example, zoning codes for light and air, urban growth boundaries, and preservation areas. Now, the challenges and opportunities from climate-change-related environmental threats to cities have unearthed new spaces of contestation. In this book, I explore the socioecological nature of contestation in cities, in particular the ways in which the trajectories of recent economic, political, and ecological processes and events have affected social and spatial marginalization. To what extent are these more recent processes, in the context of climate change and early twenty-first-century urbanization and globalization, different from those of the past?

According to urban geographers such as David Harvey and Neil Smith, processes of urbanization, driven by cycles of capital accumulation, proceed on the basis of uneven development—the creation and sustaining of urban social and spatial inequalities.[47] The "city," as such, is not a neutral container in which inequality somehow happens. The processes that make up the city—its social relations—produce inequality and spatial difference. The city is not, by nature, just. Smith makes explicit the relationship between nature and capital in urbanization processes, contending that where once nature was in unity with human actions, capitalism transforms natural material into commodities imbued with an exchange value, dissociating it from its original unity and subsuming it into systems of production. Nature is transformed into "second nature," regulated by social institutions. With the rise of globalized capitalism, the differentiated outcomes of uneven development are now extended to a global scale.[48]

Researchers of urban political ecology further elaborate on these relationships, building on Smith's arguments as well as Raymond Williams's ideas of nature as reflections of society and William Cronon's on the economic and ecological links between the city and the frontier.[49] They show how systemically unjust power relationships in the capitalist city determine the processes through which environmental harms and benefits are distributed. Contests over urban space—such as the creation of parks or the paving over of "natural" areas; the transformation of "nature" into commodities, such as in the control and distribution of municipal water; and the spatial networks through which such transformation occurs, such as the drains, pipes, and wires—are determined by intertwined sociopolitical, economic, ecological, and technological factors, often manipulated toward the material gain of political and economic elites.

These researchers assert that urban social and ecological changes are wrought together, codetermined and coproductive, as part of processes of urbanization.[50] Going beyond refuting the distinction between society and nature, they focus on the interrelationships that produce the city as a hybrid space between, and involving, society and nature, a "cyborg city."[51] Urban ecologies are formed through a dialectical relationship between social and ecological change.[52] These ideas offer an ecological analysis of neo-Marxist theoretical frameworks that link the production of urban space with capitalist accumulation. Urban political ecology brings theoretical frameworks centered on urbanization as a political-economic process to scholarship on environment, urban politics, and justice.

Alongside such notions of urbanization, society, and nature, theories of the relationship between biophysical and sociopolitical factors of change reaffirm the importance of the material and physical aspects of urban ecology. Here, Anne Rademacher's work on what she terms the "social ideas and practices of urban ecology" offers an important refocusing of a historical, critical lens on urban biophysical and socioecological change.[53] Investigating river restoration in Kathmandu, Nepal, Rademacher untangles the complexities of place, society, and nature by conducting an ethnography of biophysical change in relation to social practices and historical cultural ideas. Her research enables an understanding of how broader environmental changes might relate to place-specific practices and historical, cultural meanings in urban landscapes.[54]

In this book I extend further these urban socioecological frameworks, with a particular view to the historical relationships of power, including the role of the state, and the emerging global socialities of climate change.

Nature of Flows: The Scales and Interconnections of Urban Socioecological Change

Urban researchers have long emphasized interconnectivities of capital and information across geographic scales[55] and the material and social conditions of networked societies.[56] They've questioned the assumed stability of the urban scale as a concept.[57] Environmental researchers recognize emerging cross-scalar and multilevel institutions of global climate governance, such as transnational city-to-city networks,[58] observations heightened by accelerated globalization and what is often asserted as the diminished importance of national borders. And yet, much discourse around urban climate change responses still approaches the city as a distinct, analytically bounded entity, neglecting interconnections across space and processes of globalization, urbanization, and geopolitics. In this book, I focus on the emerging geographies of climate change response, exploring the nature of flows of ideas, influence, and capital through new global and urban networks.

Critical urban theorists and researchers of "relational geographies" respond to the problem of dynamic, interconnected sites by tracing urban space as spatial and temporal flows and relationships beyond territory—cities as "spatial formations" understood in relation to each other.[59] Ananya Roy, building on efforts to reframe, resituate, and otherwise destabilize theory from positions of privilege,[60] proposes the concept of "worlding" to counter the dominant narrative of global or world cities, in which a small number of so-called command and control cities define the global urban condition.[61] Roy asks that urban researchers shift our points of view to the myriad "urban experiments" playing out across the world. Ananya Roy and Aihwa Ong assert the "city as a field of intervention," a "nexus of situated and transnational ideas, institutions, actors, and practices" that might be simultaneously problem solving at the very lowest level and world changing at the highest.[62] Without losing sight of global forces—globalized capitalism driving urban development, the variable but global impacts of climate change—how would different views of the world, seen from different places—Dutch economic strategy seen from a kampung riverbank in Jakarta, for example—renew, revise, or extend our understanding of global and local relationships?

Researchers of policy mobilities, such as Jamie Peck, assert that policy-making processes are increasingly mobile, crossing horizontally over national and local geographic scales and vertically between hierarchies of institutions, and accelerating, shortening the timespan between policy development cycles.[63] Peck illustrates how new geographies of "policy mobility and mutation" are characterized by pragmatism, iterations of practice, the increasing presence of intermediaries, and the use of evaluation science. More than a "transfer,"[64] it is a "relational interpenetration of policy-making sites and activities," including "global policy 'models', transnational knowledge networks, and innovatory forms of audit, evaluation, and advocacy."[65] Harriet Bulkeley stresses a parallel observation specific to emerging global environmental conditions, that what is happening in climate governance reflects a broader trend in global politics, with the fragmentation of authority and shifts in responsibility to local governments and nonstate entities.[66]

Such concepts remind urban researchers of the interrelationality of ideas, actors, and institutions across space and time. Particular place-based conflicts, although often revealing in and of themselves, may well be conditioned by a broader and longer-term set of relationships. Such a view contests simple case studies and comparisons of actions, cities, or places in cities, often the primary mode of urban research. This point is not so much to claim that everything is interconnected and relative, but to assert that historically specific power relationships, often demarcated across space and time, still constrain struggles in places, even—or especially—in a world of flows. At the same time, this work reminds us of the problems that seem to transcend scales and levels and novel organizational structures, such as the continued social and spatial marginalization that appears to be reproduced across different scales, through various institutional structures.[67] This is particularly important given the historical and present-day disparities in the causes and consequences of climate change. Mobilities across scales and levels do not mitigate inequalities and inefficiencies in governance.

Plans and Counterplans: The Design Imaginaries of Urban Spatial Politics

Design in climate change research has been overlooked. But design—urban, landscape, architectural, and infrastructural—is often the platform through which contesting spatial agendas are visualized and prioritized. This is crucial given the difficult choices that initiatives to respond to climate change necessarily bring up. Design offers visions of alternate urban futures. The marshaling of design not only shows the desired physical outcomes but also exposes the sociopolitical motivations and fault lines behind power relationships in cities.[68] In this book I look into the sociopolitical dimension of design in the production of climate responses and the making of plans and counterplans in envisioning urban futures. I focus, in particular, on the ways in which design is itself a terrain of contestation, invoked and harnessed to legitimize and to resist planning efforts.

As a practice concerned with making urban built environment, design is positioned among urban planning, architecture, and landscape architecture. As a field of study, it shuttles between the modes of knowledge production in the social sciences and the protocols and practical concerns of the design professions. In research, the object of design is elusive. It is empirical, yet projective, about conditions yet to come. Broadly stated, social science research is to understand and explain. Design is to envision new possibilities and futures. This is a somewhat reductive way to make the distinction, but not a trivial one. Further, design is not simply the intended physical form—at whatever scale—of a project. For designers, it is often considered a process and a way of thinking. It is necessarily iterative, and not exclusively spatial. Investigating urban design and climate change, therefore, brings up discordant ideas and exposes disciplinary silos in ways that have not only methodological but epistemological implications.

A just and accountable inquiry into designing urban climate change responses, cognizant of the interrelationships of society and nature, and multiscalar global and urban processes, needs to deal with the politics of envisioning urban spatial change.[69] In *The Production of Space*, Henri Lefebvre takes aim at both an absolute, rational space and conceptually messy, limitless appeals to "the space of this and/or the space of that . . ."[70] Lefebvre proposes the concept of the "social production of space"—that space cannot be understood as a neutral plane or container, but that it is, rather, a product of social relations. He illustrates three concepts of space: (1) *spatial practice*, that is, perceived space, the relationship between specific actions and physical spaces; (2) *representations of space*, that is, conceived space, the conceptualized space of knowledge, of scientists, planners, and technocrats; and (3) *representational space*, that is, lived space, the social space of symbolisms, imagery, and art.[71]

Lefebvre's ideas present an approach to problems in urban research that revolve around multilevel questions about space and, in the circumstances explored in this book, have been overly defined by disciplinary emphases, inherited methods, and enforced categories. To take some concrete examples—say, the riverbank along an informal settlement in Jakarta or the urban landscape around a public housing project in New York City—these concepts offer an understanding of how space is simultaneously "real" (in the sense that we might visit and "see" a place), political (subject to contestation based on competing knowledge, expertise, rules and regulations), and imagined (reenvisioned in relation to physical space and fairly long-term projected physical and environmental changes). They enable us to weave our way between the "real," the social relationships locally and globally, and the ideas, symbols, and images that are invoked and mobilized.

These concepts of the multivalent production of space underlie the politics of urban spatial interventions. They shape, as Edward Soja asserts, how space matters in urban social justice,[72] and they shape, as Lawrence J. Vale explains, the ways in which contests over political power can be manifest in struggles over physical form and symbol.[73] In this book, I frame design as the processes, practices, and imageries through which intertwined, multiscalar urban social, spatial, and environmental changes are envisioned, contested, and conducted.[74] And I look specifically at the ways in which climate change and climate changed institutions of urban planmaking are transforming these processes, practices, and imaginaries of designing urban environments.

On Privilege and Justice

It becomes clear, as I describe ways of thinking and knowing, that many of the conceptual approaches to urban space and environment delineated here come from those researching and writing from the privilege of vaunted, relatively wealthy Euro-American academic institutions, often from prominent white, male scholars. This is a problem for two reasons. The first is that knowledge production about climate change and urban spaces remains exclusive and often exclusionary, an unjust condition in and of itself. The second, following, is that so many of the issues brought up through the work in this book concern the struggles of marginalized urban people who confront not only climate change but policy and planning responses born of exclusionary claims of expertise and systems of knowledge production, and whose voices and actions have been systemically undervalued. Climate change brings up core questions about human beings' place in the world. But not in universal ways.

In the research and writing of this book I focus on centering and elevating the voices of activists and community members from whom I've learned. I also take cues from, and strive to do justice to, the growing research on alternative epistemologies and decolonial approaches to resilience and environment. Acknowledging and developing ideas about different positions, situations, and responsibilities of knowledge production offer ways to conduct research that is more inclusive, just, and reflective.[75]

. . . A Political Ecology of Design

How are contesting visions of urban futures produced and how do they attain power? The final writings in this book take place in 2020, during the raging global coronavirus pandemic, and amid the immediate echoes of US national and global protests against systemic racism and police brutality. These events cut right to the heart of the issues raised, on the relationship of society and nature, and of power and space. They do not displace the problems of climate change and urbanization—indeed, they accentuate them. This book takes on the question in a moment when new urban futures are imperative, when the old ones—any of the old ones—just won't do. But these imagined futures must proceed from existing social conditions, what anthropologist James Holston calls the "ethnographic present."[76] Through this multivalent view of space and based on the crosscutting analysis, I explain how the urban interventions and sociopolitical conflicts examined here constitute increasingly important ways that cities are responding to climate change. And how they present pathways toward different urban futures.

Book Structure

This introductory chapter contextualizes contemporary contestations around space and environment in cities. It provides a conceptual framing of urban futures in the context of climate crisis and poses the possibility of urban climate justice. It presents the analytical framework of the book. Chapter 1 details the context, problem, and the sites and strategies investigated, and

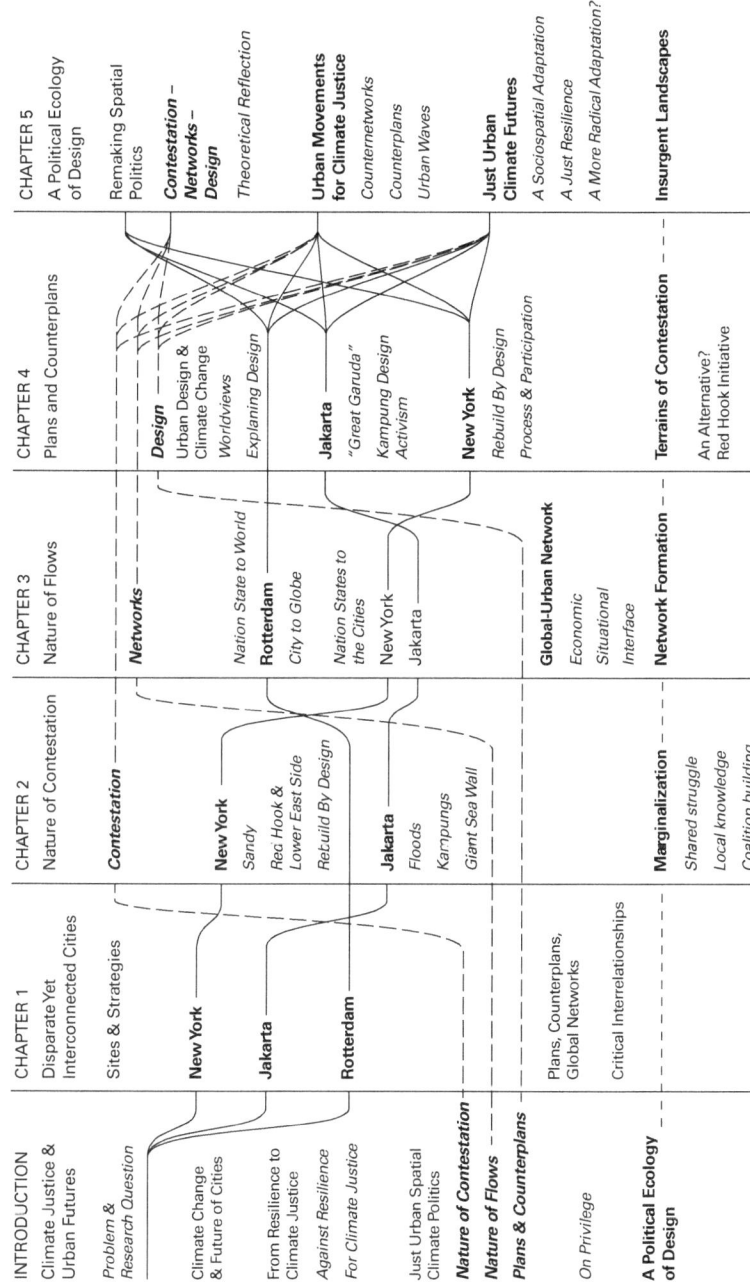

Figure 0.1
Diagram of the book structure.

explains the conceptual explorations. It discusses the research approach and methods, and previews the findings.

The next three primarily empirical chapters look at, in sequence, the three broad topics of the book. Chapter 2 conceptualizes the interrelationships between environmental initiatives and uneven urban development. It explains how contests over environmental futures have always been intertwined with capitalist urban development in New York and Jakarta, and how climate change has shifted these trajectories, creating new types and spaces of risk, and opening new fronts in planning and development. Chapter 3 follows the formation of global and urban networks behind climate change planning, tracing the multiscalar, multilevel connections among agencies, firms, and individuals across the various sites. It develops the concept of "network formation" to understand the terms of these interconnections, and shows how Rotterdam, Jakarta, and New York represent exemplary formations of a new wave of urban environmental planmaking. Chapter 4 examines the sociopolitics of designing urban resilience. It looks into the role of design and designers in the production and legitimization of climate change plans, and shows how design represents a terrain of contestation over which visions of urban futures are fought.

Chapter 5, the concluding chapter, synthesizes the conceptual strands and sites in the book, and looks to the future. It shows how the findings in the book present new ideas about resistance against hegemonic urban systems, and explains the development of "counterplans" and "counternetworks." It builds on the synthesis to reframe critical concerns of urban climate responses, presenting a sociospatial typology of urban adaptation and the notion of a "just" resilience. And it presents the terms of a critical design thinking and practice of "insurgent urban landscapes." The book concludes with developing a framework toward a theory of designing just urban climate futures (figure 0.1).

1 Disparate Yet Interconnected Cities

> You leave you come back to the shell left empty all this time. To claim to reclaim, the space. Into the mouth the wound the entry is reverse and back each organ artery gland pace element, implanted, housed skin upon skin, membrane, vessel, waters, dams, ducts, canals, bridges.
>
> —Theresa Hak Kyung Cha, *Dictee*

New York, Jakarta, and Rotterdam seem like disparate cities, with radically different sociopolitical, economic, and spatial contexts (figure 1.1). The challenges of climate change each city faces, the plans posed in response, and the conflicts over the future vision of the city appear as well to be distinct—locally defined, place-based, and historically specific. But they take place amid a set of generalized processes of global change. And, on closer view, they are interrelated, the goings-on in and between each offering new understandings of the others.

Sites and Strategies

New York

New York City seems to bear the weight of its urban history quite literally—particularly in the ever-densifying buildings simultaneously defining and leaving behind Manhattan's 210-year-old street grid. With 8.4 million people in the city proper, and 19.2 million in the larger metropolitan region,[1] it is the archetypal metropolis, the preeminent—if not original—Global City. It is also the place where, right now, the aging model of the metropolis of the twentieth century confronts the questions of what it is that makes the new city of the twenty-first.

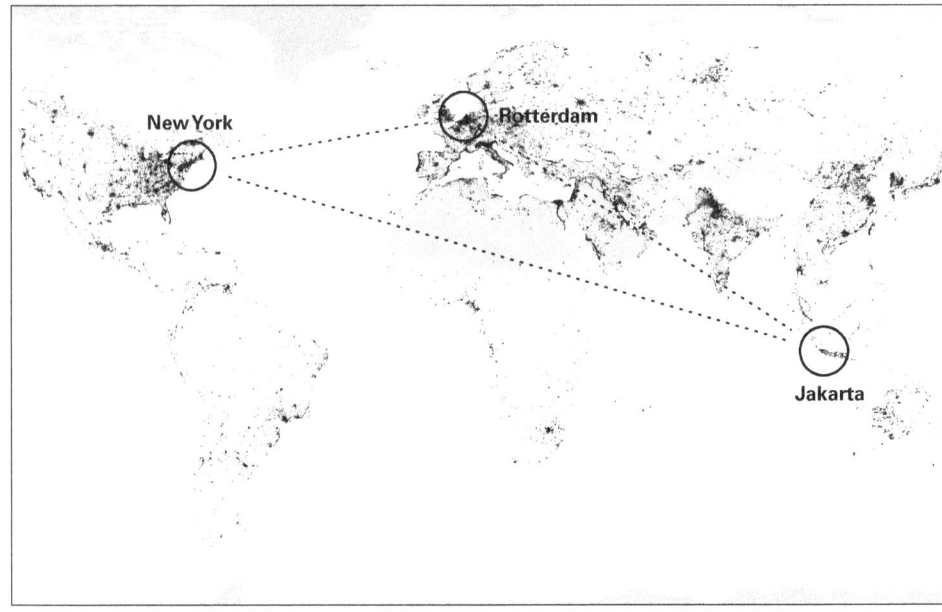

Figure 1.1
Sites: New York, Jakarta, Rotterdam. By author using NASA base image.

Many New York urban histories have rightly focused on its remarkable extents of building and people, diversity of social and cultural practices, its concentration of urban life. These histories are iconic: urban form and zoning regulation made imageable in Hugh Ferriss's charcoal ziggurat drawings;[2] urban megaprojects and community resistance of the 1960s epitomized by Jane Jacobs battling Robert Moses;[3] culture, modernity, and urban citizenship showcased in the two World's Fairs of 1939 and 1964;[4] and disaster and security intertwined, and buildings as icons and targets, in the days, weeks, and years after 9/11.[5] New York has also been the archetype for a number of key concepts that highlight the sociospatial factors of urban inequality. These include foundational concepts of gentrification including the "rent gap" and the "revanchist city,"[6] the marketization of urban lifestyles in "loft living,"[7] and multiple modes and narratives of contestation in the face of urban development.[8]

But many others have noted too the city's surprising *naturalness*. Art and environmental historian Jean Gardner observes that New York City's native natural environment—in its bays, bluffs, beaches, marshes, meadows, and forests—is the most varied of any American city.⁹ This is clearly a more literal assessment of urban nature. Other researchers have stressed, as well, that even in the extreme built-up environments of cities like New York, the transformations over time are socioecological—social and natural change wrought together. How could one forget the potent mixing of parochial moralizing, public health advocacy, environmental planning, and landscape architecture in the original New York "green grab" of Central Park, where the city evicted and demolished settlements including Seneca Village, the first African American landowning settlement in the city?¹⁰ Matthew Gandy, in probing the production of urban nature in the city, details the institutional power grabs and battles over race and class that underlie the making of municipal water networks and green space.¹¹ He makes the point that ecology in the city cannot be understood without its interactions with politics and capital. As David Harvey provocatively proclaims, "It is, in practice, hard to see where 'society' begins and 'nature' ends . . . there is in the final analysis nothing *unnatural* about New York City."¹²

New York has as well witnessed a kind of urban-nature renaissance in the last two decades that strongly links the workings of capital, urbanization, and environmental transformation. Beginning with, arguably, the initial wave of private capital and nonprofit agency-driven takeover of prime city parks by organizations such as the Central Park Conservancy in 1980 and the Bryant Park Corporation in 1988, this elaborate symbiosis of urban nature and real estate economics has been accentuated in the last two decades. The creation of the Hudson River Park on the west side of Manhattan in the late 1990s precipitated a building boom along West Street (figure 1.2). A residential building designed by the Swiss architects Herzog & de Meuron and the new Whitney Museum by Renzo Piano Building Workshop are recent examples of this development. A state-owned park, it is operated by the private Hudson River Park Trust, formed in 1998. Recent efforts at development in the park have attempted to revise longstanding zoning rules by proposing that air rights be transferrable to another block, across a street.¹³ Two other high-profile, "elite parks,"¹⁴ the High Line and Brooklyn Bridge Park, involve new public-private funding models that, ultimately, offer high-profile and high-cost (and yet, "free" to the city) urban nature in return for the acceleration of property values for privatized, high-end residential condominium development. And in Greenpoint and Williamsburg, Brooklyn, where the city has undertaken a large-scale rezoning

Figure 1.2
The Hudson River Park with new condominium towers, June 2010. Photograph by author.

of the waterfront area from industrial to residential, the legislative mechanism is different, but the physical outcomes similar.

These environmental initiatives are all framed and promoted as part of a larger goal of urban sustainability—to bring nature to people, and to reclaim the edges from highways and industry. But they are all unquestionably tied to dramatic real estate transformation, often by design. And they often test the boundaries of what constitutes "public." These developments are all widely seen as part of a longer-term citywide recovery from the dire 1970s, during which New York teetered on the edge of bankruptcy, the economic recession of the early 1980s, and the 1987 stock market crash.

In this light, climate change planning can be seen in the context of a broader focus on environmental and sustainability initiatives in the city. New York's climate change planning effort was not especially early, but was well underway in the first decade of the new millennium. Then mayor Michael Bloomberg released the city's sustainability plan PlaNYC in 2007.[15] PlaNYC was comprehensive, with emphases on housing and infrastructure to cope with projected population growth, attention to providing green space and protecting and improving waterways, and increasing energy efficiency—with a nod to climate change mitigation and adaptation.[16] As part of PlaNYC, Mayor Bloomberg convened the New York City Climate Change Adaptation Task Force in August 2008. To support the task force, the Mayor's Office, in partnership with the Rockefeller Foundation, established the New York City Panel on Climate Change (NPCC), a group of climate scientists and legal, insurance, and risk management experts. The charge of the NPCC was to provide the city's adaptation planning with "sound science and a thorough understanding of climate change,"[17] particularly for the context of the New York metropolitan region, its "infrastructure shed."[18] The panel released its first report, "Climate Change Adaptation in New York City: Building a Risk Management Response," in 2010. The city codified the NPCC in August 2012 as Local Law 42, establishing the panel as an ongoing body, to meet at least twice a year to review scientific data on climate change.[19] Alongside, the city's waterfront revitalization program, "Vision 2020," released in 2011,[20] called further attention to climate change, and in program updates included explicit stipulations that climate change projections be incorporated into project proposals seeking discretionary actions or waterfront planning review.[21]

The NPCC released its second report in 2015.[22] Of course, in the intervening years, everything had changed in New York.

Coming one year on the heels of Hurricane Irene in 2011, the impact of Hurricane Sandy on New York City in October 2012 was a watershed moment. Scenes of vulnerability—such as the images of Lower Manhattan in darkness, one taken by architectural photographer Iwan Baan for the cover of New York magazine in a story as mythic as the image (figure 1.3)[23]—brought the city palpably in confrontation with monumental environmental disaster. But it was not the first time the city had envisioned facing such watery threat. Even as the adaptation task force grappled with the science of climate change and the city, the Museum of Modern Art presented *Rising Currents* in 2010, two years before Sandy. The high-profile exhibition, also supported in part by the Rockefeller Foundation, showcased architectural and urban design strategies for the New York harbor area in response to sea-level rise. Post-Sandy, this institutional and cultural foundation was further reinforced with the formation of President Obama's Hurricane Sandy Rebuilding Task Force, led by the US Department of Housing and Urban

Figure 1.3
Lower Manhattan in darkness after a blackout caused by an explosion at a Con Edison power plant, November 1, 2012. Photograph by Iwan Baan / Reportage by Getty Images.

Development (HUD), and New York State governor Andrew Cuomo's NYS 2100 Commission.[24] Beyond the institutional context, these efforts brought highly influential individuals such as Shaun Donovan, then secretary of HUD, and Judith Rodin, then president of the Rockefeller Foundation, to aligned objectives in the post-Sandy urban region.

This confluence of factors focused climate change responses in New York in a distinct way, particularly in the context of US urban governance. In June

2013, the Hurricane Sandy Rebuilding Task Force, under the oversight of HUD, launched Rebuild By Design, a design competition that commanded federal and local political attention, and included Dutch spatial planning leadership, New York–based climate expertise, and high-profile philanthropic attention. Rebuild By Design was tasked with finding "innovative" and "implementable" resilience design proposals for the Sandy-affected region.[25] Competition organizers selected ten multidisciplinary, designer-led teams to conduct research and produce proposals, working with localities in New York, New Jersey, and Connecticut. Six winning teams and projects were announced in June 2014, just one year later, with $930 million in federal rebuilding funds allocated through Community Development Block Grants–Disaster Recovery (CDBG–DR).

Rebuild By Design presented an unusual and innovative response to burgeoning urban environmental challenges. Unique at the time, it was a prominent international design competition focused on urban responses to climate change, conducted under US federal government auspices, with federal funds apportioned for project implementation. A novel institutional and funding arrangement enabled this: Rebuild By Design was overseen by federal agency HUD, partially funded by private philanthropy the Rockefeller Foundation (which was the primary funder of the competition phase and supported the inception of the Rebuild By Design organization), and coordinated within the institutional home of the Institute for Public Knowledge at New York University (NYU).

At the same time, Hurricane Sandy exposed the unevenness of vulnerability in the urban region.[26] Systemic inequities related to poverty, joblessness, and access to housing and services in the city were accentuated in the aftermath of the storm. But the immediate post-Sandy period also illustrated the ways in which community social relationships might be linked to broader environmental resilience. In places like Red Hook, Brooklyn, and the Lower East Side, Manhattan—both coastal and low-lying, with substantial populations of low-income residents in public housing—community organizations such as the Red Hook Initiative (RHI) and Good Old Lower East Side (GOLES) played key roles, and indeed often led the way, in poststorm recovery efforts.

It was this latter observation that drew my attention to the questions and concerns in this book in a direct and personal manner. I had been working as an architect and urban designer in New York in the first decade of the new millennium. In 2010, I designed a community center building for the Red Hook Initiative. My team, working closely with RHI, converted a warehouse building just adjacent to the Red Hook Houses, the largest public housing project in Brooklyn, into offices and spaces for events, gatherings, and programming, installing skylights over the double-height spaces and large glazed roll-up doors at the loading docks, opening out to the sidewalks. Youth living in the Red Hook Houses and surrounding neighborhood are the primary constituents of RHI's education, health, and job training programs. The RHI community center quickly became a center of social life, a place in which community members felt they belonged. So, I was particularly concerned when Hurricane Sandy hit and much of Red Hook was badly affected. The RHI building emerged relatively unscathed, just feet from the edge of the floodwaters. In the days following, led by staff members and buoyed by a vibrant social media effort, the organization took on a critical role, with the building serving as a neighborhood recovery command center and soup kitchen (figure 1.4).

These community organizations, RHI and GOLES, emphasize the importance of long-term community building in grassroots-based social and

Figure 1.4
Red Hook Initiative as storm recovery center and soup kitchen, the Sunday after Hurricane Sandy, November 4, 2012. Photograph: Red Hook Initiative.

environmental resilience. "People from a community have the power to create their own social change . . . ," says Jill Eisenhard, founder and then executive director of RHI.²⁷ In the aftermath of Sandy, they as well demonstrated the potential of coordinated social media and community-based technology initiatives. These ground-up initiatives—alternative ways of thinking—run in parallel to the high-profile, large-scale plans in New York City, and city officials alternately ignored them, paid lip service to them, and sometimes suitably held them up and engaged with them. As we observe, in the poststorm years, the various Rebuild By Design projects slowly making their way through government planning and procurement processes, these alternative initiatives take on greater importance, models for bottom-up climate change responses that build on community organizing and building, often outside and in spite of institutional and systemic challenges.

Jakarta

A sprawling megalopolis on the island of Java, Indonesia, situated between the Jakarta Bay on the north, and volcanic mountains to the south, Jakarta exemplifies the critical problems of rapid urbanization, burgeoning inequality, and threats from climate change. Within DKI (Daerah Khusus Ibukota, or Special Capital Region) Jakarta lives 10.3 million people, with 33.4 million in the larger metropolitan region.²⁸ It is considered among the top five cities in the world most vulnerable to climate change, according to one report.²⁹

Jakarta has historically dealt with flooding problems. Forty percent of the city lies below sea level. Thirteen rivers thread through it. Climate change, compounded by rapid urbanization, has exacerbated this. Sea levels in the Jakarta Bay are rising.³⁰ Land subsidence, primarily attributed to unregulated groundwater extraction and increased impermeability due to urban growth, is causing sinking at rates of between 3 and 10 centimeters per year, and up to 12 centimeters per year along the coast. Parts of the city had sunk 2.6 meters between 1998 and 2014.³¹ The subsidence rate is much larger than sea-level rise, a point I return to later in this chapter. The sinking land, rising seas, failing infrastructure, and clogged rivers have resulted in increasingly frequent and harmful floods—a severe one roughly every five years, serious ones occurring sometimes several times a week during the wet season. Massive inundations occurred in 1996, 2002, 2007, and 2013.

Jakarta is also the capital city of a country that is a political and ecological hybrid. Indonesia is particularly susceptible to tsunamis, earthquakes, and rising seas. At the same time, the country is often targeted by environmental activists for extensive logging and forest burning. It is the most populous Muslim-majority nation, with relatively stable religious and racial diversity, and it was also witness to Suharto's dictatorship, lasting half its postindependence period, including, in that time, a brutal invasion and occupation of East Timor.

On the ground, Jakarta exhibits an accelerated patchwork urbanism, what geographer T. G. McGee called *desakota*—hybrid regions merging aspects of city and country.[32] Extensive urban development envelops less developed areas, producing the distinct landscape of "villages in the city." The extreme spatial differentiation—islands of glassy towers nudging against the variegated fabric of the informal *kampung* settlements, all encircled by chocked highways and polluted rivers—is echoed in its stark socioeconomic inequality.[33]

The history of Jakarta's postcolonial urban development has been to turn away—from the coast, from the water, and from the colonial city. Waves of development pushed the center of the city further south.[34] This history can be seen moving north from the new gleaming skyscrapers in Kebayoran Baru (initially planned in the late-colonial years as a new satellite city), through the weighty postindependence administrative buildings and nationalist monuments in Medan Merdeka, and finally to Kota, the Dutch colonial city, with large swaths in picturesque ruins (figures 1.5 and 1.6). Since 1995, there have been sustained efforts, including presidential decrees, to refocus development toward the north and to develop a waterfront befitting a megacity with Global City aspirations.[35]

Urban development in Jakarta has proceeded largely unchecked. It has been characterized as "governance failure" in just and balanced infrastructure provisions, particularly in the highly uneven water and sanitation sector.[36] One encounters an air ranging from insouciance to despondency when talking to everyone from city officials to community activists in the city. Development happens—often haphazardly, often against or bending government plans and regulations, often by the large, powerful private development companies, in a context of fragmented urban governance and ineffective planning.[37] Within this rampant development, the plight of the urban poor has been a major flashpoint in debates about the future

Figure 1.5
Looking south from Medan Merdeka, July 2013. Photograph by author.

of the city. The rhetoric about the poor, from the highest circles of city government down, has often been relentless. The poor are blamed for the conditions of the rivers and canals, even as activists and researchers point to large-scale illegal dumping along the banks of waterways.[38]

The January 2013 floods—reinforced by scientific reports of severe land subsidence in the city, discovered after the 2007 flood—highlighted the city's failing infrastructure and the plight of residents, particularly those living in kampung settlements along the city's thirteen rivers. Jakarta's predicament, epitomized by the notorious Ciliwung River (figure 1.7), became a cause célèbre of sorts, and precipitated a surge of action. Then city governor Joko Widodo, newly elected, popular and populist, promised change, and enlisted the help of the South Korean government and engineering conglomerates to envision the future of the Ciliwung. Ongoing river dredging and "normalization" projects by the World Bank and Japanese technical cooperation agency JICA took on renewed urgency. Beyond the infrastructural works, the problem commanded broader attention from international

Figure 1.6
Ruins in Kota, January 2013. Photograph by author.

experts. Scientists from the Singapore-ETH Center sent drones down the river to capture point cloud data for three-dimensional hydrological models. World-renowned architects joined efforts to design ambitious "vertical kampungs."

But the most eye-opening response appeared more than a year later, in April 2014. On a visit to Jakarta, Melanie Schultz, then Netherlands minister for infrastructure and the environment, announced the draft masterplan for a massive urban development and infrastructural project—a new "sea wall city," developed by Dutch consulting firms. Officially named the National Capital Integrated Coastal Development (NCICD) masterplan, it is colloquially known as the Giant Sea Wall. From the air it resembles the Great Garuda, the mythical bird that is Indonesia's national symbol (figure 1.8). The masterplan envisions a new city for 1.5 million people to be built on newly reclaimed land right in the Jakarta Bay. In addition to addressing flooding, the plan promises to ease congestion, function as a freshwater reservoir, and provide a new central business district.[39]

Disparate Yet Interconnected Cities

Figure 1.7
Ciliwung River at Kampung Pulo, Central Jakarta, July 2013. Photograph by author.

The Giant Sea Wall masterplan, reminiscent of so many modernist, iconic plans such as Brasília, the (also winged) Brazilian capital, combines older notions of iconic design and hard infrastructural feats (land reclamation and sea walls) with updated hydrological ideas and technology to confront contemporary urban environmental problems. Often referenced as a response to sea-level rise, it is more a "sinking city" plan.[40] The "wings" of the Garuda form an arc across the bay to keep out the sea and create massive retention lakes behind them, to be pumped low enough to enable drainage from the rivers and canals in the fast-subsiding city. The land reclamation strategy reflects a long history of cities' claiming new territory in a battle for development and against nature. Here, it links public infrastructural needs with privatized urban economic development, with leases on the new land meant to fund its construction.

On the ground, far from the meeting rooms in which teams of international consultants—engineers, designers, economic planners, and trade specialists—met with city and national leaders, kampung activists were

Figure 1.8
Rendering of Jakarta National Capital Integrated Coastal Development (NCICD) Giant Sea Wall masterplan, October 2014.
Source: NCICD, urban design by KuiperCompagnons.

fighting to keep their homes. The river dredging and normalization projects entail the eviction of poor urban residents from settlements along coastlines and river edges, throwing thousands into an uncertain near future. The Giant Sea Wall masterplan hastens and intensifies this threat, with the proposed retention lakes necessitating clean water flowing into them from the rivers. In some of the threatened kampung areas, poor urban residents, led by community and nongovernmental organizations such as Ciliwung Merdeka (Free Ciliwung) and the Urban Poor Consortium (UPC), have resisted. Kampung activists pushed back against city officials' claims about their presumed illegality and blame for the floods. They asserted that proposals such as the new seawall megaproject simply continue a long lineage of plans to create a modern urban waterfront, with little regard for coastal ecologies or social lives, and that the river dredging and eviction efforts are meant to reclaim valuable central city land for development.

The real problem, activists pointed out, can be traced to a longer history of Jakarta's social and spatial marginalization—including the segregation of functions and ethnicities during the Dutch colonial period, followed by the relegation of poorer residents to low-lying, risky coastal and river edges during postindependence nation and city development—and ongoing rampant urban development and inattention to urban ecological conditions, such as ground permeability and open space. Kampung activists, working alongside community architects, urban sustainability advocacy groups, and students and researchers from local and foreign universities, organized and proposed "counterplans" to business-as-usual eviction and relocation efforts. They utilized urban planning and design strategies and tools, legal arguments, and community advocacy and organizing. These kampung design activism efforts are locally specific, but they are representative of a broader program of grassroots social and spatial movements in the region.

I first arrived in Jakarta in late January 2013, barely a week after the flood. It was extraordinary to see a city from which images of inundated streets and neighborhoods had streamed across global news channels just days before feel so bustling and normal. Having grown up in nearby Malaysia, I was intrigued by Southeast Asian cities, with their lush yet threatened urban ecologies and contentious political histories, so often neglected in studies of urbanization and environment. But if my cultural and geographic background and intellectual interest in fragile urban environments brought me to Jakarta, my encounters with these oppositional geographies— transnational urban environmental megaproject planning and seemingly local and grassroots kampung activism—defined the terrain of my investigation. They led me to an emerging story that transcended space and time, borne of a longer history of contestation, and shifting in the face of new environmental challenges and sociopolitical imaginaries.

Rotterdam
In September 2014, the second "Deltas in Times of Climate Change" conference was held in Rotterdam, the Netherlands. It was jointly organized and hosted by the Netherlands government, the Dutch Knowledge for Climate research program, the Rotterdam climate program, and C40 Cities. In one room, Henk Ovink, principal of Rebuild By Design, and previously director of spatial planning and water affairs in the Netherlands Ministry of Infrastructure and Environment, moderated a panel on cross-sector collaborations with panelists from the US HUD (the federal department in charge of coordinating the Rebuild By Design initiative), New York–based Municipal Art Society, New Orleans–based Waggonner and Ball Architects, and the Netherlands Ministry of Infrastructure and the Environment. In another room, Paul van Koppen of the Netherlands Water Partnership chaired a

series of presentations by senior Indonesian government officials and the Dutch project leaders of the Jakarta NCICD masterplan. In booths in the main gathering area, Dutch environmental agencies showcased their pedigree of delta and water management in the country, and Netherlands-based private infrastructure, engineering, and project management firms touted their work in far-flung reaches of the globe. Outside the conference halls, officials led tours of projects around the city, including large-scale infrastructure like the Maeslant storm surge barrier, a part of the Delta Works, and small-scale urban interventions like "water squares," designed by Rotterdam firm De Urbanisten (figure 1.9).

One can quickly discern the deep engagement of the Netherlands with climate change-oriented initiatives in New York, Jakarta, and beyond. In New York, in addition to Ovink's position on the leadership team of Rebuild By Design, six out of the ten finalist teams participating in the competition include Dutch design and engineering expertise. In Jakarta, the NCICD masterplan is being conducted with Netherlands government funding, and

Figure 1.9
Watersquare Benthemplein, Rotterdam, June 2014. Photograph by author.

authored by Dutch infrastructure and engineering firms, urban designers and landscape architects, and economic development specialists. In a sense, this is not so surprising. The Netherlands has long been held as a beacon for spatial planning and water management—epitomized by national infrastructural projects such as the Delta Works—and has a history of global, international engagements that span trade relationships to colonialism.

However, in recent decades, two factors—economic restructuring and climate change—have been changing the Dutch sociospatial and policy landscape. Economic liberalization has led to initiatives to decentralize decision making and embrace more market-driven approaches to spatial planning and development. In 2008, the global financial crisis reached the Netherlands, and its effects were very much felt throughout the country in the years after. Also in 2008, a new Delta Commission, formed the year before and charged with long-term safety against climate change, released its advisory report. In addition to proposing to increase flood protections of diked areas, the commission recommended more flexible responses, including "Room for the River," a program to allow occasional localized river flooding. This new approach to "building with nature" is at once technocratic and ecological, a self-described "paradigm shift" in Dutch environmental planning.

Many environmental projects are now being conceived on a more local scale. The city of Rotterdam promotes itself as a model for urban climate change adaptation. City officials show off plans and model projects to address climate change causes and protect against its impacts. At the same time, there is an outward focus on international relationships. Connecting Delta Cities, a program initiated and coordinated by the Rotterdam Climate Initiative within the C40 network, promotes cooperation and knowledge sharing among ten coastal cities. The Rotterdam program helps organize conferences, such as the one in September 2014, at which Dutch climate and water agencies and major engineering and infrastructure firms are able to meet with delegations from other countries.

Rotterdam is in many ways an unlikely foil to New York and Jakarta, the two other primary cities in this book. Located in the province of Zuid-Holland (South Holland), it straddles the Nieuwe Maas River on the Rhine–Meuse–Scheldt delta, a key gateway to the German and Central European trading cities. Six hundred and sixteen thousand people live in the municipal boundaries of Rotterdam, with 1.2 million in the larger urban region.[41]

It is not even the largest city in the Netherlands, whose total population of 16.5 million[42] in the entire country is markedly smaller than that found in the metropolitan regions of New York and Jakarta. Rotterdam, along with Amsterdam, the Hague, and Utrecht—the four largest cities in the country—loosely ring a polycentric region known as the Randstad (literally "border city"), at the center of which is the Groene Hart (Green Heart), consisting of agricultural areas, nature preserves, and recreational areas.

While quite different in terms of its scale of agglomeration and size of population, two factors make it somewhat less unlikely that Rotterdam plays such a significant role in the urban environmental futures of both New York and Jakarta. First, the Netherlands, in particular the Randstad, has for a long time been perceived, represented, and planned as a dense, urbanized region. Rotterdam is in many ways the economic trade engine of a broader urban system. The city's port remains Europe's largest, and for many years claimed the title of the world's largest before being eclipsed by a growing number of Asian ports, primarily in China. It is also a city of reinvention, its historic core almost totally destroyed during the Second World War, and emerging in the years after as a center of architectural and urban design experimentation. Second, the Netherlands itself has had a long, checkered history in international affairs, through its colonial period and beyond.

Indeed, my first experience in Rotterdam was reflective of these local and global dynamics. I spent a summer in the city in the late 1990s as an intern at the architecture firm MVRDV. I was then a student originally from Southeast Asia in a US architecture school. Rotterdam was the global center of design at that time. A thriving architecture scene, globalizing not for the first time, led by the iconoclastic work of Rem Koolhaas's Office for Metropolitan Architecture, built on and challenged the functionalism of Dutch modernists such as Johannes van den Broek and Jacob Bakema, who were influential in the city's postwar reconstruction. The architects of turn-of-the-millennium Rotterdam questioned form, regulation, scale, constructions of nature, and dictates of taste.[43] They set in play ideas about designing the future city that would be enduring as new economic and climate challenges emerged in later years.

On another level, Rotterdam poses an interesting counterpoint to the two other major cities studied here, especially in regard to the issue of social inequality. A 1999 study found ethnic and wealth segregation between large Dutch cities and their surrounding wealthier suburbs, and warned about "the growing spatial concentration of ethnic minorities and low-income groups in the cities."[44] As the primary port, Rotterdam has historically functioned as a working-class, immigrant city, largely poorer than the surrounding region. City managers in Rotterdam are unhindered in their welcoming of gentrification in the city. One of their stated agendas is encouraging wealthier people to live in the city center. In some ways, this ties back to the new national policies relegating urban development issues to the localities. One official, pressed about the link between inequality and environmental vulnerability, claims that there is no such link in Rotterdam. To her, there is an inverse relationship. The vast majority of social housing is located in the city center, within the protective dike ring; it is the wealthier residents who tend to live in riskier areas along the river.[45]

For the Rotterdam Climate Proof program, "resilience" includes (1) protection against flooding, (2) a "comfortable, liveable and attractive city," (3) continued accessibility of the port, (4) limited disruption by precipitation, (5) residents' awareness of climate change, and (6) economic strength and a strong image for the delta city.[46] The second point about livability and attraction, and the latter point about economy and image, are particularly important. Rotterdam's climate adaptation program is precisely a spatial and economic development initiative.

In terms of spatial, physical implementation, Rotterdam's adaptation initiatives have focused on projects to address flooding caused by increasing rainwater, urban heat island effect, and new urban plans beyond the primary dike ring. Besides the larger infrastructural works such as the outer and inner dikes, the built projects so far have included the water square at Benthemplein (completed in 2013); underground water storage facilities, such as the one under the Museumpark garage (2011); a showcase floating pavilion in the Rijnhaven, a harbor basin adjacent to the fast-redeveloping Kop Van Zuid area (2010) (figure 1.10); and a number of green roofs and green walls completed and under construction. The city has also initiated plans for "floating districts" in Stadshavens, another area previously dominated by port activities. Compared to other cities' adaptation plans, Rotterdam's is tightly focused on physical urban design interventions that are highly "imageable" and on initiatives that have significant marketability, whether physical or otherwise.

Of course, the Dutch connection in both New York City and Jakarta long predates contemporary efforts at climate adaptation, spatial planning, and

Figure 1.10
Floating pavilion, Rijnhaven, Rotterdam, June 2014. Photograph by author.

water management. Both cities served formative periods as Dutch colonial settlements—New York as Nieuw Amsterdam from 1624 to 1664,[47] Jakarta as Batavia from 1619 through the mid-1900s.[48] Jakarta, like its colonial city peers, continues to bear the physical, social, and institutional marks of colonization. It is not an accident that the so-called Dutch Golden Age of the seventeenth century—an era of accelerated urbanization and reclamation in the low countries—coincided with the rise of Dutch colonialism worldwide. My investigation here is concerned with not so much the historical stories or artifacts but the ways in which present-day relationships in each of these places are related to a broader and longer trajectory of Dutch landscape order and pragmatism, and outward-looking internationalism, born of collective threat and trust in the state.

Plans, Counterplans, Global Networks

The environmental initiatives outlined in the three cities represent differing visions in response to social and environmental challenges, often

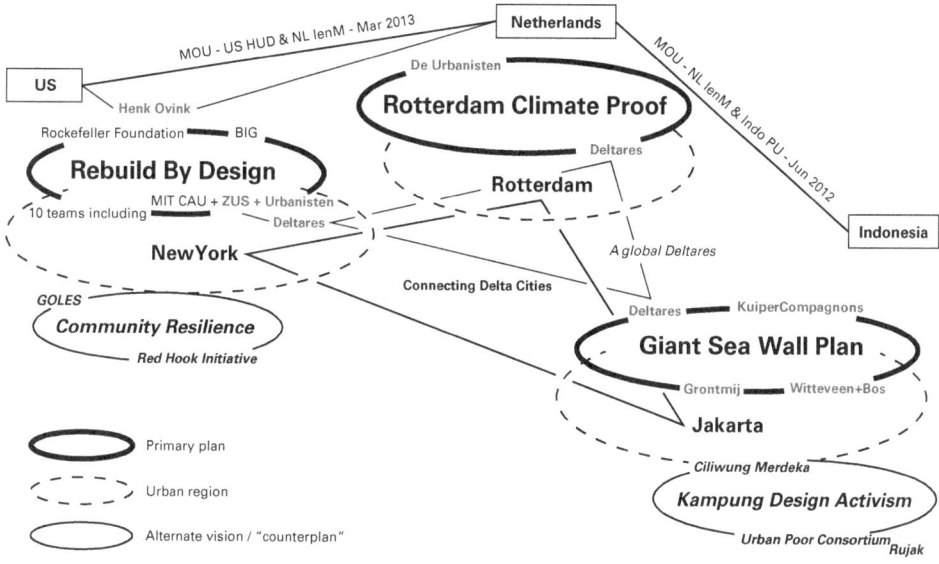

Figure 1.11
Sites, strategies, and networks: urban regions and interconnections among primary plans, led or supported by state or city, and alternative visions or "counterplans."

with oppositional priorities, methods, and objectives. They bring to light institutional power relationships, geopolitics, histories and geographies of marginalization, systemic oppressions of class and/or race, and the political economy of place—urban spatial politics, in a new context of global environmental change. They also indicate a new type of global interconnectedness in policy and design responses to climate change, in which networks of urban, national, and transnational entities work at multiple scales and levels to produce visions of urban futures. In the sense that these visions of the future are often contested, and represent alternatives in relation to local and global power structures, they might be seen as well as acts of domination or consolidation, and resistance—plans and counterplans in the context of climate change. How do urban researchers and planners make sense of these contestations and contradictions in urban responses to climate change?

The disparate cities of New York, Jakarta, and Rotterdam are interconnected in more ways than one would expect (figure 1.11). It's a bit of a trope in urban research to claim that one's object or site of analysis is complex—everything is complex. But in this case, the way we research and practice—our disciplines, fields, and inherited methods—might actually be impeding the possibility of our really understanding what is going on. Cities like New York, not necessarily lacking in financial or governance capacity, or those like Jakarta, frequently cited as lacking effective governance, but with avenues for intense growth and private investment, present new and fast-moving scenarios for this scholarship. The role of countries like the Netherlands and cities like Rotterdam, present across this interrelated set of stories, and of new global institutions and networks in the making of adaptation plans in various locales around the world also demands attention.

The complexities of the strategies and sites, local and global conditions, the interconnections and place-based contestation, all bring up a set of intertwined problems: the need to analyze power relationships locally and regionally, and globally, across national boundaries; the mechanisms and processes of urban planning and design, and those of concept mobilities, the way ideas move and transform; and the ways in which the production of images confers legitimacy and power.

As I show in this book, global, national, and urban scales are increasingly intertwined, with new institutions and frameworks of connectivity linking policies, practices, and interventions across the range of scales. These "network formations" are propelled by interactive economic and environmental conditions, and are historically and situationally defined. Dominant, state-led and state-supported plans, including Rebuild By Design in New York City and the Giant Sea Wall in Jakarta, though globally linked and constituted, tend to be reformatted by and to the sociospatial conditions in which they are embedded. They reflect the modes of urban development, constitution of market force, levels of governance, cohesion of climate policies, and patterns of institutionalized community participation. "Global" values and objectives recursively transform in "local" places. Further, climate change motivates relationships and plans, but plan objectives transcend climate-specific goals. Climate, in fact, exposes and enhances motivations and contradictions in global relationships, and facilities new avenues for capital exchange and accumulation.

In parallel to the ways in which dominant climate responses deform to account for structures of governance and modes of development, the counterplans too take different forms. In Red Hook, Brooklyn, and the Lower East Side, Manhattan, neighborhoods socially and economically sidelined yet continually romanticized and targeted for redevelopment, the imaginaries and practices of community organizations offer localized, community-specific approaches to social and environmental resilience—not so much a direct substitute for the "big plan," but ways of conceiving resilience that emphasize the agency and voice of their constituents. In the kampungs of Jakarta, confronting myriad direct and diffuse threats, activists developed innovative coalitions and tools to produce social and spatial form alternatives to "business as usual" in an entrenched top-down system, to forge new platforms for organizing and negotiation. In each of the sites, the counterplans envision transformative urban social and spatial change as part of environmental resilience.

And so what? True to the nature of the global problems we face, the book moves beyond an accounting of what is at stake. In concluding the book, I offer two broad conceptual takeaways: first, a sociospatial typology of urban climate change responses, categorized in terms of organization and form; and, second, speculations on an insurgent, networked, urban ecological design practice. I argue that, in order to "scale up," as it were, alternative social and spatial practices—the counterplans—urban researchers and planners need to look not at the strategy itself, but at the specific urban processes in which these strategies are constituted. If exploring design as a terrain of contestation reveals underlying power relationships and fault lines, then the marshaling of an explicitly insurgent, critical urban ecological design possibly disrupts such systems.

Ultimately, this book opens productive pathways toward a critical theory of designing urban climate change resilience, one that prioritizes issues of justice, centered on the production of alternative visions. Such a theory is an imperative. We know that the future will be urbanized, and that the urbanized future will be defined by climate. The field of urban climate change responses, in scholarship and practice, has so far observed, analyzed, and formulated bundles of strategies and frameworks best suited for specific circumstances—rich and poor, north and south, infrastructure and governance, physical and sociopolitical, designed and whatever might be termed "nondesigned." However, new approaches are taking shape that are not easily grasped in terms of such dichotomies. And our concepts of resilience, adaptation, and design remain chaotic, variable, and ill-formed. A critical theory of designing urban resilience would engage the spectrum of approaches, with a view tuned to the disparate power structures shaping the social, spatial, and historical interrelationships under which such approaches are proposed.

The next three chapters lay out the crosscutting topics that span sites and strategies. Aligned with the framing of the problem, each topic is multisited, multiscalar, and multilevel. Alongside the conceptual investigations such a problem provokes, we confront, as well, important methodological questions of case selection and research approach.

Critical Interrelationships

Each of these sites might present itself as a critical case.

In New York City, Rebuild By Design represents a major milestone. It is high profile; disasters in New York, rightly or wrongly, take up an outsize share of the global imagination. Its initial phases are funded and backed by the Rockefeller Foundation, a powerful global philanthropic foundation setting the agenda for urban resilience around the world. In the US context, it is notable as an environmental initiative using public, federal funds for climate change projects. It is also innovative in its embrace of the competition format. This format is now being used in, or has inspired, a number of significant initiatives (all of which involve the Rockefeller Foundation): the Changing Course competition in New Orleans; the National Disaster Resilience Competition, announced by President Barack Obama in June 2014, inviting localities that have been impacted by disasters to compete for almost $1 billion in federal CDBG–DR funds, "building on the successful model set forth by HUD's Rebuild by Design competition";[49] the Global Resilience Partnership, launched in September 2014 by the Rockefeller Foundation, joined by the US Agency for International Development (USAID) and the Swedish International Development Cooperation Agency (Sida), inviting teams to propose resiliency projects in the Sahel, Horn of Africa, South Asia, and Southeast Asia;[50] and the Bay Area: Resilient By Design Challenge in the San Francisco Bay Area, launched in 2017.

In Jakarta, the NCICD Giant Sea Wall masterplan is one of the most far reaching, in size and scope, municipally and nationally supported urban adaptation projects in the world. It is one in which the symbolic nature of the project rivals its infrastructural ambitions. It is also critical in that Jakarta poses possibly one of the worst-case scenarios for the confluence of rapid urbanization, environmental degradation, and urban inequality—making it, unglamorously, a testing site for an urban future that confronts many cities around the world. The organizational and financing structure of the NCICD masterplan, while not unique, is notable when seen in conjunction with the ambition of the project. The masterplanning was funded by the Dutch government, and produced by Dutch private firms and research institutions, while the implementation is planned to rely on very large private real estate investments. This case provides a prime example of how more cities confronting climate risks will likely choose to proceed, in a global context in which the disparate power of colonial and postcolonial relationships still matters, and privatized urban development is often seen as the preferred and sometimes only means to get things done.

Rotterdam, certainly, is different. New York City and Jakarta, on the face of it quite dissimilar, are both large, dense, socially and economically diverse urban agglomerations. They are both cities within significant urban regions, with associated administrative and environmental incongruities—city(ies) and watershed(s) unaligned. Both are undertaking significant adaptation plans in response to a set of recent disasters. Rotterdam is the key city in the key country when it comes to models for urban, spatial planning in response to environmental change. Its role in convening international forums like the "Deltas in Times of Climate Change" conferences, and its centrality as a place in which (1) design concepts for adaptation are implemented and through which (2) the actors involved in such implementation bring such concepts to other sites like New York and Jakarta, make Rotterdam a critical site.

There is, as well, the more general issue of specific, and heightened, risks to large coastal cities.[51]

While each of these sites and sets of strategies is noteworthy as a case in and of itself, the *interrelationships* between them are pivotal to understanding what is going on. It is clichéd to say we live in an increasingly global and interconnected world. But it is imperative to state that none of these adaptation initiatives happen in a vacuum, in bounded time and space. The initiatives in New York, Jakarta, and Rotterdam form particularly critical network relationships, in part because of each site's prominence but also because of the nature of the network itself. New York and Jakarta are commonly referred to in a set of very large urban regions, although in different ways. New York is often seen as a "command and control" global city (along with cities such as London and Tokyo),[52] and Jakarta as a quintessential megacity (along with so many others, including Mexico City, Lagos, Bangkok, Dhaka, Mumbai . . .).[53] Rotterdam is an emerging example of a "modeling," outward-oriented city (accompanied on this stage by Singapore, perhaps as well on a different level by Curitiba in Brazil and Medellín in Colombia).

The research approach in this book pays specific attention to the matter of interrelationships.[54] The intersecting narratives here depict one particular set of sites and strategies, but this set represents the formation of a kind of network that, I argue, will increasingly be the kind we see in global and urban initiatives in response to various manners of environmental threats, including climate change.

2 Nature of Contestation

> Yes, I move—perhaps I am seeking
>   Storms, suns, dawns, a place to hide.
> What are you doing here, pale and polished—
>   You, the stone in the path of the tide?
> —Alfonsina Storni, "Running Water"

In New York, Jakarta, and Rotterdam, the challenges and the opportunities arising from climate change impacts and the imperative to respond have unearthed spaces and actions of contestation. In New York, a high-profile disaster and a high-profile response have ignited imaginations. At the same time, uncertainty and unevenness of implementation, amid increasing attention to rising inequality, cloud the outlook for the immediate future. In Jakarta, an ambitious megaproject is proposed to solve a multitude of longtime urban problems and new environmental challenges. And yet, it seems to start by dodging the key problems, while leaving the existing city behind. In Rotterdam, city leaders maintain the profile of a well-run, well-designed, modern city, a model for spatial planning and urban hydrological design. Pulling aside the well-ordered physical surface reveals further motivations, in large part centered on global and local economic challenges. In each of the sites, the imperatives of climate change expose fault lines and accentuate fissures in the social, spatial, and environmental operations of these urban centers.

To what extent are these contestations different from those found in the history of cities to date? This chapter explores the interrelationships between environmental initiatives in the context of climate change and uneven urban development. It focuses on the impacts of and responses to climate change and on the interrelated nature and production of social and spatial contestation in cities. There are two ways to look at this chapter. The first is that it relates contemporary forces of marginalization, in the context of climate change, to the history of uneven urban development. The second is that it brings a critical urban theory framework to an analysis of urban environmental politics. Here I develop in detail the context of sociospatial marginalization and environmental initiatives in New York and Jakarta, two cities at opposite ends of the spectrum, as far as large urban centers go, but both facing rising social stratification, environmental threats, and the pressures and opportunities of global capitalism. (In the following chapter, I look specifically at the Dutch city of Rotterdam, which is in many ways quite distinct from both the large metropolises here, but, as we will see, has come play a key role in their environmental narratives.)

In developing the analysis of each site and strategy, I build on the urban regional contexts and the substantive historical factors behind spatial and environmental development and differentiation introduced in the previous chapter. I discuss the current state of environmental threats, both climate- and non-climate-related. And I trace the challenges faced by specific localities and communities, and the primary government or municipal initiatives enacted in response to these threats. I then develop a more generalized view of the nature of contestation in each site, illustrating modes of conflict, marginalization, activism, and alternative points of view or approaches.

New York

Hurricane Sandy

When Hurricane Sandy hit the New York area on October 29, 2012, it was not necessarily in the context that disaster could happen, but that disaster *would* happen. Hurricane Irene had made landfall in the US Northeast a year earlier, in August 2011 (by that time downgraded to a tropical storm). It reaffirmed that tropical cyclones could take a tremendous toll this far north along the Eastern Seaboard. New York City, which had taken the unprecedented step of ordering mandatory evacuations of coastal areas and shutting down the subway system, was largely spared by Irene. But Sandy, one year later, proved just how vulnerable the metropolitan region was.

Sandy hit New York City as a Category 2 storm and was the worst "natural" disaster in the city's history. Forty-three New Yorkers died, with another ten casualties in the rest of New York State, thirty-four in New Jersey, and four in Connecticut. The storm caused about $19 billion in losses for New York City alone.[1] It damaged more than 69,000 residential units, and left thousands looking for shelter.[2] Subway tunnels and stations were flooded, taking days for service to be partially restored. Coastal areas such as Red Hook in Brooklyn and the Lower East Side in Manhattan were submerged. The most striking visible damage, alongside the darkened Manhattan skyline, torn-off façades, and floating cars in underground garages, was the stretch of scorched and leveled houses in Breezy Point, Queens, destroyed by a raging fire as floods kept firefighters at bay (figure 2.1). In late 2012, New York State governor Andrew Cuomo asked the federal government for $42 billion for Sandy recovery.[3]

Sandy not only revealed the weaknesses in the city's infrastructure, institutions, and buildings. It exposed and accentuated its underlying inequality. In what researchers have called a "tale of two Sandys,"[4] the storm "exacerbated crises which existed before the storm and continued afterwards in heightened form," including longstanding problems such as poverty, lack of access to affordable housing, and lack of employment. On the ground, this

Figure 2.1
Houses destroyed by fire in Breezy Point, Queens, November 7, 2012. Photograph: Andrea Booher/FEMA.

implied that, in the outlying neighborhoods pummeled by Sandy, the city's Build It Back program, already slow and spotty, might simply end up reconstructing existing spatial inequities. In addition, maintenance at the New York City Housing Authority (NYCHA) public housing projects impacted by the storm has been delayed. Boilers, other mechanical equipment, and lobbies remained unfixed years after the storm. It was only in the spring of 2015, two and a half years after Sandy, that Mayor Bill de Blasio announced that the Federal Emergency Management Agency (FEMA) would give $3 billion to NYCHA to repair and protect thirty-three public housing developments.[5]

These shortcomings in recovery and rebuilding have taken place in the context of some of the most dramatic urban development transformations in recent New York City history. As historian Sam Bass Warner reminds us, American cities have always been centers of conflict, oppression, and inequality.[6] That has certainly been the case in New York from the start. Yet, new modes and extents of social, economic, and spatial disparity have emerged in the era following the city's near bankruptcy, as it transitioned from a center of industry to one of finance,[7] and the continued repercussions of urban economic restructuring result in consolidating a "dual city," a "capital of capital."[8] The process of the financialization of the built environment now reaches from its most visible, in the explosion of very tall residential skyscrapers—more than eighty stories, with $100 million penthouses, their fantastic heights enabled through the accumulation of air rights, as much as anything pure extrusions of capital[9]—to its most everyday, in the expansion of the private equity investment purchasing of rent-regulated housing.[10] The contrast of the supervisible "supertalls" and the largely invisible transformation of the rental market, how most New Yorkers live, is an apt metaphor for the rise of income inequality in the city.[11]

Red Hook
Red Hook, Brooklyn, spans waterfront port infrastructure along the New York Bay on the southwest and west, to the elevated Brooklyn-Queens Expressway and Gowanus Canal on the northeast and east. Along this short span, it traverses what might seem like alternate worlds: art galleries, wine stores, and cafés along Van Brunt Street; the expanse of the Red Hook Houses, the largest NYCHA public housing project in Brooklyn, completed in 1939, including thirty buildings and covering 39 acres; the Red Hook Ball Fields, famous for its Latin American food trucks; and the Gowanus Canal, declared a federal Superfund site in 2010. Historically an industrial, port neighborhood, home

to immigrant communities and dockworkers, the neighborhood underwent severe economic decline in the 1970s and 80s. In 1988, *Life* magazine named Red Hook the "Crack Capital of America." For some time dodging the most acute effects of gentrification because of its relative physical isolation and lack of subway access, Red Hook now confronts clear change. The conversions of warehouses along the waterfront into art spaces and residential apartments, a wave of new stores along Van Brunt Street, the spine of gentrification in the neighborhood, and the arrival of IKEA, which opened in 2008 and paid for a waterfront park, were harbingers of things to come (figure 2.2). A controversial for-profit private school and new townhouses were built adjacent to the public housing buildings, and larger, more ambitious development plans have been proposed for the waterfront.[12]

Red Hook, coastal and low-lying,[13] was one of the worst-hit neighborhoods in the city during Hurricane Sandy (figure 2.3). Residents in the Red Hook Houses lost power and heat for weeks. Temporary boilers have taken on a sense of permanence, still there seven years later in mid-2019 (figure 2.4). But

Figure 2.2
Red Hook waterfront warehouses, with Lower Manhattan skyline in the distance, May 2014. Photograph by author.

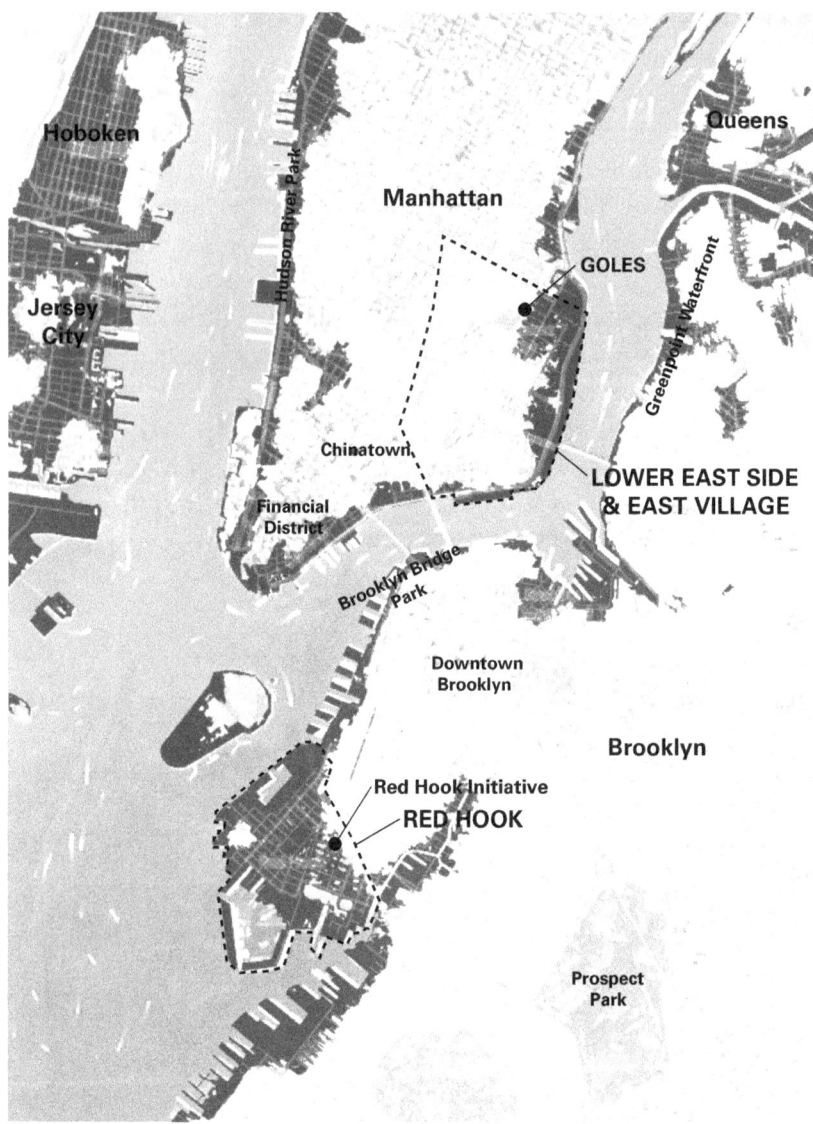

Figure 2.3
Map of Red Hook, Brooklyn and Lower East Side, Manhattan, including Hurricane Sandy surge impact, and location of Red Hook Initiative and Good Old Lower East Side. By author based on NASA aerial photo and Sandy surge mapping project by WNYC.

Figure 2.4
Temporary boilers at the Red Hook Houses, Red Hook, Brooklyn, in May 2014. Photograph by author.

in the days following the storm, Red Hook also emerged as a surprising and powerful story of community resilience and grassroots recovery initiatives. Staff from the Red Hook Initiative (RHI),[14] a local community center, members of Occupy Sandy and other local volunteers, and workers from city agencies worked together to organize recovery efforts. RHI's community space, adjacent to the Red Hook Houses, survived the storm unscathed and took on a central role, serving as command center and soup kitchen for postdisaster recovery.[15] Social media sites lit up as volunteer coordination and fundraising efforts were developed around the Red Hook efforts.[16]

RHI works primarily with Black and Latinx youth who live in public housing, targeting the systemic, intergenerational poverty that plagues the neighborhood. It provides health and education workshops as well as job training. Jill Eisenhard, founder and executive director of RHI, explains why the organization's staff members, many of whom are hired from within the public housing community, were so ready to take their place in recovery efforts:

Many of the people who were there had worked for RHI for five, eight, ten years. Our whole model is around being able to identify community need, and respond to it. Sure, it's different from a young person who's suddenly homeless. But knowing who your neighbors are, knowing how to assess a situation, knowing how to develop an action plan, an agenda . . . that isn't any different from what they are doing everyday, it's just a different kind of situation. . . . I think it's building on the social capital that's there in the neighborhood.[17]

In the days immediately following the storm, there were observations and complaints among news media, volunteers, and sympathetic New Yorkers that government agencies were not present on the ground. Eisenhard sets the record straight, noting that elected officials may not have been there on day one, but were there within a few days. NYCHA employees were on the scene, but did not communicate this fact well. At the same time, Eisenhard stresses the issues that plagued municipal and federal recovery crews, particularly confusion stemming from a lack of local knowledge. "FEMA asked us a lot of things . . . one of our board members got into a truck with [a FEMA official], because he didn't know where to go," she says. "At the end of the day, you're always going to ask someone local."[18]

Post-Sandy, there have been a number of recovery and resiliency initiatives in Red Hook. It was selected to be part of New York State's New York Rising Community Reconstruction program (NYRCR), tasked with facilitating community redevelopment planning in disaster-affected areas statewide. The neighborhood was also part of early research and design studies for Rebuild By Design, the competition launched by the Hurricane Sandy Rebuilding Task Force, although these efforts did not make it to the final round of proposals.

Local community leaders express ambivalence about these initiatives. Gita Nandan, architect and resident of Red Hook, and co-chair of the Red Hook NY Rising planning committee (now Resilient Red Hook), stresses the positive aspects of that community planning effort, including the varied and numerous educational training sessions that illustrated the key issues, problems, and potential solutions and synergies. She notes that many of the community stakeholders in Red Hook took the initiative to educate themselves about the issues. At the same time, Nandan points out the problems brought up by the disparate stakes of community members:

The critical factor, I think, is that [NYCHA residents] have no ownership over there. They have very little empowerment over their environment, and so when you're asking community leaders to put together the plan, it's very hard for residents who have never had any actionable influence to think that, whatever, they're going to sit for eight months at a table and actually make an impact.[19]

Eisenhard of RHI is more direct about the shortcomings in NY Rising's planning process:

> I don't think they did a very good job of engaging public housing residents. You start getting into discussions like, Should there be a sea wall? Or should there be floodgates? These big infrastructure questions. And public housing residents are sitting there, and they're, like, my building is still connected to a temporary boiler, and they bring gas in every day to fill it. And the diesel fumes are coming in my window. And you're talking about a sea wall? This meeting is not for me.[20]

Red Hook continues to be a focus of attention by the media, researchers, and government officials. However, while there have been efforts at community resiliency planning in the neighborhood, these institutional processes do not appear to engage fully across the diversity of stakeholders. In particular they are not effective in finding meaningful ways to include lower income residents, including NYCHA residents, approximately 50 percent of the residents in Red Hook.[21] While the critical work of community organizations in the relief efforts immediately after the storm is well recognized,[22] and efforts to reach out to marginalized residents clear, there has been little sustained attempt in the city and state planning processes to understand and build on these grassroots social support infrastructures. The postdisaster planning efforts did not, on the whole, account for the social aspects of resiliency among disparate social groups, or take into consideration the agency of those who have been disempowered. They also failed to take into account the ways in which systemic and structural barriers define the risks faced by those groups or their expectations of change.

The systemic neglect of the agency of marginalized groups manifests itself in other ways. Eisenhard expresses her concerns about "storm fatigue" on the part of Red Hook Houses residents, who have been asked numerous times since the storm to take part in focus groups on storm responses. She also points out the flip side of this kind of disassociation from the system, stating, "You talk about resilience. . . . I think for people in public housing, by December [2012], they're like, My lights are on, everything is fine, why are people still talking about this? Because when you're a low income New Yorker and you have been marginalized, stuff like this happens all the time. It's not always on the national news."[23]

There is one aspect to this story, in particular, that ties together the community social relationships, postdisaster response, and broader possibilities of planning for future resiliency. RHI launched the Red Hook WiFi project, a local mesh network, in collaboration with the Open Technology Institute (OTI), a program of New America foundation, in late 2011 as a community-led project to bring free broadband connectivity to the neighborhood. RHI and OTI first placed antennas on the roof of the RHI building and then extended the range with additional antennas on another nearby building. The network offers access to the Internet, as well as local network applications such as real-time bus tracking and NYPD relations surveys, developed in partnership with RHI participants.[24]

Hurricane Sandy left much of Red Hook without electricity and communications, but the RHI building and Red Hook WiFi stayed powered and operational. In the days that followed, it functioned as a critical communications hub for area residents. Less than two weeks after Sandy hit, FEMA officials and volunteers set up additional routers to extend the network to further support recovery efforts. Since the storm, the network has been further expanded, and RHI and OTI now also train neighborhood youth to install and manage networking equipment in a program called RHI Digital Stewards[25] (figure 2.5). The Red Hook WiFi project connects and weaves community, technology, coalition, and resilience from the ground up.

Lower East Side

The Lower East Side in Manhattan is home to some of the most illustrious and iconic narratives of New York City urban lore. The area bearing this name originally spanned 14th Street in the north to Canal Street in the south, east of the Bowery, before the area above Houston Street was recoined the East Village in the 1960s, a particularly successful campaign of cultural and real estate marketing revisionism. Historically a center of commerce and a working-class area absorbing waves of immigrants from the mid-1800s on, it has more recently been characterized by struggles over real estate development, confronting phases of gentrification from the 1970s through the 1990s and beyond.[26] The neighborhood has also witnessed diverse and conjoined movements of radical politics and avant-garde art, including the activist collectives of the so-called Peace Pentagon building, art and activism space ABC No Rio, and the work of artists Jean-Michel Basquiat and Keith Haring. The impacts of gentrification notwithstanding,

Figure 2.5
Rob Smith, an alum of the RHI Digital Stewards program, inspects networking equipment, November 2018. Photograph: Alden Parkinson/Red Hook Initiative.

the Lower East Side is still home to many lower-income residents. It contains a significant concentration of NYCHA public housing projects lining the elevated FDR Drive along the East River. These include the Smith, Rutgers, La Guardia, Vladeck, and Baruch Houses south of Houston Street, and the Wald and Riis developments north of Houston, in the East Village (figure 2.6). The East River Park, with ball fields, courts, and tracks, runs between and alongside the FDR Drive and East River.

The Lower East Side did not suffer the same extent of storm surge and flooding as Red Hook in the direct aftermath of Sandy (figures 2.3 and 2.7). However, the impacts were often invisible—in flooded basements and disrupted infrastructure stemming from a massive transformer explosion at the Con Edison power plant on 14th Street, a few blocks north on the east side of Manhattan. These impacts were particularly perilous for low-income residents living in NYCHA projects, who lived without electricity and working elevators for weeks after the storm.[27]

Damaris Reyes is a longtime community organizer and executive director of Good Old Lower East Side (GOLES), a housing and tenants' rights

Figure 2.6
The FDR Drive along the East River, with Rutgers and La Guardia Houses behind the first row of buildings, and Vladeck Houses and the East River Park in the distance, August 2014. Photograph by author.

organizing group. In the days following Sandy, Reyes found herself in a context of frenetic activity and confusion. Staff members, volunteers, and members of other community organizations were attempting to help people who were stuck in their apartments. But there was little ability to coordinate these efforts, since there was no response plan in place, and communications networks were unreliable. She recounts the realization that the volunteer activities were not organized, with disparate attention being given to different places and there not being enough knowledge of who was doing what. "That was a moment where I said, this is going to happen again and it would serve us right to figure out how to use our strength in a more collaborative and organized and coordinated way."[28]

Reyes talks about the process of forming LES Ready, the Lower East Side Long Term Recovery Group, a coalition of community groups and institutions coordinating response and preparedness planning and training for future disasters in the aftermath of Sandy: "With Sandy and disaster preparedness,

Figure 2.7
Volunteers for Chinatown / Lower East Side community organization CAAAV Organizing Asian Communities distribute supplies, November 2012. Photograph: Ken Chen via opencitymag.com.

we now have thirty-six members in the network and it's growing. We have resident associations, block associations, we have clergy, we have medical providers. That is not a coalition that you could just build around anything."

She credits her ability to bring people together to her longtime experience as a resident and organizer in the Lower East Side. "So, I knew who to call," she says, talking about her previous work on coalition building for housing and rezoning campaigns. Reyes explains some of the challenges and opportunities in building coalitions in a context where some community-based organizations are large and relatively well funded (for example, the settlement houses, which have been in operation since the late 1800s), in contrast to her own organization, GOLES, with its reputation as a group of "rabble rousers" and "trouble makers." In her view, despite—or because of—this reputation, Reyes was elected as the chair of LES Ready.

The Lower East Side, like Red Hook in Brooklyn, was selected as one of the localities for the NYRCR program. In addition, the neighborhood is the site of perhaps the highest-profile project of the Rebuild By Design competition, the "BIG U" project by the BIG team, designed to protect Manhattan from midtown down to the southern tip.²⁹ Images and descriptions of the BIG U dominated news accounts of Rebuild By Design. Its clear counterpoint to the post-Sandy photos of Lower Manhattan in darkness provokes a visceral response. The LES Ready coalition served as a key community constituent for this project. Says Reyes, "I wanted to make sure that our community was not forgotten, especially because on the surface we looked like we recovered and bounced back right away."³⁰

Reyes discusses the relationship between the design team members and her constituents. Echoing Eisenhard in Red Hook with reference to community expectations, she recalls previous planning efforts in the neighborhood that had not amounted to discernible results: "You know, this is not new anymore, the planning workshops.... People have a little bit of planning fatigue, but more than that, you have all these kind of processes that happen and they don't always result in anything concrete, so we were, like, Why do you want my opinion? For what?!"³¹

Through the course of the community meetings, Reyes was gradually convinced that they were being heard. She says, "When they showed us the final stuff when they came back the second time, I could tell by their responses. The people felt like their ideas were being incorporated."³²

Because of the high-profile exposure associated with the project, LES Ready, and in particular GOLES and Reyes, have attained a certain level of visibility in resilience design and adaptation circles. Rebuild By Design principal Henk Ovink often mentions Reyes by name, and she has participated in international panels on resiliency.

Rebuild By Design

President Barack Obama signed an executive order establishing the Hurricane Sandy Rebuilding Task Force on December 7, 2012, five-and-a-half weeks after Sandy. The task force's primary responsibility was to coordinate rebuilding efforts, strengthen the economy, understand weather-related vulnerabilities and future risks, and determine a strategy for rebuilding.³³ The president appointed US Department of Housing and Urban Development (HUD) secretary Shaun Donovan as chair of the task force. In June 2013, the Hurricane Sandy Rebuilding Task Force launched Rebuild By Design, a design competition to spur "innovative, implementable proposals that promote resilience in the Sandy-affected region." The objectives, as stated in the brief, included better understanding of the region's vulnerabilities and interdependencies;

generating regionally applicable design proposals to promote resilience; building local community and government agency capacity; strengthening collaboration within government and between government, business, academic, and nonprofit groups; spurring innovation and "outside-the-box perspectives"; and executing "world-class projects with regional impact."[34] After a call for qualifications, Rebuild By Design announced ten finalist teams in November 2013, working on design proposals for sites in New York, New Jersey, and Connecticut (figure 2.8). In June 2014, it announced the six winning teams.[35]

Rebuild By Design represented a new framework, both in organization and funding. Launched by the Hurricane Sandy Rebuilding Task Force, the management and coordination was then transferred to HUD. The task force

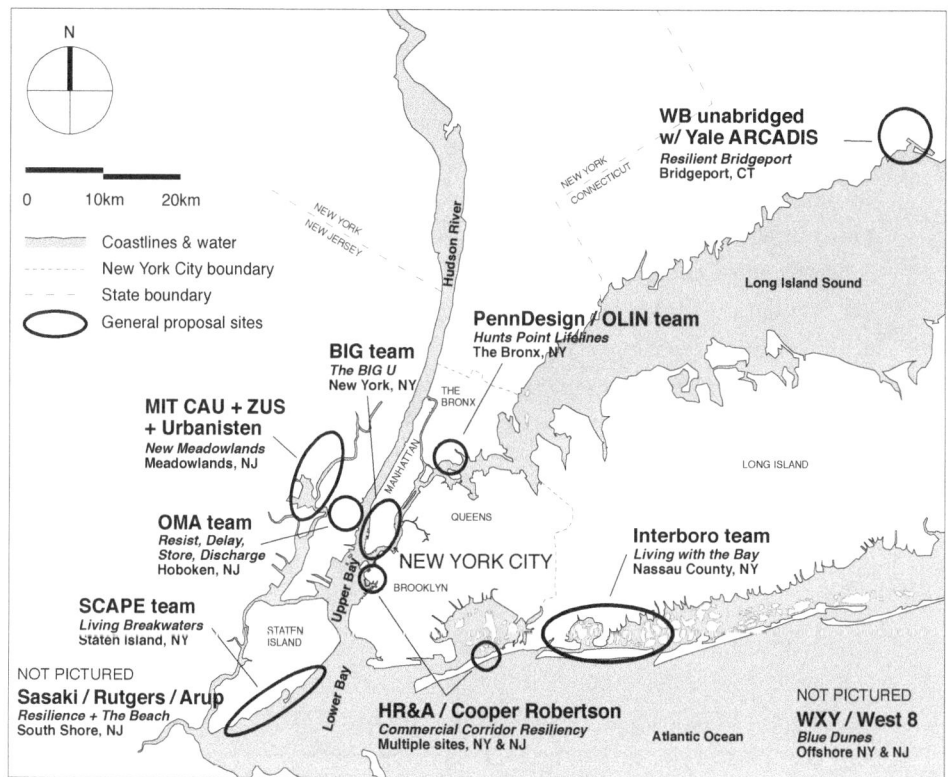

Figure 2.8
Rebuild By Design finalist teams and sites. By author.

and HUD's work were supported by a number of organizations, including the Institute for Public Knowledge at NYU, the Municipal Art Society, the Regional Plan Association, and the Van Alen Institute. The Rockefeller Foundation, a private philanthropic organization, provided a large part of the funding for the initial competition stage. Importantly, the implementation of the design proposals would be funded by $930 million in federal Community Development Block Grants targeted toward disaster recovery (CDBG–DR), allocated to HUD under the Disaster Relief Appropriations Act of 2013.[36] According to Scott Davis, then senior adviser in the Office of the Secretary at HUD, the appropriation language from the US Congress authorizing the HUD secretary to allocate the CDBG funds at her or his discretion was crucial for this step of the process. It enabled, for the first time, the use of a competition to determine the allocation of such funds.[37]

Nancy Kete, then managing director of the Rockefeller Foundation, describes the context in which the philanthropic organization decided to become involved. She cites a number of parallel factors, including ongoing Dutch economic and diplomatic missions, and the initiatives of the White House Office of Science and Technology Policy to invest in innovation and spur competitiveness.[38] "We saw an enormous opportunity with Rebuild by Design to spur something big and to help government innovate,"[39] she says. The foundation's involvement was important for two primary reasons—funding and management. While the federal CDBG funds were allocated for implementation, there were no federal funds for the competition itself. The Rockefeller Foundation was the primary funder for the competition, as well as for setting up the Rebuild By Design organization and hiring staff members. Says Kete, "HUD wasn't able to use federal or public money for anything up until the grant stage. . . . Our support made it possible to use an entirely new approach for postdisaster spends. We added a little bit of structure and back-end organization to make sure that this would work, because it needed strong project management."[40]

Beyond the organizational innovation, there were the challenges of motivation—Why take on the risk?—and the speed at which it had to happen. Kete stresses the extraordinary circumstances:

> It all happened amazingly fast, in part because Dr. [Judith] Rodin—the Rockefeller Foundation's president—had the authority to make a commitment, and also because we knew Secretary Donovan from his previous appointment here in New

York City government. It wasn't clear at the beginning exactly where all this was going to go, everything was moving at a pace I'd not seen before. Everyone felt a sense of urgency, and we knew we were writing a new script as we went along.[41]

Marion McFadden, then deputy assistant secretary for grant programs at HUD, echoes Kete's assessment of the context of Rebuild By Design. She states, "It took an extraordinary amount of work and trust, but . . . it was only possible after a disaster because the kind of compassion and goodwill you get after a disaster is unparalleled anywhere else."[42] However, McFadden as well brings up a critical point about funding, also unique to the moment: "I will say from the federal perspective, on the record, that the states and the local government—at least through my lens—were driven by the fact that there was the potential for big CDBG dollars on the back side."

The specific use of the $930 million in CDBG–DR funds substantially informed the objectives and outlook of the Rebuild By Design competition. While allowing a broad range of recovery activities, these funds are primarily targeted at low-income residents and urgent community development needs.[43] The funds would be allocated to the local municipality after the competition phase. This reinforces the necessity for community engagement, and attention to the worst impacted localities with the least capacity to respond. At the same time, it puts the responsibility to implement these designs squarely in the court of the individual localities after the CDBG funds are allocated, with their varying rules and regulations for doing this. There is no specific mechanism directly linking the competition proposals with the eventual implementation outcomes.

One of the defining characteristics of the Rebuild By Design competition was the relationship between the global—the ten selected finalist teams involved design and engineering firms from around the world (although primarily from the US and Netherlands)—and the local—the localities and municipalities that would be competing to receive the block grants. Amy Chester, manager of Rebuild By Design, recounts the pressure from funders to ensure stakeholder engagement and the challenges of making sure teams understood that they had to win local government and community support in order to have implementable projects, all in a relatively open competition structure: "So how do we take incredibly smart people that are coming from around the world and teach them about our region? . . . How do we prove to them that they need to forget everything they know? And relearn everything."[44]

Rebuild By Design, by many counts, represents an innovative new model for organization and funding. Among the questions it leaves open, unaccounted for, are the effectiveness of the proposals themselves—Will they work?—and the on-the-ground urban politics. Because of the implementation funding structure, the initiative is positioned well to address inequities in the disaster-affected region. However, it is not inevitable at all that the level of engagement expressed by design teams and the competition management results in qualitative change in the way disaster recovery and climate change preparedness are designed and implemented. I explore these possibilities further in chapter 4.

Chester expresses optimism about the community engagement process (in line with the assessment of Damaris Reyes of GOLES). She emphasizes, "Every one of them . . . we told them at the end at their jury presentation you can bring whoever you want, bring your coalition. And they all brought the local mayors and stakeholders and advocates to the jury presentation—as one team."[45]

Jakarta

Kampungs and/in the City

The word "kampung" in Indonesia, directly translated as "village," refers to a fairly variable set of settlements—often informal, often outside or straddling the bounds and regulations of municipal governance. Many have existed from colonial times, but have transformed dramatically in recent decades. In Christopher Silver's history of kampungs in Jakarta, they are described as ethnically and class-defined enclaves, increasingly drawn, spatially and administratively, into the colonial city; cleared or encompassed by urban growth during early 1900s development; increasing in size and density due to mass rural-urban migration, and variously integrated into city administrative systems in the decades following Indonesian independence; and subject to accelerated eviction and demolition in the late decades of the twentieth century.[46] It is estimated that 20–25 percent of Jakarta's residents live in kampungs,[47] largely in social and spatial circumstances that do not fit in with the aspirations of the city's leaders and economic elites for a modern, global city (figures 2.9, 2.10, and 4.2).

Government officials plainly term residents in kampungs "illegal."[48] While this is often in reference to those who live in informal settlements

Figure 2.9
Kampung Bukit Duri, Jakarta, July 2013. Photograph by author.

outside of the longer-established kampung areas, the attitude also reveals the systemic marginalization of the poorest residents of the city. Activists, in response, have pointed out the integration of the kampungs in extensive urban socioeconomic networks, including essential services and food production.[49]

The history of government interventions into the lives and homes of kampung residents has often been brutal, with routine forced evictions.[50] However, it has not been uniformly so. In the 1970s, during President Suharto's New Order, Jakarta undertook the Kampung Improvement Programme (KIP) to modernize infrastructure and services, winning the Aga Khan Award for Architecture in 1980.[51] Groundbreaking in its efforts to minimize the disruption of village settlements within the expanding city, the program focused on the provisioning of hardscape (paved roads and footpaths), water, and sanitation. While in many ways successful, the KIP did not predict the worsening environmental conditions forty years on. Nor did it prevent other threats to the settlements. Kampung areas decreased by

Figure 2.10
Kampung Pulo during a flood, Jakarta, July 2013. Photograph by author.

half in the last two decades of the twentieth century due to rapid urban development and renewal initiatives.[52] The plans to dredge and normalize many of the city's rivers and canals threaten further displacement of residents.[53] Kampungs now face double stress from climate change and increasing floods, and state- and corporate-backed displacement.

Attention to the severe flooding problem in 2013 coincided with rapid political transformation in Jakarta. Joko Widodo (known popularly as Jokowi) won the governorship of DKI Jakarta (the Jakarta Special Capital Region) in late 2012. His rapid rise was astonishing in a country that had fully embraced democracy only in 1998 and in which politicians, as a rule, came from wealthy political families. Jokowi, in both rhetoric and practice, prioritized a new kind of engagement between government and citizens, and a focus on spatial transformation. One of Jokowi's signature projects was to clear an area of kampung settlements in Muara Baru, along Waduk Pluit, a large retention basin in North Jakarta (figure 2.12). This move was ostensibly to dredge the basin and build a park. Rapidly constructed, with fledgling trees propped up, Taman Kota Waduk Pluit (Pluit City Park) became commonly known as "Taman Jokowi," even by kampung residents facing imminent evictions (figure 2.11).[54] The park is widely held as a political win, and a turning point in society-government relations.[55]

While tangible benefits for the urban poor are still in flux, one can discern the change in attitude Jokowi brought to government. Even city officials express some bewilderment at his style, but concede that he seems to be getting things done. "It's not good government, but it's working,"

Figure 2.11
Taman Jokowi, July 2014. Photograph by author.

says Aisa Tobing, chair of the Jakarta Climate Change Task Force, expressing that Jokowi's style of showing up at district offices and visiting project sites doesn't necessarily affirm his trust in city government employees. And yet, "It's working for these two years. Small progress."[56] Jokowi's habit of showing up, and his impromptu walks in various neighborhoods—*blusukan*, a term borrowed from the Javanese language, meaning, "walking around at a grassroots level," as Sylvira Azwar, of the Jakarta Research Council, explained—has shifted public imaginations about government for the better.[57]

Only two years into his governorship of Jakarta, Jokowi launched a campaign for the presidency of Indonesia. On July 9, 2014, he won, beating retired Lieutenant General Prabowo Subianto in highly factious national elections. Jokowi was officially sworn in as president of Indonesia on October 20, 2014.

Kampung Activism: Urban Poor Consortium and Ciliwung Merdeka

Even in the context of a brightening relationship with the city governor, local community organizations including the Urban Poor Consortium (UPC) and Ciliwung Merdeka (literally, "Free Ciliwung") have continued to resist the eviction of kampung residents and plans for relocation. In Muara Baru, North Jakarta, UPC, working with community architects and students from the University of Indonesia, forged a working agreement with Governor Jokowi for a new, more socially attuned social housing scheme (modern housing blocks with kampung-like formal and social characteristics), as well as a commitment to rehousing within the area for residents impacted by further evictions (figures 2.12 and 2.13)

Explaining these successes, the late Edi Saidi,[58] then coordinator of UPC, stressed the organization's three-pronged strategy, based on, first, "organizing from below . . . collective cooperation"; second, advocacy to make constituents aware of the broader issues and city rules that impact their lives; and third, coalition building and networking, bringing together various knowledge disciplines, including architecture and environment.[59] He voiced optimism about continued progress in the Muara Baru and Waduk Pluit area, and stressed the change in process he observed. I quote Saidi at length:

> In the past, the government models have been "top down." There has never been dialogue, never had participation, never had discussions with the residents. What happens, then, is that the design of the housing offered to residents could

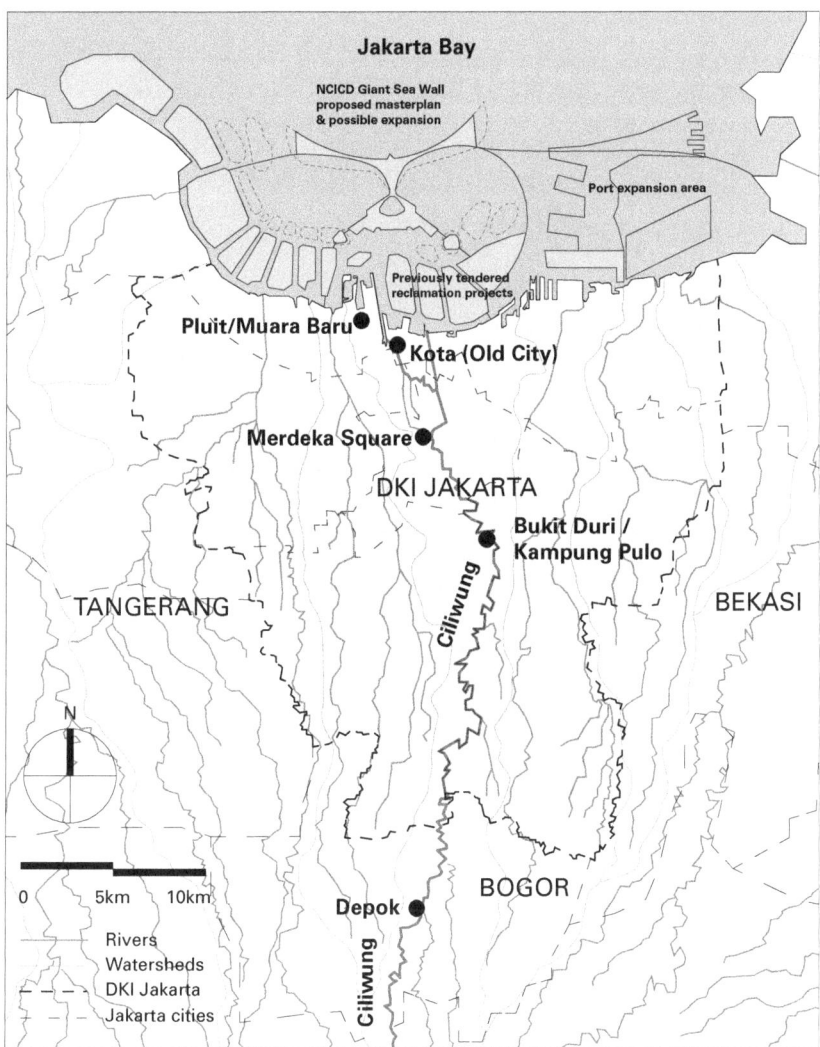

Figure 2.12
Map of Jakarta showing kampungs in relation to city landmarks and the proposed National Capital Integrated Coastal Development (NCICD) Giant Sea Wall masterplan. By author.

Figure 2.13
Organizers from Urban Poor Consortium (UPC) and Muara Baru residents, July 2013. Photograph by author.

never be a long-term prospect. In the past, residents from the area were moved to Marunda [20 kilometers away, the northeast edge of DKI]. . . . Residents were simply evicted, and forced to move. At the end . . . the residents only stayed there three months . . . three months! . . . Finally, the residents returned to where they came from. Because there wasn't any process, dialogue, or discussion. . . . I think that's different from the process happening now in Waduk Pluit. There, we have process for dialogue, participation, as well as a longer-term view; a model of housing that meets their desires and needs.

. . . Because it meets their needs, they will accept it. Location is important. The residents propose locations around the waduk, because they work around here . . . in the fishing industry.[60]

Saidi, noting that the previous city governments were "antidialogue," continued,

It's a win-win solution. The government will have an easier job, because residents won't have to be forced. They won't have to be evicted. They'll do it voluntarily. And there's a guarantee too . . . that they'll have a place [in the new housing

Nature of Contestation

nearby]. Therefore, both sides profit. The government will achieve their objectives to normalize the rivers, and the residents will have the security of a place to stay.[61]

Asked if Jokowi's imminent presidency would change anything, he expressed conviction that UPC's agreement with the governor would hold fast through leadership change and bureaucracy, and that then deputy governor Ahok would take on the responsibility of pushing forward the agreements and concepts.[62] Concrete results in Muara Baru have been spotty. In mid-2014, several new low-income housing blocks were completed, with several others under construction nearby. The new, more participatory housing typologies have yet to be seen.

Ciliwung Merdeka organizes residents in Bukit Duri and Kampung Pulo (figures 2.12 and 2.14), two kampungs that straddle a particularly flood-prone bend along the Ciliwung River in Central Jakarta, and that are facing imminent relocation (figure 2.15). Governor Jokowi had promised to visit Bukit Duri before the election for the governorship, a testament to his

Figure 2.14
Ciliwung Merdeka with designers, researchers, and Bukit Duri residents, July 2013. Photograph by author.

Figure 2.15
Ciliwung River at Jatinegara, Central Jakarta, during a flood on July 22, 2013. Kampung Pulo is on the left of the river, Bukit Duri is on the right. Photograph by author.

proclaimed populist agenda. During his meeting with kampung residents, Jokowi promised that he would support their alternative housing proposal under three conditions: that it would have majority kampung resident support, be inexpensive, and not go against city regulations.[63] The third stipulation is complicated. National government and city officials state that the rivers, including the Ciliwung, have to be dredged to 50 meters wide, with 7.5-meter easements, dimensions that would dramatically impact places like Bukit Duri and Kampung Pulo. Community organizers have continued these talks with the governor, pressing their case for alternative solutions, including conducting their own assessment of safety easement widths along the river and producing designs for new typologies of river-edge housing and rehousing in place.

Ciliwung Merdeka leader Sandyawan Sumardi explains the motivations behind the group's work, attesting to the economic relationships stemming from local kampung businesses, and the "extraordinary social model" of the kampungs. He voices frustration and optimism in the group's dealings with city government. On the one hand, Sumardi's group has had productive meetings with the governor—including his promise of support for their plans. On the other hand, he states that the process has been uncertain and unclear, and that there are disagreements and power struggles between branches of government, as well as infighting, a "pattern of conflict." In particular, Sumardi takes issue with the national Ministry of Public Works and Housing, stating that it is intent on building "megaprojects" along the river.[64]

These community-led "counterplans" by UPC and Ciliwung Merdeka and their coalitions have had some impact on public awareness and debate, including local and international media (see chapter 4). Both coalitions' designs were included in Jakarta Vertical Kampung, an international exhibition held at the Dutch embassy in 2013. At the same time, it must be noted that these two kampung areas are particularly high-profile cases, in which organizers and residents have succeeded in building substantial activist coalitions and attracted the attention of international researchers and practitioners. They are the exceptions.

2007 Flood to the Great Garuda

Jakarta's struggles with infrastructure and water likely began the first time Dutch rulers built a canal in the colonial city of Batavia. The history of Dutch control of Indonesian people and places has been long and often deplorable. Contemporary Jakarta still very much exhibits the social, spatial, and technological legacy of more than 300 years of Dutch colonization.[65] It is, in many ways, an arbitrary decision to pick up this story at a particular point in time. Yet, 2007 presented a decisive moment. That year, another devastating flood that inundated 40 percent of the city precipitated a series of developments that ultimately led to Dutch minister Melanie Schultz's unveiling of the Great Garuda plan in 2014. Hydrologists from Dutch research institute Deltares, surprised at the water level during the 2007 flood—faster than sea-level rise projections—conducted a flood hazard mapping study, and concluded that severe subsidence was dramatically exacerbating flooding conditions.[66] The "sinking city" was courting disaster.

These findings led to the Jakarta Coastal Defense Strategy (JCDS), a joint study by the Indonesian and Netherlands governments, developed by a team of consultants led by Deltares (figure 2.16). The Indonesian coordinating body for the JCDS was the Kementerian Pekerjaan Umum (PU), the

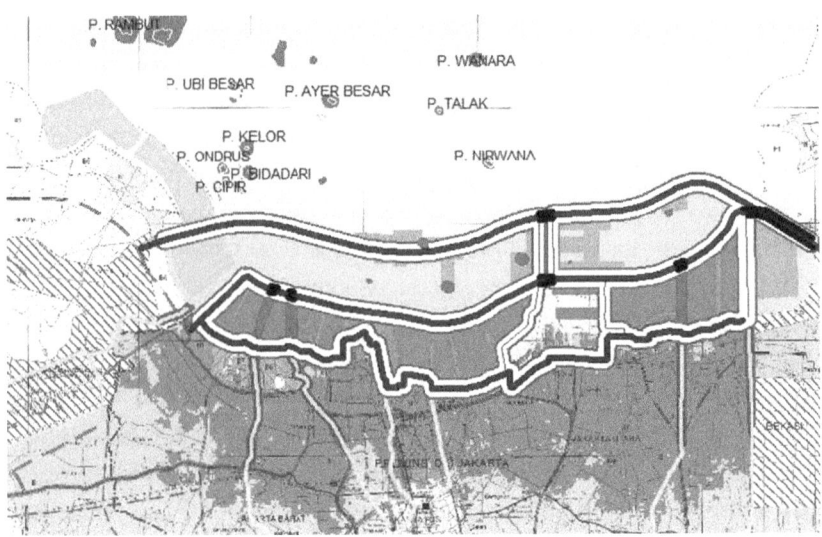

Figure 2.16
Jakarta Coastal Defense Strategy (JCDS) diagram. Bold dark lines show proposed sea walls.
Source: Indonesia, Ministry of Public Works (2011).

public works ministry.[67] The team completed its work in September 2011. The JCDS report is an extensive and detailed study of Jakarta's flooding problems. It includes hydrological conditions, social and economic ties, infrastructural networks, and governance institutions in the metropolitan region. Directed toward coastal defenses, it includes key ideas about water protections and management, including a series of parallel sea walls far into the Jakarta Bay and vast areas for water retention, making room for the water coming down along the rivers.

The findings and concepts contained in JCDS served as the foundation for the development of the National Capital Integrated Coastal Development (NCICD) masterplan in 2014, known both as the Giant Sea Wall and the Great Garuda masterplan (figure 2.17). Again it was a joint project of the Netherlands and Indonesian governments, and financed by the Dutch, though the coordinating body on the Indonesian side is the Coordinating Ministry for Economic Affairs (MENKO).[68] The consultant team is led by Witteveen+Bos and Grontmij (now Sweco), two infrastructure and urban development firms, with support from KuiperCompagnons (urban design and landscape architecture), Ecorys (an economic development agency),

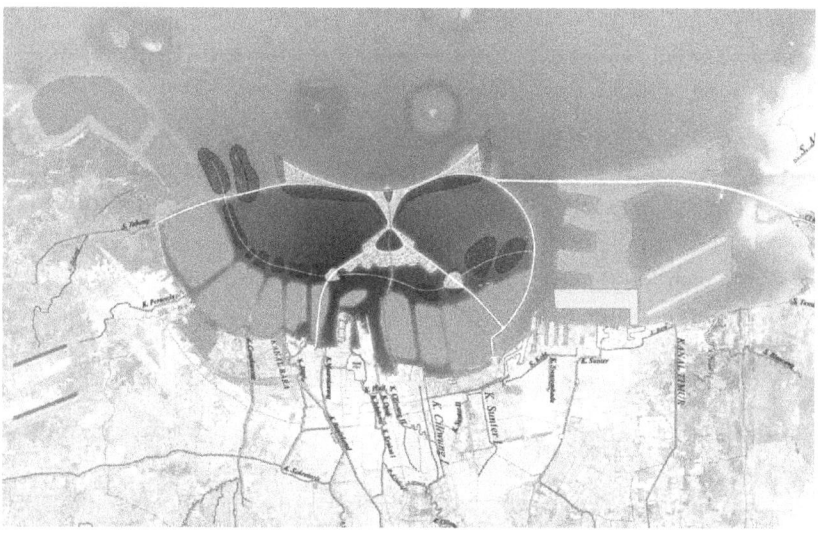

Figure 2.17
NCICD Giant Sea Wall plan. Thin light lines show the proposed sea walls along a "winged" form and retention lakes between the outer walls and coastline.
Source: Indonesia, MENKO (2014).

Deltares, and Triple-A (Indonesian counterparts). The NCICD plan develops the concept of a sea wall with new reclaimed and leasable land behind it—the figure of the Garuda—in order to raise capital for the construction. The plan is meant to pay for itself through private real estate development. Besides flood protection, the plan includes proposals for multimodal transportation, a new financial district, civic spaces and parks, and massive freshwater reservoirs behind the wings of the Garuda, into which Jakarta's rivers and canals will drain.

The reasons for the shift from a Jakarta focus to a national focus in the NCICD plan are ostensibly practical and symbolic. In practical terms, the proposed plan includes upgrades to port facilities and transportation infrastructure that are under a national purview. Symbolically, it enables the national government to take charge of a large-scale project, particularly as an economic development plan. One of the Dutch consultants involved in the hydrological research opined that the embrace of the Jakarta flood masterplan as a national project was also motivated by politics.[69] Jokowi had just been elected governor of DKI Jakarta, with rumors about a possible presidential run. The national government, at that point led by a rival party, did not want Jokowi to be able to take the credit for an important, symbolically powerful project.[70] A member of the DKI government, in an informal conversation, also corroborated the political motivations behind this shift.

Hydrologically, the masterplan is remarkable. Flooding in Jakarta comes from two sources, the sea and the rivers. The solution, therefore, involves stopping the sea from entering the city, and allowing the rivers to drain out. The team proposed a set of no-regrets measures, designed to stop overtopping of flood protections in the near future. It then offered three long-term options: (1) retreat from North Jakarta, relocating 4.5 million people; (2) onshore protections, including elevated sea wall and dikes along rivers, and retention lakes within the city totaling 10,000 hectares; and (3) a giant sea wall offshore, with retention lakes between the new sea wall and the existing coast. Conceptually, after the outer sea wall is closed, the water in the lakes will be lowered, enabling the rivers and canals to better drain into them.[71] Presented with these options, the Indonesian officials decided to proceed with the third, most extensive one.

Four aspects of the plan are worth elaborating. First, the draft masterplan acknowledges but does not include in its scope a suite of very large reclamation island projects that would line the north shore of the city. The team was explicitly told that these reclamation projects were already tendered and would not be changed or included in the new masterplan.[72] Second, the plan, particularly the creation of freshwater reservoirs in what is now the middle of the Jakarta Bay, depends on the city's ability both to stop land subsidence and clean its clogged rivers and canals. These objectives have proven difficult to accomplish in the past, and it remains to be seen whether and how this will be accomplished now. Third, the scale of the masterplan ensures disruption to local ecologies and socioeconomic networks. The plan includes narratives about replenishing mangroves and wetlands, as well as social housing (30 percent of the Garuda plan, as stated in the masterplan) and the relocation of fishermen and fishing markets from impacted coastal areas. But details about the social housing and relocation are not clear. Fourth, the implementation of the plan is fully dependent on private investment in the reclaimed land. The masterplan team has embraced a "flexible" approach. While there are concrete dates specified, like the proposed 2022 closing of the sea wall, the final shape and size of the Garuda would depend on the pace of real estate development.

The ambitious objective of turning the retention lakes into freshwater reservoirs is necessarily tied to other infrastructural projects currently under way, including the World Bank–funded Jakarta Urgent Flood Mitigation Project / Jakarta Emergency Dredging Initiative (JUFMP/JEDI) to dredge and channelize canals throughout the capital region, a masterplan conducted by the Japan International Cooperation Agency (JICA), and projects by the Ministry of Public Works to normalize and widen the Ciliwung River. This presents a significant challenge. According to Fook Chuan Eng, senior water and sanitation specialist at the World Bank in Jakarta, their dredging projects will only proceed when the city succeeds in relocating residents out of the many affected areas.[73]

As an intervention into land and environmental politics, the Giant Sea Wall masterplan resituates the arena of debate—literally outside the current city. At first glance, it could be considered the latest in the line of urban development phases that turn their back on the old city and leave it behind—"creative destruction" via adaptation.[74] Yet, its objectives are wholly tied to social and spatial changes back onshore. The pressure to proceed with the plan—a plan—will undoubtedly accelerate evictions along canals and rivers that are affected by the dredging and normalization projects.[75]

For activists like UPC and Ciliwung Merdeka, after organizing around concrete issues such as easement widths and rights-of-way, building heights, and ownership terms, the Giant Sea Wall presents a new front to their work that is somewhat abstract and distant. Its impacts on their constituents are not immediately tangible. For other groups, such as Rujak Center for Urban Studies, an urban research and advocacy center that frequently collaborates with community organizers in the kampungs, this expanded terrain now demands research not only on the infrastructure and relocation plans that directly impact kampung residents but also on the masterplans, technical reports on subsidence, flooding, and reclamation, and even broader issues such as the national laws on the permitting of sand to be used for reclamation. Activists and researchers specifically question the masterplan's basis of "knowing" what the real problem is and how to fix it. To Dian Tri Irawaty, formerly of Rujak, the Giant Sea Wall effort is entirely in line with the city government's efforts, ongoing since 1995, to encourage privatized development along the bay, often on reclaimed land (figure 2.18). The environmental scenarios, in her mind, are justifications for imposing the development plan, and the promises in the masterplan about social housing and relocation of fishermen are means of deflecting criticism.[76]

The iconic figure of the "Great Garuda" poses additional complexities. It is easy—literally by design—to visualize the massive bird-shaped new city in the bay. It is somewhat more difficult to visualize the impact of dredging and normalization along the rivers and canals. What is the difference between 35 feet versus 50 feet of river clearance? How do you "see" that impact in the dense kampung neighborhoods in which the river's boundary conditions are not always so distinct?[77]

The Giant Sea Wall masterplan is only partially a plan to keep out the rising sea. Its primary technical objective, from a protective infrastructure point of view, is to deal with the sinking city. Deltares hydrologists have asserted since the study carried out after the 2007 floods that the key threat to Jakarta comes from land subsidence.[78] Sea-level rise and stronger, more unpredictable storms will exacerbate the situation. Projected sea-level rise, as Kees Bons of Deltares states, falls within the margin of uncertainty of

Figure 2.18
Looking out over the Jakarta Bay, with the towers of Pantai Mutiara, an earlier gated development on reclaimed land, on the left, May 2017. Photograph by author.

subsidence.⁷⁹ Yet many media stories of the masterplan have stressed climate change as a motivator. Bons himself acknowledges that the invocation of climate change is the most effective way to garner attention for funding both nationally and internationally. By most accounts, subsidence in Jakarta is caused by overextraction of groundwater, a particularly acute problem in the city because of its ineffective municipal water system.⁸⁰ This condition worsens as rapid urban development continues. It is easy to see the irony—development is the problem, and, in this case, development is posed as the solution.

It would be a mistake to say that the progenitors of the plans are always their most ardent supporters. Deltares was a primary actor in evaluating the 2007 floods and authoring the 2012 JCDS plan, and now plays a supporting role in the NCICD masterplan. Well aware of the difficulty and expense of a large-scale hydrological feat such as closing off the retention lakes from the sea, Bons says, "So, just that it can be done doesn't mean that it has to be done. . . . We try to do everything not to close . . . because it's the unsustainable solution."⁸¹

Marginalization and Urban Environmental Change

The dominant state-led environmental plans in New York and Jakarta reflect the existing urban economic and sociospatial systems in which they are embedded. Rebuild By Design in New York, while created via an innovative set of mechanisms—meshing private philanthropy, targeted federal aid, and new transnational relationships—still relies on and works through a set of planning principles that are particular to the United States. It is posed as a regional initiative, but it is not comprehensively so. The funding structure of Rebuild By Design—the use of CDBG–DR funds for the implementation phase—guarantees that the individual proposals will be constrained to specific localities. The funding, often a fraction of what is necessary to implement the full scope of the plans, is intended to spur further local government funding and private investment. The objectives are ambitious, the process novel, but the overall arc fits well within the preferred mode of urban governance—each municipality to its own, increasingly reliant on public-private partnerships for large-scale planning initiatives.

Both the impacts of climate change and the making of resilience plans accentuate longstanding challenges and highlight ongoing struggles, sometimes precipitating new modes of community resilience. Organizations such as RHI and GOLES look to their histories of building community social relationships, as well as embarking on new paths, with RHI relying on and extending its social networks for mutual aid activities in the wake of the storm, and GOLES building a broader coalition on the strength of its organizing history and relationships.

In Jakarta, the NCICD masterplan is ambitious and grand in urban and environmental design, and in infrastructural terms. It is equally ambitious in its intent to capture very large-scale private investment in order to carry out the vision, in line with recent trends in urban development in the city and region. As massive as the plan is, its authors designed it to be implementable in phases, with variable end configurations, linked to levels of protection, and to the extent of real estate buy-in. Like many of Jakarta's other large-scale projects—the toll highways, stalled monorail, and canal dredging—it cannot be said to be comprehensive. The masterplan of the new reclaimed city proposes solving many problems, but it also says little about a barrage of other problems—both social and infrastructural—back on land.

As political circumstances shift in Jakarta, so has the nature of contestation changed. Community leaders like Edi Saidi of UPC and Sandyawan Sumardi of Ciliwung Merdeka agree that this is a better situation than it has been in the past. Governor Jokowi's tenure enabled more open and effective lines of communication between residents and city government, and the possibility of significant agreements. Yet Jokowi too continued the push for privatized urban development, as did Basuki Tjahaja Purnama (Ahok), his successor as governor of Jakarta. These leaders as well govern a city that is sprawling in both physical space and bureaucracy. As Sumardi states, the fragmented nature of governance in Jakarta and the often unsynchronized actions between levels of government remain significant hurdles.

In both New York and Jakarta, climate change has indeed changed the situation. In New York, Hurricane Sandy prompted the focus on issues of resilience, and reinvigorated discussions on climate change. Sandy was a "tipping point," as Cynthia Rosenzweig, co-chair of the New York City Panel on Climate Change (NPCC) recounts, which led Mayor Michael Bloomberg's team to contact Rosenzweig to reconvene the NPCC and update the climate projections for the city. Beyond the science, the wake of Sandy and the prospects of greater risks arguably paved the way toward different structures of organization. The Hurricane Sandy Rebuilding Task Force's "Hurricane

Sandy Rebuilding Strategy" report explicitly focuses on existing threats and those related to future climate change.[82] Rebuild By Design, launched by the task force, has clearly helped put not only design but also climate change in government and public focus.

In Jakarta, the 2007 and 2013 floods brought on the specter of (at least partially climate-induced) environmental catastrophe for the city. This realization is entangled with the long-running objectives to change the narrative of the city, to build, in this case, a world-class waterfront and riverfronts befitting a global city. What remains ongoing is how organizations such as UPC and Ciliwung Merdeka continue their fights on a local community level in the face of new kinds of threats that emerge across an extended spatial and scalar terrain. These include, now, both the actual impacts of climate change and environmental catastrophe and also the invocations of such threats, the powerful narratives of urgency that drive projects such as the Giant Sea Wall.

Spatial marginalization is inextricably intertwined with the impacts of urban environmental change in both New York and Jakarta. This is not always because of geographical conditions, for example, low-lying coastal conditions, but also by the socioeconomic factors that accompany such spatial differentiation. In Red Hook and the Lower East Side in New York the location of public housing areas exacerbated the impacts following Hurricane Sandy, particularly with problems of access during the immediate recovery period, and with longer-term repair and maintenance issues. The scale and concentration of housing projects in these two neighborhoods contributed to the marked susceptibility of their residents. In Jakarta, many at-risk kampung areas are located in precisely those places that are most susceptible to flooding, perched on riverbanks or along retention basins and the coastal floodwall. In places like Muara Baru in North Jakarta, and in Bukit Duri and Kampung Pulo along the Ciliwung in Central Jakarta, the continual influx of migrants to the city, coupled with the pressures of development on the shrinking kampungs, have resulted in increasingly precarious conditions, socially and physically.

Of course, marginalization in New York and Jakarta are quite different. New York does not exhibit the same scope of informality that one finds in Jakarta (even though there are clearly informal living situations, contributing, for example, to the suggested undercounting of residents in public housing in Red Hook). Conversely, even though class and economic struggles play out in very real ways, the urban poor in Jakarta's kampungs do not face the kind of systemic racism and violence that plague many residents of New York's public housing and poorer neighborhoods. At the same time, both cities exhibit increasing socioeconomic and spatial inequities in the face of rapid urban and economic development, and both have a stated imperative to address socioenvironmental issues with "green" projects.

In terms of resistance to and organizing against marginalization, three critical points are common across the sites in New York and Jakarta. These are the relationship between shared struggle and resilience, the organization of local knowledge, and the building of broad-based coalitions.

Shared Struggle and Resilience

First, a collective understanding of shared struggle matters. Histories of marginalization and organizing against marginalization have been central to the potential for social and environmental resilience in Red Hook and the Lower East Side in New York, and in the kampungs of Jakarta. Jill Eisenhard's observations about RHI staff members' shared experiences in facing adversity explain how they were able to respond quickly and effectively immediately after Hurricane Sandy. Damaris Reyes echoes this in her thoughts about the role of GOLES's long-term struggles for housing rights in the Lower East Side and how the organization's reputation as rabble-rousers—born of a willingness to pursue contentious political action—became an asset in organizing a broader community coalition.

In Jakarta, poor urban residents face a withering onslaught: uncertain tenure rights, rampant and rapid urban development, increasing environmental threats, and social stigma. These oppressions continue even with repeated observations that stress the social and economic vitality of kampungs, their integral but often less visible ties to the fabric of the city. And yet, there exists long-running, cohesive organization among kampung activists and residents against the threats they face. In the key examples of Muara Baru, Bukit Duri, and Kampung Pulo—kampung areas facing the most immediate and disruptive evictions—UPC and Ciliwung Merdeka succeeded in partially resisting or delaying demolition, putting together coalitions and proposing community-led alternatives, and maintaining effective lines of communication with city authorities. This resistance is based at least in part on the shared struggles, constituted spatially and socially, faced by kampung residents.

We often talk of low-income housing in the United States, particularly public housing projects, in terms of segregation and isolation, and view it as something of an anachronism at a time when privately developed, mixed-income projects are the norm. We also often hear about the resilience of poor people confronting adversity. But these examples suggest a more proactive, positive (in its definition of affirmative or inclusive) approach to weaving together social and environmental resilience. It will not do to fetishize poverty or oppression, but it is critical to know how solidarity emerges from a collective understanding of shared histories of marginalization.

Importantly, this understanding of collective struggle and shared history offers a way to consider physical *form*—both urban form and settlement form—as a part of social and environmental resilience. Aspects of form in discussions of resilience have so far resided largely in building structure and technology, landscape ecologies, and infrastructure. Eisenhard of RHI emphasizes on multiple occasions that it is the *place-based* nature of the organization's community building that matters.[83] RHI's constituents' *location*—spatially and physically among the Red Hook Houses, a public housing form that is by design bounded and territorially specific—and *position*—with the socioeconomic and cultural context of public housing residents in a gentrifying southwest Brooklyn—are interrelated, functioning together as formative pieces of community-based social and environmental resilience.

Local Knowledge
Second, the organization of local knowledge is significant and powerful. In New York, this is particularly the case in the days immediately following a disaster like Hurricane Sandy. Eisenhard's statements about FEMA's and government officials' reliance on RHI staff members to lead them around the neighborhood and Reyes's realization about the need for coordination among the many long-running community groups in the Lower East Side illustrate two aspects of this. In Jakarta, the local knowledge integral to the kampungs—particularly how kampung residents, historically marginalized and in many ways made invisible in the modern city, are essential parts of important social and economic networks—largely forms the basis for organizers' deliberations with government officials. Activists, too, consistently

invoke the *lack* of attention to such local knowledge in their resistance to the Giant Sea Wall plan.

These examples offer a powerful yet not complete response to Sheila Jasanoff's assertion about the discordances between abstract scientific and specific experienced climate knowledge.[84] Here, local, embodied, and experienced knowledge forms not only the basis for knowing the problem but also the grounds for resistance and alternative views. But they are not necessarily sufficient on their own. Among the kampung activists in Jakarta, such knowledge and actions are augmented by the advocacy-oriented research work done by Rujak, which collects, synthesizes, and disseminates broader, often more abstract levels of knowledge in close collaboration with activists who are part of pro-poor organizing groups. The frameworks for broader and more generalized knowledge production and dissemination, often involving researchers and networks far beyond the localities most at risk, are critical for the building of local knowledge as a part of organizing and resistance.

Coalition Building

Third, forming broad-based coalitions is critical. In Red Hook, RHI's Red Hook WiFi exemplifies one manner of this work. The broadband access project was launched on a very local level, developed through community participation and the partnership of a technology and information nonprofit organization, transformed in imagination and significance by a major disaster event, which then led to the development of more sustained organizational capacity for broader and longer-term change. The work of Reyes of GOLES, in the Lower East Side, exemplifies another. There she mobilized LES Ready as a proactive coalition-building initiative based on her organization's experiences during the initial chaos wrought by Hurricane Sandy. She recognized that the preponderance of community-based groups in the neighborhood would not alleviate confusion without such a coalition.

In Jakarta, UPC and Ciliwung Merdeka have been particularly effective at forming broad, diverse coalitions. These include local community designers, academics, students, and policy advocates. as well as researchers from around the world, whose engagement with the community organizers on the ground in Jakarta reinforces global attention to the political conflicts underlying issues of flooding. This ability has been important in building knowledge, developing awareness, and maintaining the coalitions' struggles through news cycles and political shifts. The attention and engagement necessary for coalition building have no doubt been aided by the high-profile nature of the flooding and social conditions in the city. For example, backlit photographs of kampung houses along the Ciliwung adorn the walls of the International Architecture Biennale Rotterdam, presented as a kind of Ground Zero of one extreme of the global urban condition. The "picturesque" "slums" combined with the dramatic deluge have proven to be irresistible to media, advocates, researchers, and designers alike, a kind of "disaster scenography." While this long-emerging phenomenon brings attention and effort to just causes, it also represents, at its core, the objectification of struggles and the reification of dominant worldviews about megacities of the Global South.

This dual condition of visibility and objectification in the face of social and environmental challenges and struggles demands some caution and critical assessment on the part of both activists who are fighting for communities on the ground and researchers who are looking for critical cases of resistance. And yet there are sustained and hopeful movements in New York and Jakarta. In all, the three points in common here—the shared struggle, local knowledge, and coalition building—depict complex terrains of contestation incited by and in response to the new conditions brought forth by urban climate change impacts and planning actions. These movements' dynamics are reflexive: inward and outward, shared and outreached. Looking from the rather disparate urban sites facing some parallel shifts in urban development and environment planning, they together offer a more generalized notion of collectivity, knowledge, and movement building.

3   Nature of Flows

Declaiming Waters none may dread—
But Waters that are still
Are so for that most fatal cause
In Nature—they are full—
—Emily Dickinson

Why, how, and under what conditions do interconnections among sites and cities form? One of the remarkable things about this story—and increasingly others like it—is the role of the Dutch. Dutch infrastructure planners, hydrologists and engineers, architects, urban designers, and landscape architects, and economic development consultants are extensively involved in New York and Jakarta. They are as well in many other parts of the world, including New Orleans, Ho Chi Minh City, and Dhaka, all places facing significant climate and water challenges. Urban climate change adaptation plans, although often associated with a specific "city" and involving a bounded physical geography, are produced in the context of spatial, political, and economic relationships that span multiple scales and levels. This chapter explores the ways in which large-scale adaptation plans are conceptualized. Who is behind them, and who stands to benefit? It focuses primarily on the actors, entities, and networks involved in the production of these plans.

Cursory studies of Rebuild By Design and the Giant Sea Wall reveal the extent of Dutch involvement. A key figure in the New York efforts is Henk Ovink, principle of Rebuild By Design and senior advisor to HUD secretary Donovan in the Hurricane Sandy Rebuilding Task Force. Ovink was formerly director general of spatial planning and water affairs in the

Netherlands. He led Secretary Donovan on a tour of water management projects in the Netherlands after Sandy. No fewer than six of the ten teams participating in Rebuild By Design included Dutch designers and engineers. The cause of the 2007 Jakarta floods, attributed to severe land subsidence, was determined in part by Deltares, a Dutch consulting firm and research institute involved in water management projects around the world. The NCICD Giant Sea Wall masterplan in Jakarta, funded by the Dutch government, was authored primarily by Dutch engineering, design, and economic development firms (table 3.1).

The triangulation between the three countries was completed when, in September 2014, the Netherlands Water Partnership (NWP), a business development coalition of public and private entities, organized a trip for a delegation from Indonesia to visit New York and New Orleans to learn

Table 3.1

Table of actors in Rebuild By Design and Jakarta NCICD Masterplan

Strategy	Rebuild By Design	Jakarta NCICD Masterplan
Site(s)	Multiple sites, New York metro region, USA	North coast of Jakarta metro region, Indonesia
Coordinating body	US Department of Housing and Urban Development	Coordinating Ministry for Economic Affairs, Indonesia
Primary actors*	Primary RBD staff: **Henk Ovink** (principal), Amy Chester (managing director), Eric Klinenberg (research director) Finalist design teams: **BIG** team, HR&A Advisors Inc. with Cooper, Robertston & Partners team, **Interboro** team, **MIT CAU+ZUS+URBANISTEN** team, **OMA** team, PennDesign/Olin team, Sasaki/Rutgers/Arup team SCAPE team, **WB unabridged with Yale Arcadis** team, **WXY/WEST 8** team	Masterplan team: **Witteveen+Bos** (engineering/consulting), **Grontmij** (engineering, now Sweco), **KuiperCompagnons** (urban/landscape design), **Ecorys** (economic/social research), Triple-A, **Deltares** Program management unit: **Royal Haskoning** (engineering/management), **Rebel Group** (economic advising), **UNESCO-IHE****

* **Bold** denotes teams and firms with Dutch participants or of Dutch origin, or Dutch individuals, see detailed description later this chapter.
** Institute for Water Education, part of UNESCO, but based in Delft, Netherlands, established jointly by UNESCO and the government of the Netherlands.

about adaptation projects. Officials from both American cities and HUD as well as representatives from the Rockefeller Foundation were part of this trip.[1]

How might we understand the relationships between the actors, institutions, and physical places of the Netherlands, renowned for spatial planning and water management, and sites of environmental challenges and adaptation initiatives in New York and Jakarta? This chapter extends theories of "relational geographies" to probe the conceptual and material landscapes of global and urban interconnectivities in the context of climate change and globalized urban development. I trace the development of emerging urban environmental plans and propose the concept of a "network formation" to understand relationships that bridge geographic scales and institutional levels. I argue that these emerging networks form in response to shifting political-economic and environmental conditions to mobilize ideas and influence across sites and boundaries. They build on economic relationships, including promises of economic growth, situational relationships, defined by historical bases of knowledge and power, and specific interface conditions, including narratives of culture and environmental urgency.

Multiscalar Multilevel Interconnections

Nation State to the World
The Netherlands has embarked on a concerted effort to promote its urban water expertise. The reasons for this are rooted in political-economic and ecological conditions at home and globally.

Much of the physical environment of the Netherlands is constructed, reclaimed from drained peat bogs and shallow seas. Almost a third of the country is under sea level, with another third requiring protections from river flooding. Historically, the region known as the Low Countries has accomplished this massive reorganization of land and water through the "polder" system, a collective social, environmental, and spatial framework through which groups of farmers contribute toward the drainage and maintenance of an area of land. The determinants of this interactive system between technology (wind-driven pumps), measures of land, and the efficient planning and construction of drainage channels and canals result in the familiar traditional polder geography, contributing to the "culture of order" of the Dutch landscape.[2] This "moral geography"[3] arising from the ongoing struggle to retain control over the environment is a key factor in the making of Dutch national identity.[4] Spatial planning is central to nation building. The Netherlands is held to be the most planned country in Europe.[5]

The region has had some form of this collective water management since 1250, when the first regional "water boards" were formed to facilitate the management of hydrological systems, with increasingly extensive and centralized flood protections and drainage infrastructure over the next 700 years.[6] The destruction caused by the 1953 North Sea flood, however, galvanized the country into even more ambitious protection schemes. In total, 1,836 people died in the Netherlands due to this flood, and 136,500 hectares of land were inundated.[7] The Delta Commission was formed, tasked with protecting the country from future disasters.[8] Based on the commission's reports, the country embarked on the Delta Works, a series of monumental dikes, sluices, dams, and storm barriers in the southwest delta region of the country (figure 3.1). These projects culminated in the Maeslant storm surge barrier in 1997 along the Nieuwe Waterweg (New Waterway) in Rotterdam (figure 3.2).[9] The Delta Plan required protection levels for a 10,000-year storm event for the most critical, highly populated areas.[10]

"No one, not living in the Low Countries and not having studied their history, can understand the struggle these placid lands have had." The words of hydraulic engineer Johan van Veen, considered to be the "father" of the Delta Works, attest to the deceptive nature of the Dutch landscape.[11] Planning for water management in the Netherlands, particularly in the wake of the 1953 flood, has been controlled by the national government in conjunction with the regional water boards.[12] It has focused, historically, on hard infrastructure and feats of hydrological engineering—"dredge, drain, reclaim."[13]

Two factors have shifted this. The first is economic restructuring in the face of stagnating growth and uncertain economic futures. National initiatives to liberalize the economy have decentralized decision making around spatial planning and urban development, leading to more locally coordinated, market-driven approaches.[14] There is now a stated *de-emphasis* by the national government on urban planning and design, leaving the "balancing of urban and green space development" to provincial and municipal authorities.[15] In 2008, the effects of the global financial crisis reached the Netherlands, precipitating an economic contraction that was very

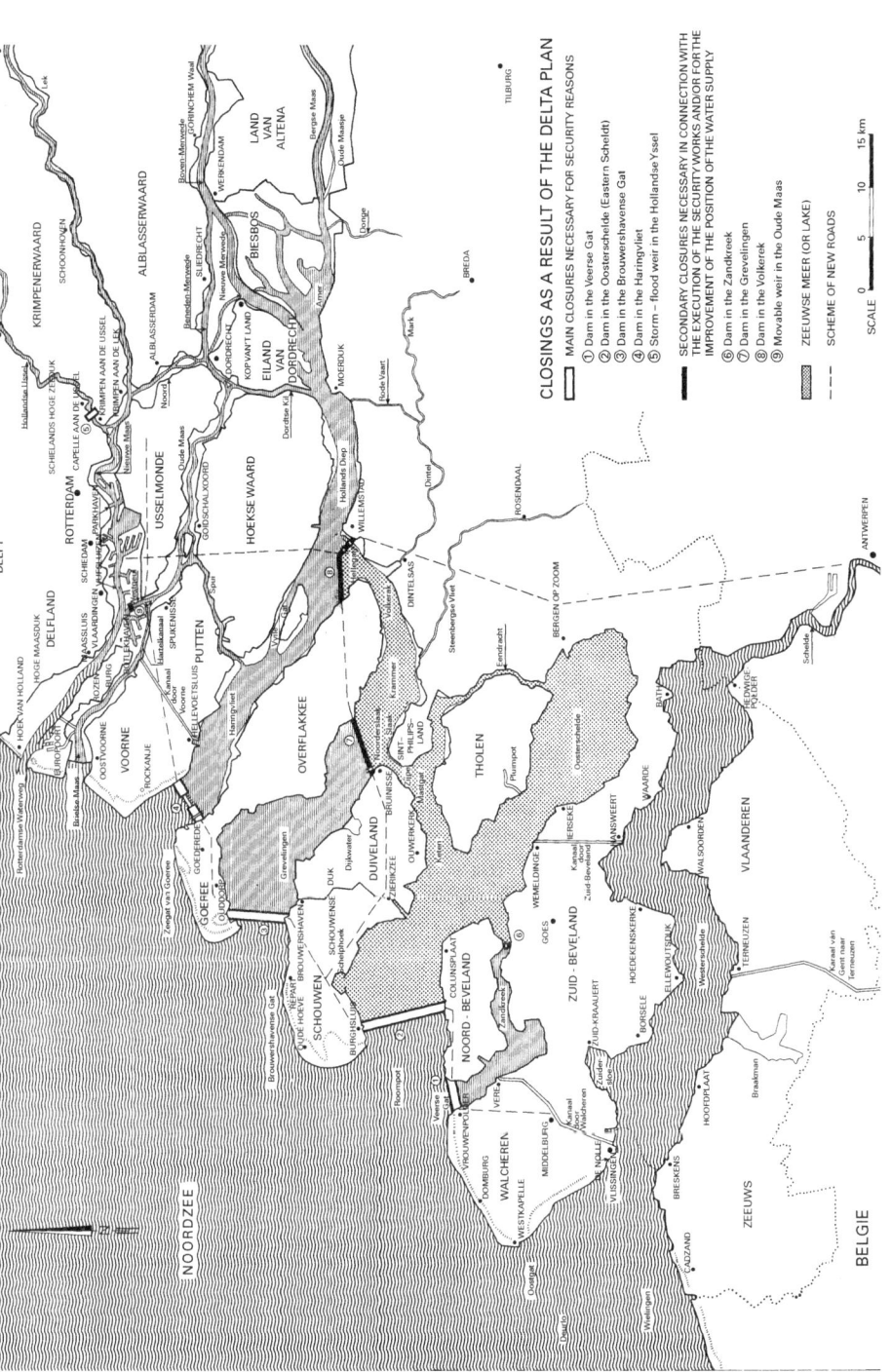

Figure 3.1
Map of Dutch Delta Works.
Source: Delta Committee (1962).

Figure 3.2
Maeslant storm surge barrier, Nieuwe Waterweg, Rotterdam, September 2014. Photograph by author.

much felt throughout the country in the half-decade after. Restructuring coupled with the impacts of the recession have meant a prolonged slowdown for architecture and engineering firms working in the country and have motivated city agencies and development firms to find different ways of conducting business and funding projects. In 2010, Dutch newspapers announced that cities had "stopped building,"[16] reflecting the pitched concern among built environment professionals and planners envisioning the future of cities in the country.[17]

The second is climate change, which now poses new threats to Dutch water management. These come not just from rising sea levels but also warmer temperatures, increasing precipitation, and uncertainty in a system dependent on balance and predictability. A new Delta Commission was formed in 2007, charged with long-term safety against climate change. In addition to proposing to increase flood protections of diked areas by a factor of ten—primary dikes raised ever higher—the commission's 2008 report recommended more flexible responses. These included implementation goals for "Room for the River," a program begun in 1996 in response to flooding around the Rhine and Meuse rivers.[18] The program involves reconstructing the banks and dikes around selected rivers to allow room for occasional, localized flooding. One example, for the Waal River in Nijmegen, relocates the dike 350 meters away from the river, creating an ancillary channel for flood water, and an occasional island with new development zones and recreational areas like beaches and parks (figure 3.3).[19] Approaches like Room for the River and the "sand engine" at Delfland—using the power of wind and waves to help distribute material—combine engineering with natural dynamics. Dutch proponents have termed this hybrid approach "building with nature." These strategies are still technocratic, yet ecological, described by their proponents as a "paradigm shift" in Dutch environmental planning.[20]

On one level, many environmental projects are now being conceived on a city, or local, scale. On another level, there is an outward shift toward international relationships. Rotterdam is a prime example of this dual

Figure 3.3
Room for the River project in Nijmegen showing "floodable" island and ancillary channel, July 2016. Photograph by author.

outlook. The city launched Rotterdam Climate Proof in 2008—tasked with ensuring climate change resilience by 2025—and promotes itself as a model for adaptation. While adhering to the Dutch emphasis on design and spatial planning, it is strongly economic in strategy—in line with the national policy trajectory of decentralization and strategic economic development. According to Rotterdam mayor Ahmed Aboutaleb, "climate change adaptation provides unique opportunities for growth."[21] City officials tout urban design pilot projects, including combined parking and stormwater storage facilities, floating districts, and "water squares"—recreational spaces that also protect against flooding from cloudbursts. These projects support the climate program's claim as a model for adaptation and are widely displayed in city material promoting Rotterdam as a desirable place to invest and as a beautiful, livable city.

Not unlike other cities, the making of the Rotterdam plan is specific to its spatial and political context, its relationship to geography, and its economic position within the nation-state. But, for Rotterdam, this origin story is further elaborated and framed in such a way that it is now tied to the fortunes of many cities around the world.

A number of key factors lie behind the Rotterdam adaptation plan's strong links to urban space and context, and its international focus. The city had developed its first Water Plan in 2001, for the first time linking the vision of the municipal government with that of the three water boards with which it shares overlapping jurisdictions. But Arnoud Molenaar, manager of the Rotterdam Climate Proof program, as well as the city's chief resilience officer,[22] and John Jacobs, strategic advisor at the Water Department of Rotterdam,[23] pinpoint a particularly significant turning point in the city reframing both its attitude toward water and its role in climate adaptation. In 2005, the city held its International Architecture Biennale, ominously or enthusiastically titled "The Flood." Alongside the Biennale, the planning and economic departments and water boards developed the Rotterdam Water City 2035 vision—a "relatively wild vision, but inspiring" says Molenaar.[24] This vision of a "water city" was then incorporated in the Water Plan 2, released in 2007, linking urban spatial development with water management.[25]

At this point, a number of significant parallel initiatives were taking place. The city launched the Rotterdam Climate Initiative,[26] its municipal climate change program, in 2006. That same year, the International Advisory Board Rotterdam (IAB), an advisory council on economic affairs and urban development, issued its annual report, recommending that Rotterdam "shake off modesty" and capitalize on its "unique selling points," including becoming "world capital of CO_2 free energy."[27] In 2007, two national programs began. The Knowledge for Climate research program, involving universities and applied engineering and research institutes, was tasked with investigating the consequences of climate change for the Netherlands.[28] The formation of the new Delta Commission in 2007 reinforced the broader focus on climate change in the country.

"Before 2005 water was a plague, and after 2005 water was an opportunity," states Rotterdam Climate Proof's Molenaar.[29] Pressed to elaborate on how and why these events and initiatives came together as they did, Molenaar talks about "serendipity . . . using the coincidences that happen." At the same time, Molenaar and Jacobs talk of working behind the scenes, urging the Rotterdam mayor at the time to take on a larger role in regional and national climate research initiatives, just as these initiatives were taking shape. They boast that Rotterdam's programs were the first municipal climate plans in the Netherlands. Says Jacobs, "We started writing our own story. We changed it all. And that is coincidence. . . . It is also because we had change agents in Rotterdam. . . . Chemistry on all levels."[30] Jacobs recalls the development of the second Water Plan in 2007—how the urban planners, tasked with the design and wellbeing of the city, had to find ways to collaborate with the water boards, who were historically in charge of water management but not necessarily concerned with city form. The plan brought water back to the city, but it could be done only when the two priorities—urban and spatial development, and water management—were brought together.

There are two distinct but related aspects to the Rotterdam planners' narrative of their city. On one hand, Molenaar refers to the fact that Rotterdam was heavily bombed during the Second World War, and the central city was almost completely leveled. "We are able to design new things, in a sense, in our city," he says.[31] It's like there are things in the DNA of the city, a propensity for or embrace of *change*. Chantal Oudkerk Pool, then senior advisor for Rotterdam Climate Proof, agrees with this, saying, "Rotterdam, within the Netherlands, we are widely known for being independent, for wanting to do our own thing and for actually doing it."[32] She gives the example of the floating pavilion (figure 1.10), a pilot project that tested the limits of Dutch planning law, "that kind of experiment which, I think, is sort of in the character of the city. Just to, you know, *try anyway*."[33] On the other hand,

Molenaar admits, "To a certain extent it's a matter of storytelling."[34] And it is both, intertwined quite neatly.

While it seems obvious that water management and urban spatial development in the Netherlands should be linked, many of the actors in this story stressed that it has not always been so. Indeed, water has played a key role in the sociocultural and spatial imaginaries of the Dutch, but not necessarily in the ways that urban space and development has progressed. Water—in the form of "protection from . . ."—has largely been under the purview of the national government and the powerful water boards. Environmental designer Florian Boer, principal of De Urbanisten, a design firm extensively involved in Rotterdam's local climate adaptation projects, and a member of one of the winning teams in Rebuild By Design in New York, affirms that the current trajectory of urban design reflects a change in understanding of water and urban spaces, as well as shifting relationships among city governments, water boards, engineers, and designers. Says Boer, "If there's more rain how could that actually become something you don't just solve by putting it away. How it could also contribute to an attractive city. . . . Why not make central collection points in neighborhoods where the water can flow to, where you can buffer the water for a little while, instead of putting it under the ground?"[35]

Boer references projects like Amsterdam's Bijlmermeer, a large postwar development of 40,000 dwellings that was constructed on a polder, as an unfortunate consequence of "modern ideology" and the sense that the country had conquered nature and was free to build as it pleased. These developments, according to Boer, were "cut loose from the underground, the soil, the *logic of the landscape*."[36] Boer illustrates the paradigm shift using his own experiences designing and constructing the water square in Benthemplein, Rotterdam, for which he was the primary designer (figure 1.9). He notes the increasing buy-in by city officials and engineers around new ideas about water:

> How can we design it in such a way also that it is still effective, from a water quality and quantity point of view, but also that it's a good space, a place actually that you can also really enjoy in such a moment. I thought it was really nice that the engineers were also very interested. They said, hey, this is interesting, because this is also giving something new to our vocabulary.[37]

Everything stated thus far explains the making of a municipal adaptation strategy—perhaps one economic and image-oriented in focus, but still

Table 3.2
Timeline of relevant events in Rotterdam

2001	First Water Plan released
2005	Key International Architecture Biennale Rotterdam, titled "The Flood"
2006	International Advisory Board recommendation to "shake off modesty"
2006	Rotterdam Climate Initiative launched
2007	Water Plan 2 released
2008	Rotterdam Climate Proof (adaptation program) launched
2010	First "Deltas in Times of Climate Change" conference
2014	Second "Deltas in Times of Climate Change" conference

produced and maintained within the institutional and jurisdictional space of traditional "city planning." How did Rotterdam's municipal climate program become so strongly linked to the international relationships fostered by the Dutch government?

City to Globe

If urban spatial visions animate the Netherlands' emerging expertise, they circulate globally through multiscalar, multilevel, and historically defined frameworks. Several entities play key roles in globalizing Dutch climate programs like Rotterdam's, linking them with global institutions and networks, and then with cities such as New York and Jakarta. One of these is Connecting Delta Cities (CDC), a network of ten cities (including Rotterdam, New York, and Jakarta), part of C40 Cities.[38] Coordinated by a secretariat in the Rotterdam climate program, CDC convenes member cities and serves as a depository of knowledge and best practices. Since 2009, CDC has published three books, each including summaries of the climate threats and initiatives in each of the cities in its network.[39]

Oudkerk Pool of Rotterdam Climate Proof, who also served as the coordinator for the Connecting Delta Cities secretariat, explains both the objectives of the network, and its potential benefit to Dutch business:

> Every city is struggling with the same thing. And it's not just knowledge; it's also about keeping things on the political agenda, or how to finance your measures in times of economic crisis, or how to involve your populations. So, the key objective is to learn, but there's also another element to it, to create economic spin-off for our city. We hope that, if Rotterdam within the Netherlands, or even within the world, is seen as a very important place when it comes to water management

and climate change adaptation, that water-related firms move to Rotterdam, or that business from Rotterdam or the Netherlands will get more access to assignments abroad.[40]

CDC is a network of cities, but not necessarily a flat, neutral one. The CDC online knowledge portal, in mid-2015, was dominated by cases and sites in the Netherlands, primarily in Rotterdam. There are a number of cases from the United States. Most of the other non-Dutch, non-US cases are from Vietnam, where Dutch entities are playing a very large role. Its examples of intercity cooperation include New Orleans and Rotterdam, Singapore and Rotterdam, and Ho Chi Minh City and Rotterdam, a clear pattern. Arguably, because of the disparities between cities, it cannot operate as a flat network even when organized as such. Places like Jakarta and Ho Chi Minh City have been conditioned—not only by a history of colonialism, but by postcolonial nation building and development aid, economic restructuring by global lending institutions, and the continuing economic inequities of global capitalism—to rely on technical and financial assistance. Changing this dynamic is challenging, as I explore further in this chapter.

According to Oudkerk Pool, the CDC, as a relatively small network of member cities and participants, increases its reach and impact by linking with larger international conferences, including the C40 summits.[41] In September 2014, the Rotterdam climate program helped organize—along with the Dutch Knowledge for Climate research program, the Netherlands ministries for Infrastructure and the Environment and Foreign Affairs, and C40 Cities—another of these larger events, the second Deltas in Times of Climate Change conference, titled "Opportunities for People, Science, Cities and Business." The conference, attended by over 1,300 people, featured panels by academics, practitioners, and industry experts, and information booths with Dutch climate and water agencies and major engineering and infrastructure firms (including Witteveen+Bos, Grontmij, Arcadis, Royal Haskoning, and Tauw). Bangladesh, Vietnam, Indonesia, and the United States were well represented by delegations. In this setting, the connections between national and local government, nongovernmental organizations, private interests, and international constituents are made explicit.

Deltares, a Dutch research institute, plays another key role in the bridging between urban climate initiatives and international relationships. The institute was formed in 2008, with a merger of WL|Delft Hydraulics (a firm that specialized in hydraulics research and consultation), GeoDelft (a geotechnical research consultancy), and parts of TNO (Netherlands Organisation for Applied Scientific Research, an independent, nonprofit research organization) and Rijkswaterstaat (itself a part of the Netherlands Ministry of Infrastructure and the Environment [IenM], formerly the Ministry of Transport, Public Works and Water Management, and now renamed the Ministry of Infrastructure and Water Management). This amalgam of private, public, and nonprofit consultation and research is central to the mission of Deltares, which maintains and proclaims its independent research status while at the same time being partly funded by the Ministry of Economic Affairs, Agriculture and Innovation and the Ministry of Foreign Affairs.[42]

"Knowledge is the core business of Deltares," states the institute's 2012 strategic plan.[43] While still operating primarily in the Netherlands, Deltares strongly emphasizes its global ambitions, as well as its intent to function in symbiotic relationships with Dutch policies in trade and foreign aid, and Dutch businesses abroad. Headquartered in Delft and Utrecht in the Netherlands, in 2015 it had offices in the United Arab Emirates, Singapore, Indonesia, and Brazil, with an affiliated office in the United States. Deltares has played a role in a number of high-profile water infrastructure projects around the world. It was involved in the Palm Islands and The World developments in Dubai, conducting coastal impact assessments, flow modeling, and beach design for these ambitious and controversial coastal reclamation projects. Delft Hydraulics, a precursor to Deltares, was involved in the Marina Reservoir project in Singapore, a freshwater reservoir created by damming the mouth of the Kallang and Marina Basins. It developed water-quality and operational management tools for the project. And Deltares was also invited, along with a number of other Dutch firms and consultancies, to participate in the Dutch Dialogues planning sessions in New Orleans after Hurricane Katrina, an effort that led to the Greater New Orleans Urban Water Plan.

Kees Bons, then representative of Deltares in Indonesia, elaborates on the institute's unique position with the water management sector, stating,

> The role of Deltares . . . is that we are what we call the expert advisor. . . . So we are in a luxury position in that we can really learn from the most challenging problems in the world. But that gives a responsibility. We are not a private firm. We are a foundation, and our task is primarily to . . . make [knowledge] available to the Dutch government and to the Dutch private sector.[44]

The NWP is a network currently consisting of 200 Dutch and Dutch-affiliated businesses, government agencies, nonprofit organizations, and research institutes. Headquartered in The Hague, its objective is to help the Dutch water sector gain greater international impact by providing a platform for networking, knowledge sharing, visibility, and influence. It prioritizes collaboration and cooperation among its participants, and building public-private partnerships.[45] An independent organization, it is largely funded by Dutch government agencies, and also partners with them on national policy initiatives.[46] For example, it is the cocoordinator of the Partners for Water program, commissioned by the Dutch ministries of Economic Affairs, Infrastructure and the Environment, and Foreign Affairs. This program offers subsidies to consortia of Dutch companies, research institutions, and NGOs working in select target countries to undertake feasibility and pilot projects in water management around the world. Targeted delta countries, in mid-2015, included Bangladesh, Egypt, Indonesia, Mozambique, and Vietnam.[47]

At the second Deltas in Times of Climate Change conference in Rotterdam in September 2014, NWP was the convening organization for the panel on the Jakarta NCICD masterplan, bringing together the leaders of the Dutch private consultants and key Indonesian national and capital city politicians (figure 3.4). Paul van Koppen of NWP, the chair of the panel, and Ad Sannen of Royal Haskoning, in charge of the program management part of the NCICD plan, were in sync, imploring the Indonesians, "Who will be the champion [of this plan]?"[48]

One can see a similar effort in the way that Singapore, the island city-state, has fostered hybrid public and private organizations, spinning off semiprivate firms that then take on consulting projects on environmental, infrastructure, and urban development in other countries. Similar to Singapore, another highly planned nation, the Netherlands in many ways sees itself as a single urbanized entity, particularly in the Randstad. The two nations have always prioritized global links—bearing in mind, of course, the vastly different timescales of their respective histories as independent nations, also interconnected.[49]

Entities such as CDC, Deltares, and NWP, alongside the national and municipal programs, provide capacities for city modeling, scientific research, and marketing. While Dutch planning is generally seen as centralized, these initiatives show a more reflexive, multiscalar operation. Shifting conditions are embraced as opportunities to rework Dutch sociospatial relationships and to retune planning and knowledge institutions to an increasingly climate-aware and alarmed global audience. The adaptations are in

Figure 3.4
At the Deltas in Times of Climate Change conference, (left to right) Victor Coenen (Witteveen+Bos), Purba Robert Sianipar (Coordinating Ministry for Economic Affairs, Indonesia), Ad Sannen (Royal Haskoning), and Sutanto Soehodho (deputy governor, DKI Jakarta) discuss the NCICD masterplan, Rotterdam, September 2014. Photograph by author.

the systems of planning as well as the objects of planning. Flood protection that has largely focused on regional infrastructure such as the Delta Works now includes coordinated urban projects. In this shift, social and spatial adaptation happens not just in response to climate change, but toward new modes of urban environmental project making. Cities are not just protected by the dikes. They are a feature of the protection.

Nation States to the Cities

On a national level, the Netherlands affirmed memorandums of understanding (MOUs) with both the United States and Indonesia. In March 2013, IenM and HUD agreed to an MOU for cooperation between the two countries in sustainable urban development and water management. Then Dutch Minister of Infrastructure and the Environment Melanie Schultz and then HUD secretary Shaun Donovan (also chair of the presidential Hurricane Sandy Rebuilding Task Force) signed the MOU in Washington, DC.[50] A year later, in April 2014, Minister Schultz was in Jakarta, Indonesia, to announce the Dutch-funded and Dutch-authored NCICD, or Giant Sea Wall, masterplan, as well as to affirm the cooperative intents behind a June 2012 MOU between the Netherlands and Indonesia on issues of water and environment.[51]

MOUs between nation states and subnational parties are not unusual. However, in recent years they have been brokered toward cooperation on sustainable urban development and water management, explicitly toward climate resilience. More often than not, they involve Dutch entities.[52]

Dutch involvement in New York and Jakarta long pre-dates these initiatives. As noted in chapter 1, both cities were Dutch colonial settlements—New York as Nieuw Amsterdam from 1624 to 1664, Jakarta as Batavia from 1619 through the mid-1900s. In Jakarta, three centuries of colonization are evident in the institutions and spatial, physical manifestations of the city, the marks of longtime Dutch efforts to modernize and rationalize governance and planning in their colonies.[53] In New York, colonial traces are more ceremonial. In these diverse contexts, present-day Dutch initiatives land with varying ease. In both cities, a specific environmental event marked a shift in longer relationships.

In New York, since Hurricane Sandy, the unique events and novel institutional arrangements that gave form to Rebuild By Design (detailed in chapter 2) empowered HUD officials to play a greater role in urban resilience conversations at local and international levels, while the promise of federal funds motivated local government cooperation and enthusiasm.[54] They also enabled a fluency and flexibility not always found in federal programs. The Rockefeller Foundation had already conducted workshops and published papers on urban resilience, and funded the Asian Cities Climate Change Resilience Network (ACCCRN) since 2008. Preexisting relationships between the philanthropic organization and HUD's leadership enabled rapid response in the wake of the storm.[55]

Rebuild By Design's institutional organization—HUD's oversight, Henk Ovink's principal role, and the Rockefeller Foundation's funding support of the competition phase—also enabled the involvement of international design and engineering firms with expertise in water management and flood protection, including many Dutch firms. The fluency of globally circulating ideas then encounters the relative obduracy of local politics and fragmented governance. Rebuild By Design aspired to be regional in scope, providing the planning and protection evident in the Dutch examples. But CDBG funds necessitate local, municipal control over implementation. There was cooperation but there were no formal implementation mechanisms between Rebuild By Design and these localities. Furthermore, Hurricane Sandy's impacts had exposed the uneven social and spatial vulnerabilities across the urban region, with systemic inequities exacerbated in the wake of the storm. Rebuild By Design's participatory process assuaged some local community concerns but, in some ways, it postponed the discontent. Notably, in late 2014, community organizers in the Lower East Side in Manhattan questioned the prioritizing of specific areas in the implementation plan.[56] In mid-2017, four years since the program's start, the winning projects were variously making their way through local public comment and tendering processes.

Dutch involvement in Jakarta environmental planning experienced a turning point after the 2007 floods (detailed in chapter 2). A flood hazard mapping study by Deltares concluded that severe land subsidence—at rates up to 12 centimeters per year—was exacerbating flooding.[57] These findings led to the JCDS, conducted jointly by Dutch and Indonesian agencies.[58] The JCDS detailed hydrological conditions, social and economic ties, infrastructural capacities, and governance roles, and it outlined strategies for floodwalls in the Jakarta Bay. Its findings became the basis of the NCICD masterplan.[59] While Dutch infrastructural interventions have been part of Jakarta's urban development since the early colonial period,[60] with institutional connections continuing past independence, the NCICD masterplanning offered Dutch engineering and design firms a high-profile urban spatial planning and water management involvement, supported by the Dutch national government under the terms of the MOU between the countries.

The masterplan's flood protection strategy—the "wings" of the seawall creating massive retention lakes pumped low enough to enable drainage of the rivers and canal—is somewhat reflective of the Netherlands, where much of the population lives below sea level, protected by dikes, canals, and pumps. But while planners there have been advocating for smaller-scale and ecologically attuned projects, the Giant Sea Wall harks back to classic, "hard" models of Dutch planning.

Broadly, the NCICD takes technical lessons from the JCDS, and creates an urban development plan in which the infrastructural "wall" is privately funded by leasable reclaimed land. The masterplan has provoked pitched debate about large-scale development, environmental protection, and social inequality. Environmentalists express concern about its impact on ecological systems and fisheries. Activists question the masterplan's claim to know what the real problem is and how it presuppose a solution that, once again, downplays or neglects the concerns of poor urban residents for their livelihoods and community networks.[61]

Global-Urban Network

We see a multiscalar, multilevel network—through which capital, knowledge, and influence flow. In contrast to a static view defined by stable external state relationships and internal national policies, and bounded, cohesive cities, a relational view reveals connections and interpenetrations across scales and levels (figure 3.5). This network is driven and defined by interrelated factors: economic relationships, historically defined situational relationships, and a set of interface conditions.

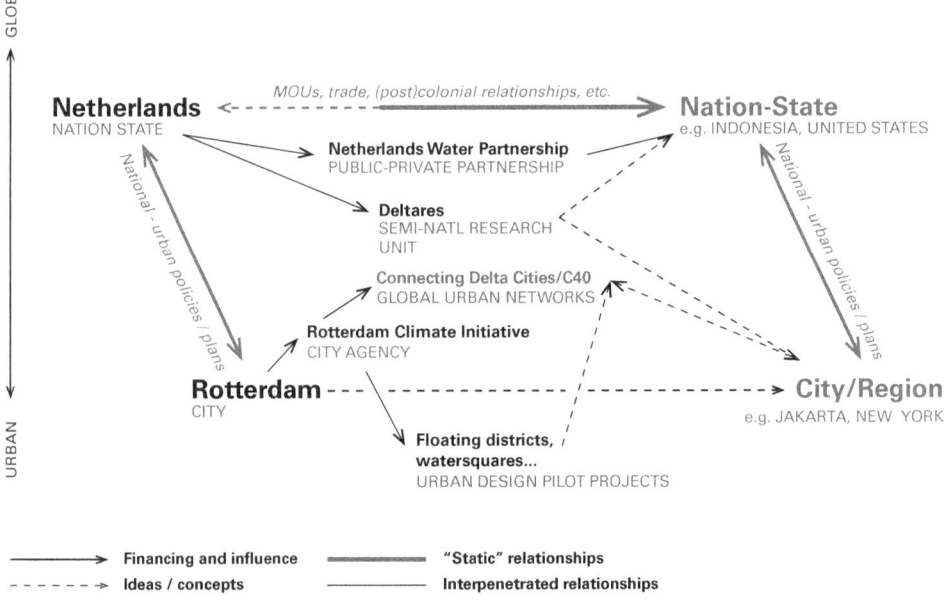

Figure 3.5
Diagram of global-urban networks.

Economic Relationships

Economic development, primarily privatized urban development, underpins Dutch involvement and investment in Jakarta and New York. The Netherlands' "top sectors," national priority sectors, include water, creative industries, technology, and logistics.[62] Planning for water is a key export in which the Dutch hold undeniable pedigree. Economic conditions at home have motivated the emphasis on global relationships. Climate change has made only more urgent the need for solutions. Water is a way for the Dutch to brand themselves to the world—at once economic development and foreign policy.

For Indonesia, Dutch officials are eager to see a relationship characterized by postcolonial influence and development aid transition into something more reciprocal in economic exchange—if not necessarily more equal in political power. The opportunities transcend Indonesian borders. A high-profile development in Jakarta constitutes a scaffold onto which Dutch firms can establish themselves in expanding regional markets. According to an NWP official, the Giant Sea Wall serves as "a vehicle for the Dutch sector to show their expertise, to be a credible partner, especially for private investors . . . also as a showcase project for the rest of Asian city development."[63]

For Rebuild By Design in New York, the federal funds for the winning proposals—a fraction of the projected costs—are meant to spur private investment. Participation in the initiative reinforces Dutch influence and expertise. This could enable the consolidation of work in the region and country by transnational engineering and project management firms such as Arcadis (involved in three of ten finalist teams). But it also creates new roles for small firms such as De Urbanisten, designer of the Rotterdam water squares. Its participation in Rebuild By Design opened new opportunities across the Atlantic.[64] This exposure, in turn, positions its designs, prominently featured in Rotterdam's climate program and Dutch water sector marketing, within a global discourse on Dutch creative industries and environmental planning.

Situational Relationships

These economic relationships highlight associated situational ones, involving historically determined and evolving geopolitical power relationships. Minister Schultz, unveiling the NCICD masterplan in Jakarta, said, "We

Dutch feel very much at home here. We feel *senang* [at ease]," a remarkable statement in a former colony.[65] The Giant Sea Wall, in many ways, conforms to traditional notions of international development, involving top-down planning, Western expertise, and a technocratic approach. Relating economic development and private investment with imminent catastrophe, it is a kind of environment-induced disaster capitalism—perhaps a projective "shock doctrine," how author Naomi Klein has described efforts to secure private profits around disasters and wars.[66] In Indonesia, where Deltares's office is embedded in the public works ministry, these processes are empowered by enduring postcolonial ties. They recast what anthropologist Ann Stoler terms "imperial formations"—the persistent ways in which past colonial relationships are reconstituted in ongoing processes of destruction—here written again in the balance of degraded urban landscapes, environmental urgencies, and aid and accumulation.[67]

And still, the NWP official describes the struggle of proving that it is the trusted long-term partner when Korean and Japanese companies are promising solutions for less money. The NCICD may be a "showcase," but its implementation has continually been in flux and doubt. In late 2015, a trilateral letter of intent was signed by Indonesia, South Korea, and the Netherlands to study joint implementation of the NCICD.[68] In mid-2016, progress had slowed due to uncertainty around governance support in Indonesia.[69] In 2017, a Deltares representative stated that the plan would no longer involve the ambitious Garuda landform, instead possibly relying on existing, tendered reclamation projects[70]—a decision later echoed by a government official.[71] While postcolonial influence continues to define the terms of environmental vulnerabilities and urban governance, it is not a sufficient determinant of the progress of particular plans.

In the United States, such explicit appeals are tempered by a sense of mutuality—perhaps a more certain feeling of being "at ease." US HUD secretary Shaun Donovan met Henk Ovink while touring the Netherlands to observe water infrastructure after Hurricane Sandy. Ovink suggested to Donovan that he help with the presidential task-force effort.[72] Ovink cites his background in spatial planning and policy, experience in public and private sectors, academic ties, and skills in building coalitions as key factors in making him the "ideal partner" for the United States. He further explains: "That combination of having the responsibility for the Netherlands when it comes to water management and spatial planning. Knowing how to bring design to that approach, and knowing how to create these alliances, made me an ideal partner for the US."[73]

The extensive involvement of Dutch firms in New York preceded Hurricane Sandy. However, the accelerated activity after Sandy illustrates the maneuverings of large firms like Arcadis in a scenario of environmental risk. At the Deltas in Times of Climate Change conference in 2014, Edgar Westerhof, senior planner at Arcadis, recounted how the firm was central to the climate change work precipitated by Sandy. Panel moderator Cynthia Rosenzweig, a climate change scientist based in and researching New York City, corrected him, calling it a "mischaracterization" to suggest that little had been happening in the city before the storm.[74]

Ovink, now essentially an ambassador with dual roles—for Rebuild By Design and the Dutch water sector—sees it diplomatically. For him, the competition created a process,

> [t]otally connected with everybody, and able to infuse all stakeholders. So it means that the people in that region now understand climate change differently. They now understand mitigation and adaptation differently than when we started. It also means that those engineers and designers from New York now understand comprehensiveness differently. And it means that those designers and engineers from the Netherlands now understand regionalism and fragmentation and community approaches differently.[75]

In Indonesia, longtime Dutch governmental and institutional relationships guide a process of problem framing and solution making. In the United States, transnational corporate and diplomatic activities are institutionally boosted after a disaster.

Interface Conditions

Economic and situational relationships are reinforced by interface conditions—specific characteristics or the dynamic between the sites or actors—including cultural narratives and invocations of urgency.

The origin story of Dutch water expertise is rehearsed on multiple levels. In Rotterdam, officials talk of writing their own narrative. In public speeches worldwide, Henk Ovink recounts the development of the Netherlands' culture of living with water, promoting its relevance for other places confronting risk (although its 800 years of societal learning is not on offer). These narratives are effective. An evaluation of the first phase of Rebuild By Design found that HUD secretary Donovan's leadership and the commitment of federal funds were critical motivators, and so were Ovink's "charisma and vision."[76] Sustaining partnerships is seen as critical in New York as it is in Jakarta.

While the overall image of globalizing Dutch water is one of coherence and organization, friction appears around specific initiatives. Critics of the Giant Sea Wall in Jakarta express fears of a "black lagoon"—sewage-laden canals draining into the proposed retention lakes. A Dutch hydrologist acknowledges these concerns and opines that closing off the wall might be considered a last resort. He did not foreclose alternatives, such as approaches similar to Room for the River, but asserted, "Indonesian problems have to be solved by Indonesian people with Indonesian solutions."[77] This sentiment is prevalent among Dutch individuals, who are mindful of past criticisms.[78] But the most ambitious version of the NCICD was carried to its launch, despite the concerns, propelled by promises of modernization, invocations of urgency by Dutch research reports and public statements about the sinking city, and the acquiescence of local officials. Says a Jakarta official: "There is no other way. If not, [we will be] increasingly flooded."[79]

Climate change researchers have pointed to "adaptation regimes"[80] and "resilience machines."[81] The "machine-like" systemic characteristics are ascribed to differential power relationships, appeals of threats and uncertain futures, and dominant modes of development. These factors are apparent in Jakarta: there is evident threat, and a draw toward modernization and infrastructural fixes; there are few alternatives to consider, and Dutch influence and long-term power relationships and urban development dynamics are hard to shake. In New York, processes are informed less by historical power relationships and more by an aligned vision of new urban futures promoted alike by government agencies, transnational corporations, and global philanthropies. Systemic, structural factors hold firm, propelled by economic-ecological shifts on a global scale. But they are enabled by situational and specific, conditional relationships.

Network Formation

The global-urban network reveals relationalities that are cross-site and multiscalar. On one level, the motivations behind the initiatives in New York and Jakarta cannot be fully understood without relational tracings to sociospatial changes in the Netherlands. On another level, the Dutch engagements in New York and Jakarta are illuminated by relational distinction from the other; generalized forces inflected to meld to historically defined sociospatial conditions. Seeing each site from the others shows how shifting, distinct political economic conditions guide the terms of engagement and the trajectory of the relationships.

New York, Jakarta, and Rotterdam comprise a sample of dynamic global phenomena—a *network formation*. This concept offers a way to see and understand the terms of such interconnected processes, and to categorize a set of relationships—not to denote a concrete and unique, or exclusive, network. Nations like the Netherlands and cities such as Rotterdam, with a convincing origin story, expertise pedigree, and internal and external motivators; cities like Jakarta, in rapidly growing economies facing environmental and social challenges; and cities like New York, already a node in global economic flows, contemplating new urban futures, represent a distinct and exemplary formation (figure 3.6). Rotterdam, here, functions as a *reflexive* site—the site itself, and the relationship between it and other

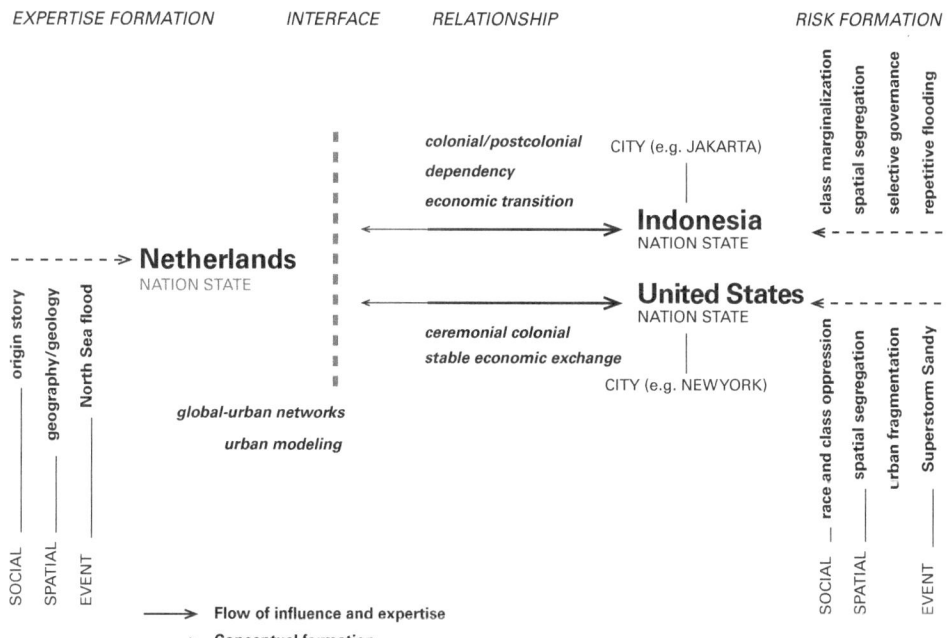

Figure 3.6
Diagram of conceptual interfaces, relationships, and formations.

sites, sharpening the analysis of each of the strategies, and the comprehension of the whole.

This view illustrates the ways in which national and corporate strategies might be operationalized through cities. The Netherlands' priority sectors are foregrounded by urban projects, municipal planning, and a web of institutions—including Connecting Delta Cities, a transnational municipal network, and Deltares, a research institute given the latitude to function as a global consultant, with public ties and private opportunities. These networks and entities, conceptually, pull the global and urban together. Besides creating symbiotic links across scales, they enable local, physical interventions such as the water square in Rotterdam to play an outsize role in international discourse, and in national and corporate strategic market making.

Recognition of the broader network is critical in light of prevalent assertions about the "obvious" importance of cities, and other invocations of the "Urban Age" that veil a large part of the motivation behind cities' environmental project making.[82] These findings reaffirm yet complicate assertions about the "metropolitanization" of climate change. We should not too quickly accept the discourse of cities as sole or primary actors, even if we agree with the precept of strategic security and economic interests as their key drivers. We should be attendant to the operations of cities as part of broader agendas and to the extent to which city-centric emphases are driven by self-reinforcing urban development visions.

Circulating ideas reflect concrete spaces. In the context of climate change and crises, the networks mobilize and transform ideas about the spaces of society and water, bringing the biophysical workings of infrastructure and hydrology into the realm of interconnected economic flows. It is a sort of sociohydrological addendum to Manuel Castells's "space of flows"[83]—ideas and images about actual or material flows of water join the organizational processes of capital, information, and technology.

The network formation framework is particularly insightful where presumably stable or long-running relationships are evolving and reconfiguring in response to external and internal factors, and where a key site or actor occupies a critical node of multiple relationships. Capturing the network in formation reveals relational trajectories behind multisited plans that remain years in evolution and expands the notion of process, enabling critical assessments of pivotal stages.

Seeing the network in formation also broaches specific possibilities for understanding alternative ideas and visions. These findings raise a critical line of questions that I will return to in the following chapter. Globally circulating ideas are not so free-flowing on the ground, and tend to be deformed and refracted in response to local political-economic and spatial conditions. In each site, historical trajectories and geographic conditions have shaped social and environmental marginalization, and contesting visions of urban futures. This contestation has given rise to protests against perceivable unequal distribution of resources or direct threats of displacement and dispossession. Have urban spatial protest movements reorganized themselves in response to global-urban networks? And if so, how have the concerns around locally and materially specific inequities been transposed to larger geographic scales and higher governance levels of planning?

In this chapter I traced the development of a kind of global-urban environmental project making. In terms of understanding places, it is neither comparative nor singular. Each site helps to reveal the others. Tracing the formation of global-urban networks transcends bounded, city-centric emphases in urban climate change research. It explains the spatial and temporal interconnections within and across sites, and the ways in which urban spatial interventions operate within broader political economies and ecologies.

As climate change threats heighten, as globalized urban development continues, and as the means through which knowledge is shared and influence peddled develop, such formations, and permutations thereof, are emerging as the crucial framework within which environmental projects are conceived and justified. I have illustrated an approach to understanding the social, spatial, and event-driven factors behind the claims of expertise and the formation of risk, and also how different historical relationships and interfaces impact such factors. As researchers continue studying how cities respond to changing environmental and geopolitical conditions, we will need to define further conceptual categories for the interfaces, the relationships, and the types of risk and expertise formation within networks such as this one.

4   Plans and Counterplans

All the things we hide in water
hoping we won't see them go—
(forests growing under water
press against the ones we know)—
—Annie Finch, "Landing Under Water, I See Roots"

In each of the sites investigated in this book, the spatial, physical forms of the plans and projects proposed invoke cultures, histories, and senses of place. Why do urban climate change responses take the forms and meanings that they do? This chapter explores the design of these plans and projects. At its heart are the confoundingly circular questions: What is the story behind what we see? And how does what we see influence the story? In interrogating urban design for climate change, I begin with a rather more general question: What, really, is design? I then explore more specific questions. How does design relate to urban climate change responses and how do we assess this? What are the motivations behind specific designs for urban climate change responses?

Urban Design and Climate Change

How has urban climate change research dealt with design? Too often it is through neglect, when design is simply not considered an object of analysis. Pivotal books on spatial planning and climate change, where one expects to find substantive discussion of design, tend to sideline the topic or subsume it into broader discussions of policy or implementation frameworks.[1] Numerous accounts of planning and climate change—on governance, policy, community, justice, and so on—often ignore spatial issues altogether, let alone the action, practice, or process of designing those spaces.

At other times, design is considered in two broad categories: first, through what might be considered responsible professionalism, and second, through *speculative* design. The first category, responsible professionalism, is exemplified by a book titled *Two Degrees*, written by principals of Arup, an international engineering firm.[2] It focuses concretely on the facts of the problem at hand—the science of climate and GHG emissions—and what to do about it, providing physical design strategies for mitigation and adaptation. It stresses an approach of "integrated design," to ensure a "harmonious whole."[3] The book ties built environment interventions to the scientific bases for action and pays due attention to planning scenarios and issues of vulnerability, uncertainty, and risk. The second category, speculative design, includes combination research-design projects such as *On the Water | Palisade Bay*, for which Guy Nordenson, Catherine Seavitt, and Adam Yarinsky conduct a prescient study of the Upper Bay of New York and New Jersey, two years before Hurricane Sandy.[4] It involves scientific studies and mappings of dynamic systems and ecological flows, hydrological analysis, histories and precedents for waterfront design, and speculative design interventions focusing on soft infrastructures like wetlands, barrier islands, and reefs to guard against rising seas and stronger storms, as well as new modes of energy production and transportation. *On the Water | Palisade Bay* served as a key background project for the influential *Rising Currents: Projects for New York's Waterfront* exhibition at the Museum of Modern Art in 2010 (discussed below).[5]

Such speculative design initiatives for climate change have surged in design schools, professional design discourse, and as part of a number of urban and regional initiatives in the United States since Hurricane Sandy.[6] Design, generally relieved of the responsibility of explanatory theories and replicable findings, finds firm footing, so to speak, as informed provocation and as a mode of influence and inspiration. This is how design tends to work best—observing problems across scales and fields and synthesizing new solutions.

Worldviews of Design
But that is not enough. Besides largely sidestepping the conditions of explanatory theories and associated responsibilities of social scientific

Plans and Counterplans 117

research, these design initiatives, provocative and inspiring as they are, rarely probe the context in which they operate. In other words, these approaches to knowing and effecting change are not reflexive. They are often underequipped to delve into the sociopolitical relevance of design in the urban settings in which they operate. They rarely investigate the contestation around their own practices or the multiple constructions and understandings of design in envisioning and making urban space.[7] Design for climate change response is still undertheorized.

It is evident from the conversations with various actors in New York, Jakarta, and Rotterdam around designed responses to urban climate change that the idea of design is vague, and the role of design is unclear. To illustrate the diverse understandings of design, I quote five figures involved in and around the Rebuild By Design effort in New York, and one from a quite different but related context.

For Henk Ovink, Dutch spatial planner and principal of Rebuild By Design, design is an expansive process, able to broach new possibilities: "You have to be able to step out of your preconceived idea about how you deal with these things, and create a place, a space in time, but also physical, in a process, where you can step outside of that reality, step outside of your normal world. This is what Rebuild By Design [was intended to be]. A process on the edge of the real world."[8]

For Damaris Reyes, community organizer and executive director of GOLES (and community participant during the Rebuild By Design public meetings), design is more about the aesthetics, the spatial, physical form of the urban proposal. Reyes states, "The design itself people like. What they don't like is what's getting done during what phase."[9] For her, the "design itself" is distinct from the process and the implementation. Design affects community; it can change their lives. It does this primarily through aesthetics and form.

Amy Chester, manager of Rebuild By Design (with a community organizing background), echoes this in the one instance, stating, "I'm interested in design as something that is beautiful . . . bringing aesthetics into the conversation. . . . It creates a sense for people who are using the building to act differently, to use space differently, to think about their workspace differently, or the way that they live differently, or their community differently. That's how I just think about design."[10] In a follow-up conversation, around Rebuild By Design's five-year mark, Chester expands her definition, stating,

"Design can be policy.... The design of policy. To us, design is the answer to whatever the challenge is."[11] She goes on to explain that the core focus of the organization is on the built environment and on enabling translation between the practices of design and the challenges of the urban built environment.

For Michael Marrella, the director of waterfront and open-space planning for New York City, design is, perhaps not surprisingly, more multivalent: "For coastal protection projects, given that the physical form that these projects take will define how the public is able to use the waterfront ... how do you physically compromise the view corridors *and* allow for direct line of sight to the waterfront edge for resiliency or public safety. How do those two get reconciled? That oftentimes comes down to a question of design." That is the procedural and pragmatic aspect of urban design. But Marrella is also in tune with design as an instrument of influence and provocation. He says, "There were two important things that came out of Rebuild by Design. One was getting climate adaptation planning literally on the front page of the *New York Times* magazine. The other is that it was using design as the means of discussing these issues."[12]

And for Florian Boer, environmental designer and director of De Urbanisten, a Dutch design firm involved in both Rotterdam's municipal climate plan and Rebuild By Design, design is similarly more complex. Design is a process that weaves together, and shows the interfaces between, infrastructural systems, ecological systems, and physical space. He says, "If you want to make a more resilient city, it should become more interactive with the surface [of the city]. ... These types of [design] measures can make the city more resilient but [they make] it also more visible, tangible. You can involve people in that. [They make] it also more comfortable and more pleasant."[13]

Anna Brown, senior associate director of ACCCRN, based in Bangkok, Thailand, explains what design might mean in working with multiple, often very different cities. She offers a parallel perspective, which appears on some level aligned with Ovink's: "I would say that design has probably been most within the process. So it's not [necessarily] that kind of physical design aspect, but I think the process that cities have gone through, through facilitation support by our partner organizations. ... This is critical particularly going into very different contexts. And needing to understand the set of different factors, how they play out in local contexts where there are physical, spatial realities, and [also] political realities, relationship realities, and ecological realities.[14]

For each of these figures, there is certainly an overlapping, broad understanding of design as the manipulation and organization of spatial form. But, evidently, they view the potential of design through their own backgrounds and ways of knowing.

Explaining Design

From broader ideas of design and the varying viewpoints expressed here, one may point to three registers, or conceptual levels, of urban design. First, at its most concrete, it is about specific urban spatial and physical places at multiple spatial scales. Second, a level up in abstraction, it is about the social practices that form how such spatial, physical places are used and given meaning. And third, more abstractly, it is about the projected ideas about the future of such places—as a proposed solution, as well as a set of ideas about what constitutes desired or preferred urban futures. That is, designing the urban necessarily intertwines physical place, social meaning, and contested visions, across levels of abstraction.

Design, indeed, is part of the production of space. Recalling Henri Lefebvre's ideas of the social production of space (discussed in the introduction): the three concepts of space—as spatial practice (the relationship of social actions and physical spaces), representations of space (the conceptualized space of planners), and representational space (of symbolisms and imaginaries)[15]—offer an analytical path into the complexities of urban design. Space is contested, as is the design of space. In urban sites in which biophysical conditions and imminent climatic, environmental changes cause damage and harm, that have been witness to histories of social and spatial conflicts, and for which designs have been proposed with projected ideas about the future, a multifaceted and reflexive way of seeing and understanding helps to explain spaces that are simultaneously "real," contested, and imagined.[16]

Within these multivalent understandings of space, what defines effective, and *affective*, design? Beyond proposing a solution that fulfills programmatic, spatial, and social objectives, design also has to work on additional levels, to legitimize itself—that is, the process and meaning of design—and to legitimize the project. More procedurally, the approach to understanding space through design includes considerations that are both *descriptive* and *analytical*. In more descriptive terms, the approach involves the delineation of the specific aspects of the spaces and designs in question. It asks questions such as: What is it, and what does it promise to do? Who is involved in decisions about its production and development? Who does it propose to serve? Does it appeal to precedents? What are they? And, how is it paid for (both the production of the design and the implementation of the project)? In more analytical terms, the approach inquires into the ways in which such spaces and designs might be understood as forms of practice, as social relations, and as imaginaries. It asks: How might forms of urban climate change responses be categorized? How are the social relationships formed, and whom does it exclude? How does the design address the actual or stated problem, and to what extent is there a gap between what is needed and what is envisioned? And how is design—and discourse around design— used to legitimize the plan? How is design used to contest the plan?

Building on the overarching framing of climate justice and urban futures through this approach, the analysis here focuses on the forms of exclusion and resistance that emerge across the sites.

Jakarta

Great Garuda
The NCICD Giant Sea Wall masterplan is likely one of the largest municipally and nationally supported urban adaptation projects. It is also one in which the symbolic, formal nature of the project rivals its infrastructural ambitions. Aerial renderings produced by Rotterdam-based urban design and landscape architecture firm KuiperCompagnons depict the new city and seawall as a bright bird with open wings protecting the dark city behind it (see figure 1.7). Gleaming white towers trail off into green parkland and the cool blue of the retention lakes. On the surface, references to the winged Brasília, and the feeling that this is a happier, softer version of utopian, modernist visions, are hard to shake. The renderings present an idealized society living smoothly through the transition of environmental change, with ample prosperity, recreation, and urban nature on the other side. The words in the masterplan echo this vision: "Formed by the laws of nature, flow and efficiency, this elegant foil-shaped waterfront city resembles a great bird, an eagle spreading its great wings to protect the people of Jakarta, the national capital."[17]

The initial design sketches of the Garuda design, by landscape architect Gijs van den Boomen of KuiperCompagnons, show a slightly different

Plans and Counterplans

side. They are large, immediate, and gestural, the contradictions of scale, ecology, and politics smoothed over by the broad marker strokes. In their roughness and indeterminacy, the sketches are aspirational in and of themselves. A large printout of one of van den Boomen's sketches hangs on the wall in the NCICD planning office, located in the Indonesian Ministry of Public Works building (figure 4.1). The sketches are visions of the future yet to be interrogated or contained by the precision of the digital renderings (let alone the sociopolitical conditions on the ground). When asked about the design, van den Boomen chooses to show these sketches first.

On a technical level, the design of the Giant Sea Wall refers quite directly to a number of hydrological strategies apparent in water management infrastructure in the Netherlands, and to other large-scale reclamation and damming projects around the world. The inner, existing sea wall is first reinforced. An outer sea wall is then built in the bay, keeping out the sea. The wings of the Garuda are created by landfill along the outer sea wall, with a typical cross-section of 400 meters (although this can vary by scope of eventual development). This creates large retention lakes (of a minimum of 7,500 hectares, about twenty-two times the size of Central Park in New York City) between the outer wall of the new city and the current coastline

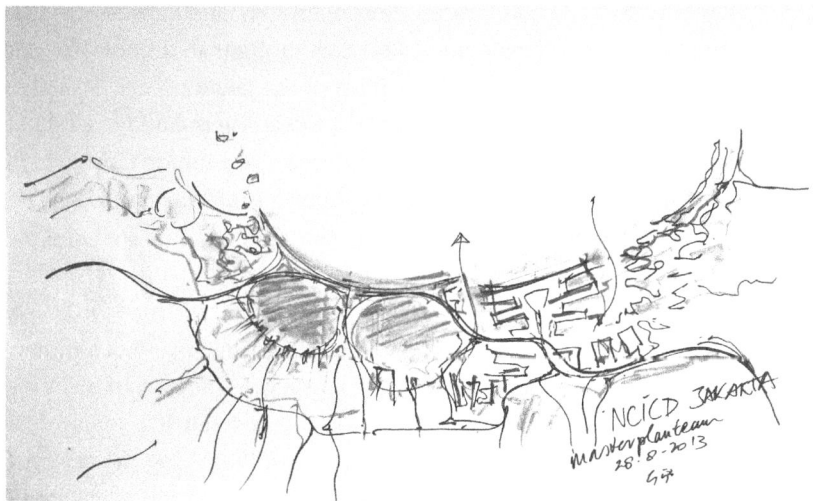

Figure 4.1
Great Garuda sketch by Gijs van den Boomen, August 2013.
Source: KuiperCompagnons.

(see figure 2.17). The water levels in the retention lakes will be allowed to fluctuate by 2.5 meters. Excess water will be pumped out to sea—730 cubic meters of water per second, according to projections, slightly larger in magnitude, incidentally, than the average discharge of the Hudson River at New York.[18] This pumping keeps the lake levels lower than the water levels of the existing canals in the city, allowing the canals to drain out.

Simply put, the plan calls for a large enough body of water that can be pumped low enough so that the canals and rivers running through Jakarta might be able to drain into it during the heaviest rain and the highest tides—the largest sink in the world, drained by the biggest pumps in the world. In addition to controlling flooding, these lakes are meant to become freshwater reservoirs in the future, as captured seawater is gradually replaced by freshwater from the canals and rivers. This, of course, will depend on whether the canal and river waters are suitably unpolluted. The Giant Sea Wall marries large-scale, iconic reclamation projects like the Palm Islands in Dubai and complex hydrological works like the Marina Reservoir in Singapore—both, not coincidentally, projects involving Dutch research institute Deltares (as discussed in chapter 3).

The dynamic behind discussions on the design of the Great Garuda is revealing. In a video on the Jakarta work, JanJaap Brinkman of Deltares, a key figure in the post-2007 research on hydrology and subsidence, talks about how "bright architects came in and they thought about how this dike should look . . . they saw wings in the form of the Jakarta coast."[19] Design, for him, comes after the engineering, after the decision to build coastal protections. At a presentation at the Deltas in Times of Climate Change conference in 2014, Victor Coenen of infrastructure firm Witteveen+Bos, the project manager of the NCICD masterplan, half-jokingly said that designer van den Boomen was "playing with his iPad . . . while we were working very hard on serious matters."[20] Van den Boomen, in his office in the Van Nelle Factory building in Rotterdam—the building itself a kind of temple of modernism, designed by Johannes Brinkman and Leendert van der Vlugt and completed in 1931—speaks about how he covered the walls of his Jakarta hotel room with large sheets of paper while making the sketches, and going at it freehand. "I literally demolished the hotel room," he says.[21] It is back to basics, urban designer as rock star.

Nevertheless, van den Boomen strongly emphasizes the necessity of local stakeholders in Indonesia to embrace the Giant Sea Wall. For him, it is critical for it to be an Indonesian project. He says, "Our role was also to capture . . . the technical processes, and integrally shape them in such a way that the people of Jakarta, our counterparts in the process, could become enthusiastic about the initiative." Well aware of the parallels with Brasília, he brings up the comparison himself in presentations to Jakarta's officials, posing the question to them: How will Jakarta be different? He contends that the project is not really about a dike, but about "changing the city."[22]

If anthropologist James Holston had asserted that utopian modernist design did not take seriously existing social relationships,[23] then what van den Boomen is advocating for is a kind of *post*modern design (not in the usual architectural sense, but as a process). It is a time in which the designers, so mindful of modernism's checkered history, both in design and in development, have themselves adapted to a new global environment. The new design doctrine is one that negotiates capital, authority, and participation. It will no longer be Le Corbusier proclaiming the "prodigiously true" nature of his Plan for Algiers,[24] but the Dutch urban designer and landscape architect inviting a shared possession of the legitimacy of his vision. As if to say, why wouldn't you want to take ownership of this? Why wouldn't you want to be behind the vision to a new kind of city? Dutch designers, engineers, and economic development officials alike affirmed this approach and point of view.

The complex ways in which the various actors invoke the symbolic form of the Great Garuda emphasizes the necessary, indeed powerful, element of design in the building of legitimacy in such a project. But it is not well understood. Design is regarded, alternately, with dismissiveness, bemusement, and detachment. This confusion presents both hurdles and openings for those who are in the design role.

Kees Bons of Deltares recalls the pivotal role of the design:

> If you go to the meetings before [the design] it was all rather technical. And so the image contributed to people realizing that this was more than just a number of technical activities. They started to see the city and the whole activity as something else. From a collection of technical activities, it became one new icon for which several technical activities were necessary. That's the shift that happened.[25]

Bons then stresses the key point powerfully. The Garuda design, he states, turned a *Dutch development aid project into a national ambition.*[26]

I will restate it more explicitly. At its most stripped down, the Giant Sea Wall is merely that, a wall. It is an engineering project, a "defense strategy"—born out of disaster and motivated by the specter of worse disasters. It is an expensive fix for decades, if not centuries, of bad decisions. This was, in essence, what the JCDS embodied, authored largely by hydrologists from Deltares two years before (see the discussion in chapter 2). But, formulated as the Great Garuda, it is proposed as a national development plan—a step into a different kind of world citizenship. Here, we see one important aspect of the broader terrain: adaptation to urban environmental change is at once social and spatial. Initiatives of adaptation have to negotiate multiple measures, experiences, and representations of space, essentially shuttling around the Lefebvrian conceptual triad of perceived, conceived, and lived spaces.[27] It is a kind of *political ecology of design*, in which the visions of biophysical and ecological constraints and possibilities are messily mapped to the socioecological struggles of urban change. Here, design achieves a critical objective. Design connects the pragmatic to the emotional.

Kampung Design Activism
But design also connects the emotional to the pragmatic.

Many of Jakarta residents most vulnerable to floods live in the informal kampung settlements along the thirteen rivers and coastline, especially along the notorious Ciliwung River. Kampung residents, basically synonymous with the urban poor in Jakarta, are plainly called "illegal" by city officials. These officials blame kampung residents for the floods, saying that their actions degrade the waterways, while turning a blind eye to illegal garbage dumping and uncontrolled development, two much more likely causes.

This is where the ambitious Giant Sea Wall plan intersects with the plight and struggle of the kampung residents. The plan to create large retention lakes between the outer wall of the new sea wall city and the current coastline, and to turn them into freshwater reservoirs, counts on clean rivers and canals flowing into the retention lakes. These rivers and canals have long been clogged by sediment and refuse, and increasingly overstressed by stormwater runoff attributed to the decreased ground permeability caused by rapid and rampant urban development.[28] This places renewed urgency on projects by the World Bank and Japanese agency JICA to dredge and widen canals and rivers—to increase their flow, "normalize" them, in the words of city officials. The dredging and widening projects directly threaten the displacement of kampung settlements, many of which are perched at or over the edge of water bodies (figure 4.2; also figure 1.7). A presentation

Figure 4.2
On the edge of Waduk Pluit, July 2013. Photograph by author.

by the Regional Development Planning Board of DKI Jakarta shows 1,183 houses to be impacted just in the two kampungs of Bukit Duri and Kampung Melayu along an approximately 3,450 meter (2.2 mile) stretch of the Ciliwung.[29]

The work on the NCICD masterplan coincided with a number of resistance initiatives among kampung residents and activists on the ground. Both the UPC and Ciliwung Merdeka succeeded in forging working agreements with city officials for alternatives to the kind of forced evictions and displacement that have characterized recent struggles in Jakarta (discussed in chapter 2). Both organizations achieved this through innovative coalition building and design initiatives.

In Muara Baru, adjacent to Waduk Pluit and where Taman Jokowi replaced a stretch of demolished kampung houses (see figure 2.11), UPC's coalition includes community architects, students from the University of Indonesia, and researchers from Rujak. Coordinator Edi Saidi recounts how UPC's organizing strategy and its use of broad-based coalitions, including designers, started in the aftermath of the Indian Ocean tsunami in 2004. At that time, Saidi worked alongside Marco Kusumawijaya, an architect and director of Rujak, Yuli Kusworo, an architect from Arkomjogja (Jogja Community Architects), and local community network Uplink Banda Aceh to help design and rebuild communities.[30] UPC, Rujak, and Arkom continued their collaboration on the Strenkali project in Surabaya, Indonesia, a notable example of community-led "upgrading in place" along a riverfront—where residents, to avoid displacement, proactively reconfigured and reoriented their houses to face the river, allowing for widening and infrastructural improvements (figure 4.5).[31] In Muara Baru in Jakarta, UPC's design departs from the previous upgrading-in-place strategies, partly in recognition of the challenges in remaining directly along the retention pond amid the political and environmental pressures. UPC's design comprises five-story apartment blocks, with collective spaces for economic and social uses on each floor (figure 4.3). Organizers also secured promises from Governor Jokowi that the new housing would be built on nearby land.

Ciliwung Merdeka organizes residents from Bukit Duri and Kampung Pulo in Central Jakarta, two of the most threatened kampungs along the Ciliwung. Ciliwung Merdeka built a coalition that included, at one time, Kota Kita, a citizen planning group, designers and planners from Harvard Graduate School of Design and the Bartlett Faculty of the Built Environment of University College London, and housing advocacy organizations like the Asian Coalition for Housing Rights. Ciliwung Merdeka has also been in talks with city officials and has continued to press its case for alternative solutions, including proposing designs for new typologies of river-edge housing and rehousing in place. In their vision for a "humanitarian vertical kampung" for Bukit Duri, they proposed to conduct community-led mapping of the kampung and river, to determine the best course for river widening, and designed new stacked, higher-density kampung dwellings to house selectively relocated residents within the existing area, maintaining neighborhoods and livelihoods (figure 4.4).[32]

These initiatives by kampung activist coalitions bring up clear provocations and questions about the relationship between design and social justice. In recent years, there has been a fair amount of attention paid to humanitarian design—*design like you give a damn*, in the words of the founders of the now-shuttered organization Architecture for Humanity.[33] These efforts are motivated, in large part, by the premise that the skills of

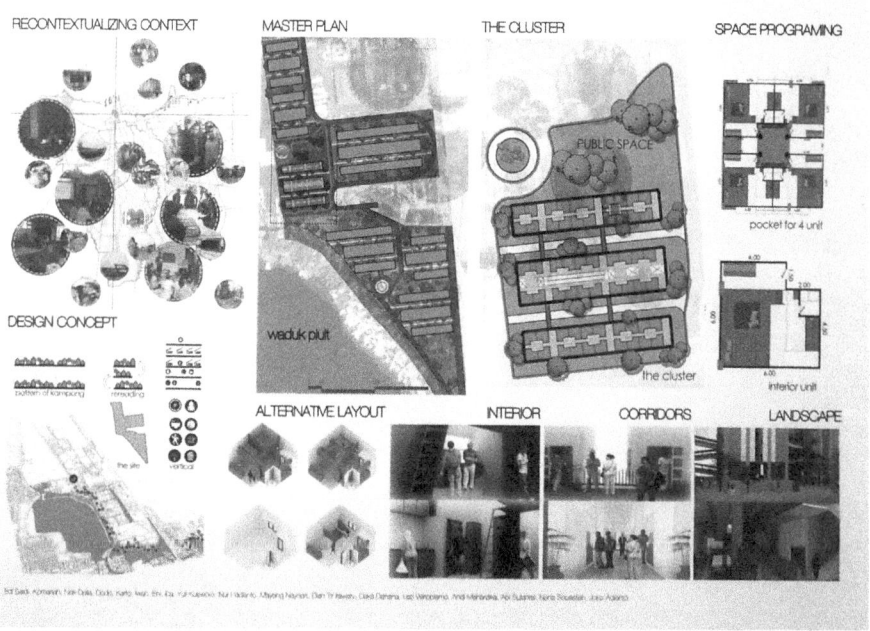

Figure 4.3
Participatory design concept by the Urban Poor Consortium for a new kampung typology at Muara Baru, exhibited at the *Jakarta Vertical Kampung* exhibition at the Dutch embassy in Jakarta, July 2013.

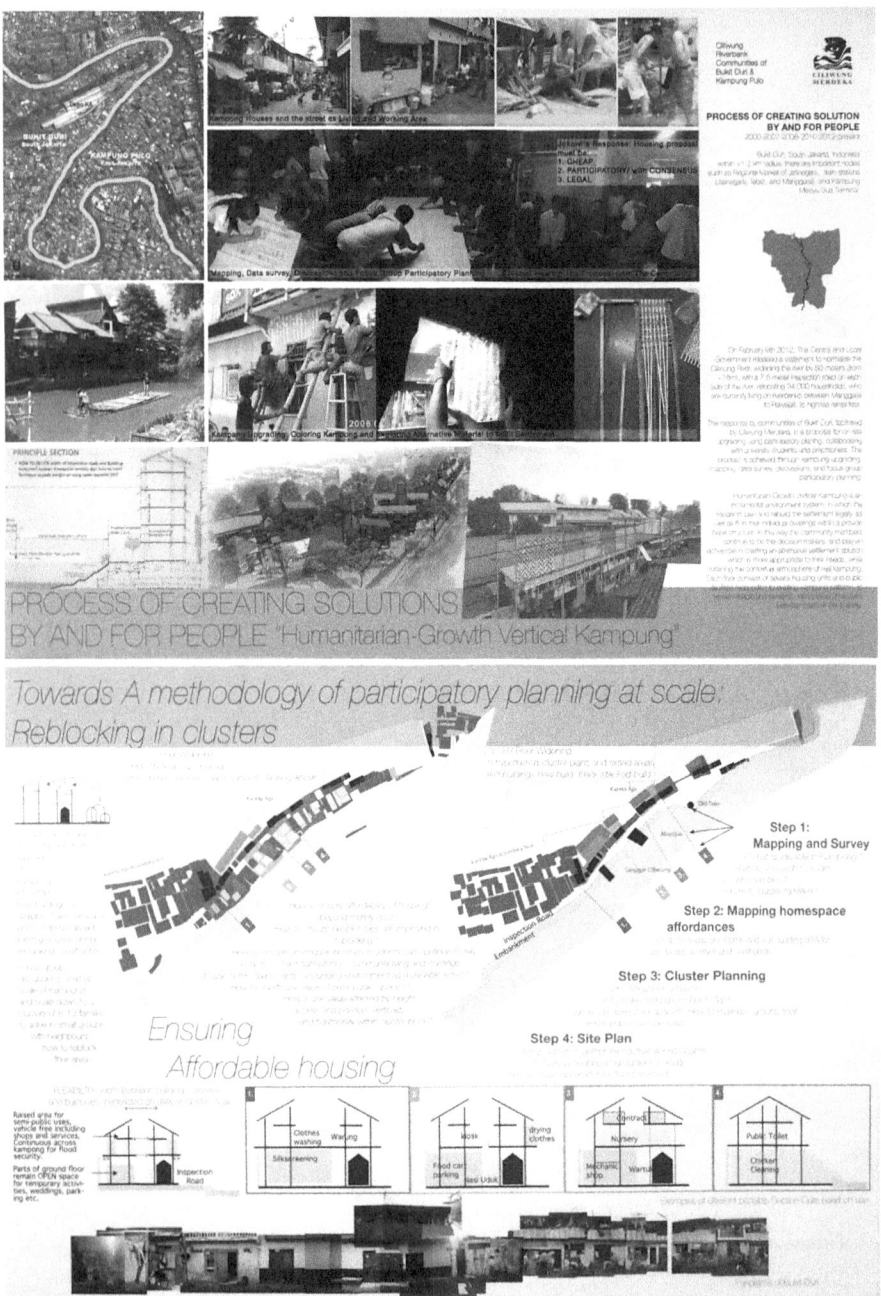

Figure 4.4
Ciliwung Merdeka's design for a "humanitarian vertical kampung," exhibited at the *Jakarta Vertical Kampung* exhibition at the Dutch embassy in Jakarta, July 2013.

Figure 4.5
Strenkali upgrading project in progress in Surabaya, July 2014. Photograph by author.

professional or trained designers are much needed in, and yet often neglect, the places with the most pressing social and environmental problems. One often sees projects like schools and clinics in Africa and South Asia designed by young architects, usually from the United States or Europe, sometimes from more local places, subscribing to these ideas and practices.

But the alternate visions in Jakarta—these counterplans—are not simply examples of humanitarian design. Nor are they a design-driven form of the "entrepreneurial" slum dweller, à la Hernando de Soto,[34] kampung residents individually empowered to take their fates (and their homes) into their own hands. It is more coherent, collective, and multilevel. Kampung organizers build on the exigency of real, shared struggles, conditions of notoriety, a history of political activism, and the vision and ability to form new coalitions. Design, in effect, becomes part of a *platform for organizing*. Design makes political vision tangible—documents, numbers, urban and architectural forms—to explain and negotiate. Both coalitions' visions were presented in an exhibition titled *Jakarta Vertical Kampung* in the Dutch embassy in 2013, and they have succeeded in building a working, if tenuous, relationship with city officials.

Says Sumardi of Ciliwung Merdeka,

> For years, the urban poor in Jakarta had a very negative stigma, that they were lazy, passive, illegal, only taking welfare, and didn't want to participate, didn't want to be organized. We proved that a collective planning process, with plans and mappings, could be made by the community themselves . . . that they had the imagination to form the ideals for their own kampung, in ways that were concrete.[35]

Design connects the emotional to the pragmatic. It gives form—and legibility, a design equivalent of hard copies—to what might have been summarily dismissed as emotional appeals or fought off as political activism.

Ariel Shepherd, then a community architect with the Asian Coalition for Housing Rights (ACHR), who spent more than a year living in Bukit Duri and working with Ciliwung Merdeka, agrees with this assessment, and adds some complexity. In her view, design does legitimize and give form to organizing. But if the work of design is done too quickly, without organic, broad-based community support, it can overplay a sense of completion and diminish participation.[36]

New York

Rebuild By Design

The development of design as a central concern in the New York context is complex and enlightening. It is partly due to timing, prior research, and the fortuitous connections of powerful people, including HUD secretary Shaun Donovan, Rockefeller Foundation president Judith Rodin, and Henk Ovink, Dutch director of spatial planning and water management. One should be reminded: this is not a typical thing, having innovative design for climate change as the focus of a US federal program.

Nancy Kete, then managing partner of the Rockefeller Foundation, the primary funder for the Rebuild By Design competition phase, discusses the "resurgence of the design perspective" around their work immediately following Sandy. I quote her at length:

> My colleagues at the Rockefeller Foundation had funded the *Rising Currents* exhibit at MoMA [in 2010]. I see that as the precursor to Rebuild By Design, because it helped people think differently both about how to live with water and the role of

Plans and Counterplans   131

> design in finding innovative ways to do just that. When Dr. Rodin was asked to co-chair the NYS 2100 Commission, and pulled a few of us in to contribute, the first thing I did was look back at *Rising Currents*. It had an interesting history: Guy Nordenson was one of the NYS 2100 commissioners. He had won the Latrobe Prize, and [with Catherine Seavitt and Adam Yarinsky] produced the *Palisade Bay* book. Then they teamed up with the head of architecture for MoMA and ran the *Rising Currents* contest. The Foundation then made a relatively small grant, for us, to support the MoMA exhibit. In a certain way the full value of that support wasn't obvious until Sandy hit. Everybody on the NYS 2100 Commission had either seen the exhibit, or heard about it.
>
> It made my job much easier on the land use and environment subcommittee [of NYS 2100]. Because while there were some commissioners who were saying, Okay, Sandy proves we need these big gates, others said, Well, what about all those ideas from *Rising Currents*? So the commissioners and a lot of the press, they had this design memory; they had this visual vocabulary, and this spatial vocabulary, that I don't think most people would have had if it hadn't been for *Rising Currents*.[37]

Kete is careful not to overplay her own role or that of the Rockefeller Foundation more broadly. But she stresses this moment without hesitation:

> And you know, frankly, I made sure people remembered it. We got copies of the exhibition guide from MoMA, we gave them to all the commissioners, and [we included] the language in the 2100 report. . . . Because it had been so visual, because it had been at MoMA. . . . It really informed the recommendations in the land use chapter of the NYS 2100 Commission report, which were to use nature and nature-based solutions as your first line of defense. Which was pretty good![38]

Ovink was also part of bringing this focus on design and the built environment. As someone who, at a moment's notice, can go into detail about the history of and motivations behind Dutch spatial planning and water management—what he calls a culture of "living with water"—he stresses the need to bring in line the process and the outcome, and for comprehensive planning, stating,

> [t]his is something we developed in the Netherlands over time, which is that, on a regional scale, there are interdependencies when it comes to infrastructure. And those interdependencies make it very clear that if you put them on a real agenda—if you make a plan—you gain a lot. You see missed opportunities, you can bring benefits together and investments together to create more benefits. You can define the process in a comprehensive way so you don't lose out in the implementation.[39]

We see this in the six winning proposals themselves—New York's version of that idealized society post-climate change.[40]

The **BIG** team proposed "The Big U" for Lower Manhattan, a series of buildings, landscape elements, and demountable protections that wraps around Manhattan (figure 4.6). While the conceptual scheme envisions a very big "U" looping around the island from East 42nd Street, along the East River, down around the Financial District, and then back up to West 57th Street, along the Hudson River, the competition proposal itself focuses on the southeast third of that, from East 23rd Street down including the Battery-Financial District. The team's design documents stress the "needs and concerns of the Island's diverse communities" and "integrated social and community planning." (The team was awarded $335 million.)[41]

The **Interboro** team takes a comprehensive view of Nassau County's South Shore. Titled "Living with the Bay," the team's plan stresses a regional approach, looking systemwide at the south shore of Long Island before focusing on the area around Long Beach and Mill River (figure 4.7). The team proclaims a process that intersects a "systems approach" with a "community approach." Its proposal is explicitly ecological in strategy, with wetlands and a combination of soft and hard infrastructure. It also takes on issues of racial segregation, affordability, and governance, although the implementation of ecological infrastructure is better defined than its social and governance objectives in the proposal. (The team was awarded $125 million.)

Figure 4.6
Rendering of the "Big U" proposal at the south tip of Manhattan by BIG team, 2014.
Source: Rebuild By Design.

Plans and Counterplans

Figure 4.7
Aerial rendering of "Living with the Bay" proposal by Interboro team, 2014.
Source: Rebuild By Design.

The **MIT CAU + ZUS + URBANISTEN** team's "New Meadowlands" project in New Jersey is set in a context in which fragile wetlands ecosystems abruptly meet expanses of concrete, asphalt, and steel—the support systems for the New York City area urban agglomeration. The team's proposal encompasses strategies ranging across the environmental to the economic (figure 4.8). A nature reserve serves as the backbone of storm protections, while enhanced transportation networks and recreational spaces offer impetus for more urban-scale densification and residential development. (The team was awarded $150 million.)

The **OMA** team, addressing Hoboken on the New Jersey shore west of the Hudson River, proposed a strategy to "resist, delay, store, discharge" water (figure 4.9). In line with the lead architecture firm's approach—what might be called a rhetorical pragmatism—the plan proposes a series of enhanced hard and soft infrastructure protections along the coast (to resist), permeable areas within the city (to delay), a set of storm water holding areas within the city (to store), and pumps and drains (to discharge). "Defended Coastline," it proclaims in its briefing book. It appears that the OMA team stresses least, at least in explicit terms, the sociopolitical and community relationship matters, compared to the other winning proposals. (The team was awarded $230 million.)

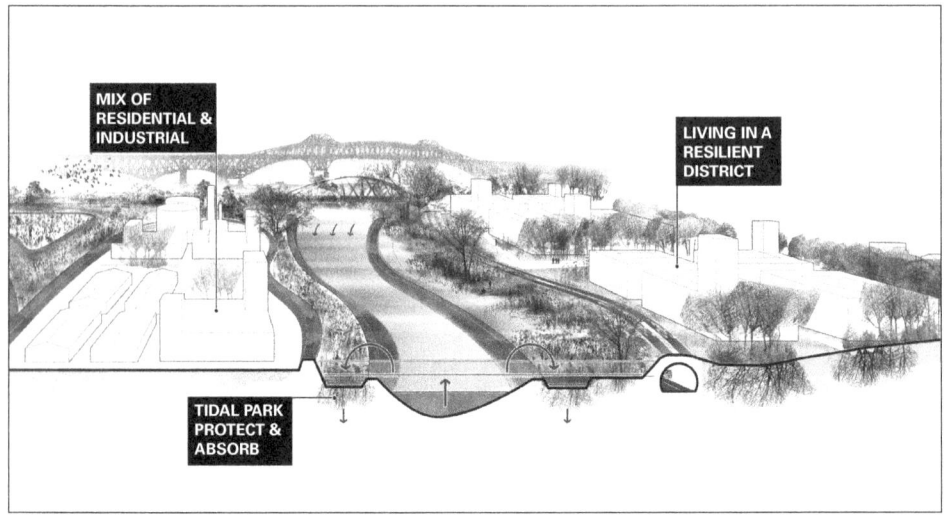

Figure 4.8
Concept drawing of "New Meadowlands" proposal by MIT CAU+ZUS+URBAN-ISTEN team, 2014.
Source: Rebuild By Design.

The **PennDesign / OLIN** team, looking at Hunts Point, in the Bronx, zeroes in on the specific challenges of the neighborhood, one beset by poverty, environmental vulnerability, and undesirable land uses (figure 4.10). It also stresses the strengths of local activism, including the work of groups like Sustainable South Bronx, who have led local EJ and green jobs initiatives. The proposal, called "Hunts Point Lifelines," seizes on the fact that the neighborhood is host to one of the largest food distribution hubs, and it highlights opportunities for effective community-based planning, new jobs, new methods of intermodal food and supply distribution, and local economic development. Livelihoods matter as much as flood protection. (The team was awarded $20 million.)

The **SCAPE** team proposed "Living Breakwaters" for the eastern coastline of Staten Island (figure 4.11). Eschewing conventional "hard" protections, the proposal entails a series of breakwaters—submerged and exposed partial barriers—to dissipate storm surges. These are built of hybrid construction, a combination of proprietary "ECOncrete" blocks and gabions to encourage oyster habitats and other marine life. SCAPE also stresses the community links, making the point that these developments would provide educational

Figure 4.9
Rendering of "Resist, Delay, Store, Discharge" proposal for Hoboken by OMA Team, 2014.
Source: Rebuild By Design.

and cultural opportunities for local residents. A diagram on its design board depicts "culture," "risk reduction," and "ecology" in relation to each other. (The team was awarded $60 million.)

The operative scales of the proposals are rather divergent. The OMA and BIG teams proposed designs for highly urbanized areas. The MIT team looked at a very large, industrialized and urbanizing landscape. The SCAPE team, led by landscape architects, took on more of a coastal protection and community engagement project, rather than a more broadly comprehensive scheme. The PennDesign / OLIN team explored a somewhat smaller scale, a neighborhood.

Each of the teams emphasizes community engagement in its process. Each tries to make this engagement an evidently discernible part of its design. At the same time, these scales, and the scope of the projects, bring up clear issues in terms of the engagement objectives. When your list of

Figure 4.10
Aerial rendering of "Hunts Point Lifelines," South Bronx, proposal by PennDesign / OLIN team, 2014.
Source: Rebuild By Design.

Figure 4.11
Rendering of "Living Breakwaters" proposal by SCAPE team, 2014.
Source: Rebuild By Design.

stakeholders includes ten New York City municipal departments, four city council districts, four state senate districts, six state assembly districts, eight US congressional districts, three New York State departments, numerous federal agencies and departments (including Army Corps of Engineers, Coast Guard, Homeland Security, Interior, Transportation, Environmental Protection Agency, General Services Administration, and National Parks Service), as well as various real estate developers and property managers, nonprofit organizations like Friends of the High Line, Battery Park Conservancy, and community groups such as Asian Americans for Equality, as the BIG team's BIG U proposal does, who, actually, are your stakeholders?

According to Ovink, Rebuild By Design attempted to bridge two cultures, to merge "entrepreneurship, individualism, winning, and competition, with a collaborative approach, this polder model, and a focus on the common." This is an ambitious task in the urban spatial politics of New York City. Ovink himself recognizes this: "So, collaborative, inclusive, competition. That's actually impossible!"[42]

Process and Participation

The Rebuild By Design award process was set up in a very specific way. Federal community development block grants targeted toward disaster recovery (CDBG–DR) were assigned to local municipalities (as detailed in chapter 2). The CDBG–DR funds are specifically meant to aid low-income communities after disaster.[43] Given this structure, design teams had to win the backing of a broad group of local stakeholders in order to win the project. Design, then, was tuned toward a particularly communicative fashion—aligned with normative planning principles.

For example, in the BIG U proposal by the BIG team for Lower Manhattan, designers explicitly attempted to hybridize Robert Moses and Jane Jacobs—promising to reconcile the two iconic, almost mythical figures who are often caricatured as the despot and darling of New York urban development fights, Moses's craving for freeways, bridges, and urban renewal programs posed against Jacobs's love of 1960s' Greenwich Village streetlife and protests against the demolition of historic buildings. The team presented design drawings that proposed meshing top-down and bottom-up, large-scale infrastructure and community relationships. One could argue that the designers attempted this Moses-Jacobs meshing on two levels. The first in terms of the spatial objectives of the design itself, combining waterfront infrastructure, prominent cultural buildings, and spaces for local gathering, and the second in terms of their own practice, necessarily engaging with a broader "public" on a city-scale (after all, this team had the highest-profile site), and attempting to bring community groups on board with their proposal.

The community stakeholders here, including longtime Lower East Side housing advocates, ended up quite happy with the vision and their participation. But they did not start out that way.

"We have a history of seeing beautification further exacerbate gentrification," says Damaris Reyes, the executive director of GOLES and chair of LES Ready. She explains her concerns about the community design process,

> Let me give you some background. The west side gets everything, okay? The west side gets everything, they get everything! So, here is this moment where the "BIG U," you know, is moving forward for all of Lower Manhattan and they're now directed by the city to focus on our community. That was like flag number one. People are, like, what, oh, really, now you want to come over here? You know, they start looking at you, you know, side eyed, like of course they want to protect the land there because they want to make sure that they can still sell it, that's what people think and so yeah, people drew those conclusions.[44]

Reyes here brings up longstanding issues in Manhattan urban politics. The west side of Lower Manhattan, including the West Village, Tribeca, and

Battery Park City neighborhoods, has for some time been affluent and influential. The disparities she mentions are quite obvious. The dismantling of the elevated West Side Highway made way for the new Hudson River Park; yet the also-elevated FDR Drive on the east side remains, community and recreational uses in the surrounding area much less developed, after multiple planning initiatives. And after the 9/11 attacks, the Chinatown area adjacent to the Lower East Side was hit particularly hard, first by the immediate economic impact, then by inequitable distribution of housing and job-creation funds[45] and spatial segregation by security barriers and rerouted transportation from the Wall Street area.[46]

So, the fact that the BIG team was focusing on her community was not immediately a positive. Yet, Reyes and members of her coalition were heartened by the involvement of Amy Chester, the manager of Rebuild By Design. Reyes says,

> Amy [Chester] in her role was a significant factor because she's been an organizer, she's from New York, she knows the challenges so she knew immediately what I was talking about. You know, I can't tell, you know, the designers before this, where they were at, if they're inclined towards these things. I understood that they were designers and really that I want them to do was to be prepared to listen and then act from that space.
>
> After we made the agreement to work together, our focus quickly shifted towards making it successful . . . [47]

Chester herself notes the challenges of making this connection between the designers and the community stakeholders. She recalls going to three-quarters of all the public meetings, introducing herself, and stressing to the audience, "We are here today because the teams have to get your feedback and have to prove to us that your feedback was taken into consideration."[48] Rebuild By Design ensured a level of community engagement on the part of the design teams by enforcing this link between the outcome of the competition and community and political support. After a process that was, to Damaris Reyes, both contentious and productive, LES Ready convinced elected officials to support the BIG team's plan.[49]

Two of the challenges to the Rebuild By Design strategy are directly linked to the very innovation it is credited for. The first is the uncertain relationship between the competition phase and the implementation phase. After the winning teams were declared, HUD released the CDBG–DR funds either to the city or state in which the effected localities reside. Then, each city or state body began their own program to manage the funds and move the projects forward, subject to the local and state politics and legislative processes. By mid-2015, a fragmented picture of this emerged across the localities with winning proposals, including states and cities issuing requests for proposals, conducting environmental reviews, holding further community workshops, and continuing the refinement of project design scopes.[50]

In the New York City case, Michael Marrella, director of Waterfront and Open Space Planning, notes,

> With Rebuild by Design in particular, there's so much political and public attention to these projects, we're certainly not looking to shift course dramatically—in part because Rebuild by Design did a very good job of building public anticipation, public desires for these projects.... I think what it really amounts to is determining the scope of the project given the funds that were allocated ... the city is not going to be able to take the money and change course drastically.[51]

The BIG team's BIG U proposal was awarded $335 million in CDBG funds—a lot of money, but a fraction of what it would take to build defenses surrounding Manhattan, from midtown down. The initial award, in line with the broader Rebuild By Design strategy, is meant to spur further private funding, to create a "new form of public-private financing mechanism."[52] After the competition phase, HUD released the funds to the city, which then started its own planning and implementation process. One part of the city-led planning process, for what is now called the East Side Coastal Resiliency (ESCR) project, retains largely intact the primary design team members from the BIG U project.

Early in the implementation phase, in the fall of 2014, there was already debate and contestation over which areas are protected first. Community members in low-income areas in the Lower East Side—the very ones who helped bring the elected officials on board to support the project—contend that they are not being prioritized, even though their neighborhoods were the hardest hit, and the lowest lying.[53] This situation proceeded through mid-2015 as the city began new public meetings for this project. Another conflict between the city planners and community members would emerge later, in late 2018, when the planning team for the (now) ESCR project changed the physical design strategy and phasing for the plan, ostensibly without further community agreements.[54] These contestations illustrate very well what is perhaps the key challenge of the Rebuild By Design initiative. Design works to engage communities, "win" block grants, and capture

Plans and Counterplans 141

imaginations. But in this case, the integrated, regional planning aspirations did not translate into a larger attempt to change social relationships and political systems in the city in transformative ways. Power relationships and governance structures remain.

Chester, deep in the implementation phase, four years after the conclusion of the competition, underscores the problem and offers an assessment:

> We're not having the conversation about how to protect the entire city any longer, because we are focused on how to get this project built or that project built.... How do you keep both conversations at the same time? Because you want to stick up for the Lower East Side and you want to stick up for every community and you want them to get what they want. And what Rebuild was able to do in the research stage was have this regional conversation that then ended when it became project based....
>
> I don't fool ourselves that we were able to change the system, but what I do think we were able to do is disrupt the system for a little while to create projects that would have never been created otherwise, and to give communities a voice and a vision and a hope to have the words literally to talk about what they want to see, which after Sandy, no one knew.[55]

Ovink, for his part, notes, "Very comprehensive, innovative, inclusive proposals on the table of institutional partners had to be taken apart because they did not fit the system." He rues what he observes to be a reactive response among some of the implementing agencies, which then entailed revising the proposals to meet competing interests and needs instead of fixing the system itself. But, speaking in the spring of 2019, he sees some commonality emerging through the protracted process in the Lower East Side, a path forward. It takes time, government ownership, and an inclusive process for projects like these to succeed, he stresses.[56]

Not shy about grand pronouncements, Ovink is nevertheless modest about envisioning social transformation. "My goal is to change the world," he says, "but it's not me who will change it."[57]

Terrains of Contestation

My objective in this chapter is in part to unearth the complexities behind what is often (mis)understood as a rather straightforward proposition—to design. What constitutes design depends on the worldview of design thinking one refers to; it also depends on the audience, or the recipient of design ideas. Often, what is seen as a multilevel process by urban designers is understood to be the aesthetic, desired outcome by the community participant or the politician. But my objective is also to reveal the power in design. That is, the ways in which the processes and production of envisioning alternate social and spatial futures are able to confront and challenge dominant modes of urban development, or accepted protocols of professionalized urban spatial practices.

In Jakarta, the Giant Sea Wall masterplan—the Great Garuda—shows off its intentions and its affectations. It is eye-opening, this plan, in this location. There is an almost simplistic narrative to be wrought: the sophistication of the hydrological plan meets the obduracy of the canal conditions; the immediate, figural Garuda, a cultural symbol, in a plan that has not yet allowed any public participation. If one were doing a straightforward design review, one might critique harshly this overbearing use of symbol and figure to achieve design goals. But the plan eludes such easy dismissal. In political terms, balancing Dutch vision and Indonesian aspirations, the Great Garuda design achieved an important goal. It garnered the political support of city and national government officials—even through a contentious election and transfer of power that changed both the city and the nation. The design gave form to a previously technical process. It allowed officials to see beyond a wall, even beyond a real estate development project, to national ambition.

Will it work? Work for whom? On one level it may already be working. In chapter 3, I explained the Dutch objectives in developing the masterplan, and asserting themselves as the credible, long-term partner. They look to strengthen their position in Indonesian regional and broader Asian urban development. The first phase of the NCICD plan broke ground in October 2014. The flexibility in scope and extent, as well as the hydrologists' and planners' earlier options to do less, suggests to me that parts of the masterplan will likely be built, even if confronted by less than perfect economic and political conditions. The question of whether it will work, in this regard, hinges on whether the project moves forward in a productive manner, regardless of final scope, accomplishing some of its key objectives; whether other objectives, including the canal dredging, move forward productively, perhaps with successful kampung rehousing initiatives; and in what ways the Dutch consultants and governmental organizations will proceed along with it.

In Muara Baru, and in Bukit Duri and Kampung Pulo, community organizations UPC and Ciliwung Merdeka along with their coalitions have

Plans and Counterplans 143

marshaled design toward productive protests against evictions-as-usual and agreements with then governor Jokowi. Design here enabled kampung residents to give form to a sociopolitical campaign. The visions and the measures afforded by the design process and documents enabled new platforms for negotiation between organizers and city officials. The continued challenges of resisting evictions and demolitions in kampung settlements, and the persistent incapacity on the part of the city government to build different models of socially oriented housing, attest to the difficulty of changing longstanding, unjust systems. Few examples of concrete, positive changes on a notable scale have emerged. And yet, these design-fueled countermovements, these sociospatial alternatives, have helped to sustain and grow a long-range political movement.

In New York, Rebuild By Design promised to do something quite extraordinary: to develop a comprehensive design strategy for an urban region facing climate change impacts and deliberative process of community engagement—at least in a somewhat simplified form merging Dutch spatial planning and water management with US urban politics. Its centering of design in urban climate change responses revealed both the possibility of the moment—following a major environmental disaster in a major city— and the maneuverings of individuals and institutions who harnessed their connections, expertise, and influence.

Organizers for Rebuild By Design intently foregrounded community participation, ensuring a level of engagement between design teams and community stakeholders. At the same time, each team's proposal reveals priorities that reflect both the local sites it is designed for and the intentions and disciplinary and expertise makeup of its team members.[58] Among the winning design teams, the BIG, Interboro, and SCAPE teams proposed designs that explicitly intended to form a bridge between ecology and infrastructure, on the one side, and community inclusion, on the other. It is worth remarking that this particular dualism is perpetuated even in the projects that attempt to bridge it. That is, ecology-infrastructure and social-community are posed as distinct and typically in tension, needing to be brought together, and not seen as intrinsically intertwined within urban processes. The MIT CAU+ZUS+URBANISTEN and OMA teams privileged infrastructure and economy, while PennDesign / Olin stressed socioeconomic goals.

The teams took inspiration from the initiative's broader regional aspirations. But in each case, the final proposals tend to be rather bounded in scope and scale, largely conforming to the political and regulatory structures of municipalities and the social relationships of communities on the ground. Amid the ongoing work, design's negotiation of the disparate power relationships, the different points of view, the marginalized voices and positions remains only partially accounted for. The framework of community organizing is brought into a role of mediation, between professionalized, expert knowledge on the part of the design teams and the community interests and local knowledge among constituents. But design is not yet harnessed in a role of accomplice, working to challenge oppressive social structures in cities.[59]

In one particular way, it may be surprising that designers in Jakarta and New York did not take even stronger cues from the Dutch exemplars. They could have looked at how, for example, agencies and firms in the Netherlands work across multiple levels of governance and institutions of public and semipublic charge to marshal relatively small-scale and singular models of urban design projects, such as De Urbanisten's Rotterdam water square (discussed in chapter 3), into what are posed as transformative examples of urban social and ecological interventions, to be learned from around the world. It bears remembering that a project such as the Rotterdam water square exists not only within the multiple levels of Dutch governance and public and private institutional structures, but also within the spatial, territorial context of Dutch national spatial planning and water management, more than half a century after the beginning of the Delta Works. Singular works of design are particularly powerful when situated within aligned social, spatial, and institutional contexts.

Could the design projects in Jakarta and New York be similarly contained, spatially, and yet have such far-reaching influence, conceptually? It seems, for now, that the answer is no—with the possible exception of the SCAPE team's "Living Breakwaters" project for Rebuild By Design, the ideas for which date back to the lead firm's work on "oyster-tecture" for the 2010 *Rising Currents* show at MoMA. The notion of "living"—constructed and "natural," more softly protective—physical environments coupled with social engagement and learning continues to kindle interest among designers and commentators for more environmentally and socially attuned urban spaces.

An Alternative? The Red Hook Initiative

To conclude this chapter, I offer one example of an alternative approach, a project with which I am very familiar. In 2010, my design firm SUPER-INTERESTING!, of which I am a cofounder and principal, designed a community center for the Red Hook Initiative in Red Hook, Brooklyn. The RHI space was designed in a collaborative process, by and for the community (figure 4.12). We made a collective sense of ownership by participants a priority. When Hurricane Sandy hit the New York region, Red Hook was one of the worst-hit neighborhoods in the city. RHI's space survived the storm, and in the days after, emerged as a hub of grassroots recovery efforts (figure 4.13; see elaboration on this in chapter 2).

In Red Hook, community building, social and environmental resilience, and space and design were inextricably intertwined. It serves as an example for how designers can engage with deeper aspects of justice and equity. Eric Klinenberg, NYU sociologist and research adviser for Rebuild By Design, explicitly made this connection when he brought members of the selected design teams to the RHI space, asking: "Can we design spaces like this?"[60]

Figure 4.12
Red Hook Initiative, designed by SUPER-INTERESTING!, March 2010. Photo by author.

Figure 4.13
Red Hook Initiative during Sandy recovery, November 2012. Photo by Red Hook Initiative.

It is a rhetorical question. Of course we can and do! Left unsaid in such a question, but nevertheless implied, are larger questions about the relationship between Rebuild By Design—and design more broadly—and grassroots resiliency initiatives.

How did the RHI space remain safe after the storm? I can offer some thoughts about this. One aspect was luck and topography. The flooding reached the streets adjacent to the RHI space, but did not go beyond. Another was a matter of architectural design and economy. The building was built by the developer and owner as a warehouse space—involving relatively inexpensive building materials and structural system, with a concrete, slab-on-grade floor construction. It does not have a basement. Our team designed the space in such a way that the mechanical systems were placed on the roof and mounted on the walls, out of the way of floodwaters. (Mounting critical equipment above the ground floor is now a standard architectural design recommendation for storm surge and flood resilience. The Red Hook Houses buildings, just across the street, do have basements with mechanical equipment, and did not fare quite as well.)

These observations explain how the space stayed relatively dry, and how the electricity remained on. What happened after is just as important. How did the space, along with the staff members and volunteers, become a recovery hub in the wake of Sandy? In my view, three points stand out. First, our design team paid particular attention to the relationship between spatial design and social organization. We prioritized openness, transparency, and accessibility—aligned with RHI's approach as a community space—as well as a diversity of spaces to account for the fast-changing and often unpredictable uses. This included leaving the large warehouse doors as glazed, roll-up doors. In the days after the storm, this enabled volunteers to set up a soup kitchen service just inside the doors, with lines spilling out onto the sidewalks. The flexible, open spaces accommodated the stocking and organizing of supplies and meetings for coordinating relief efforts. Second, the location of the building, "catty-corner" to the Red Hook Houses, allowed the RHI space to function as it was intended—as a place by and for the community. Public housing residents impacted by the storm could come by without leaving their neighborhood. Volunteers patently knew the community they were working to help. Third, associated, there had been "buy-in" from the community members—the staff and participants, almost all of whom have ties to public housing. The RHI space, completed only two years before the storm, had become a center of social life. Jill Eisenhard of RHI relates stories of youth participants exclaiming in wonder that it was the most beautiful building in the neighborhood, and that it was *theirs*.

A project like the RHI space does not replace the kind of large-scale infrastructural and landscape design projects that Rebuild By Design envisions. There is a space for big plans like that, especially in circumstances in which there is broad consensus for high levels of physical protection, embraced as part of the sociocultural and economic lives of residents. But the RHI project allows us to consider that crucial weaving of social and spatial factors—in ways that are particular to the place, position, and agency of systemically marginalized urban residents.

So it is not that one project changes much—but this one project is successfully embedded in a broader process of organizing for social and political change. *People from the community have the power to create their own social change.* . . . Jill Eisenhard, executive director of RHI, continues, "You have to create opportunities for people to take action ahead of time, you can't wait until there's some kind of disaster."[61]

Design connects the pragmatic and the emotional; it bridges social and spatial. But it is not neutral. Design is political, and intertwined with foundational ideas about society—concerning symbol, image, identity, power, and legitimacy. Design opens terrains of contestation. When invoked, understood, and practiced as part of building a movement for political change, it can take its place in visualizing and countering the structures—both physical and systemic—that bind people and places in precarious social and environmental conditions. Design can be a part of resistance, a mode of political organizing.

5 A Political Ecology of Design

> so beautiful in her eyes;
> water will come again
> if you can wait for it.
> she feels what the desert feels.
> she waits.
> —Lucille Clifton, "water sign woman"

On August 20, 2015, Jakarta security personnel began the forced eviction of residents in Kampung Pulo and the demolition of their homes along the Ciliwung River. This followed a sequence of contradictory announcements and news stories—with Governor Ahok first agreeing to rehouse residents in place and then apparently changing his mind.[1] In the lead-up to the evictions, kampung residents were termed squatters (in Bahasa Indonesia, *pemukim liar*, literally "wild residents"), with no legal rights . . .

In the years after Hurricane Sandy hit the New York region and floods inundated Jakarta, things changed and things did not.

In Jakarta, the forced evictions of the kampungs in 2015 reset relationships between the capital region government and poor urban residents, offsetting some of the goodwill that had been developed during the early days of Jokowi's governorship. The evictions were followed by a period of tumultuous politics in the city. Jokowi's deputy, Basuki Tjahaja Purnama (known by his nickname Ahok), assumed the governorship of Jakarta and, later, was found guilty of blasphemy after making a speech for which he was accused of insulting Islam. Ahok lost the Jakarta gubernatorial election of 2017, which took place just before his trial, to Anies Baswedan. Anies campaigned on a promise to stop land reclamations in the Jakarta Bay. His camp also signed a political contract with a coalition of urban poor residents and activists, including UPC and Rujak, around kampung land tenure and the rights of street vendors and rickshaw drivers.[2]

In late 2018, I conducted follow-up fieldwork in Jakarta. I again visited sites I had first researched six years before. Stretches of a reinforced sea wall were evident, under construction along the north shore of Jakarta near Muara Baru. This is part of the first phase of the NCICD masterplan. But the ambitious Garuda vision is gone. The planning process continues between the Indonesian Ministry of Public Works and Housing and its Dutch and Korean partners to develop an outer sea dike, albeit in a modified, scaled-back form. In Bukit Duri and Kampung Pulo, where the force of evictions and demolitions of 2015 and 2016 still show in the ragged edges of walls and floors of some houses left partially standing, new concrete embankments and an access road cordon off the Ciliwung River (figure 5.1).

Compounding the still-uncertain futures of these and other vulnerable sites in the city, President Jokowi announced in August 2019 that the

Figure 5.1
New embankment and access road along the Ciliwung River, at Bukit Duri and Kampung Pulo, Jakarta, May 2017. Photograph by author.

Indonesian capital would be moved from Jakarta to a new city on the island of Borneo. The near- and far-term implications of this dramatic decision are still very much unknown.³

In New York, the moments of relative enthusiasm among many planners and design practitioners during and following the Rebuild By Design competition phase settled into the slow and unsteady amble of individual municipality review and procurement processes. Many of the finalist projects are still in progress. But, as of 2019, it was hard not to think that not much has been done. The initial proposals, already constrained to localities, have been further fragmented. The area covered by the BIG U proposal for Lower Manhattan is now divided into two city-led projects: the East Side Coastal Resiliency (ESCR)—with retains some core ideas and team members from the BIG team—and the Lower Manhattan Coastal Resiliency (LMCR) projects. Two projects, the portion of the BIG U now named ESCR and Living Breakwaters in Staten Island have promised start dates of 2020.⁴

Mid-2019, in Red Hook, Brooklyn, "temporary" boilers sit outside the red brick buildings of the Red Hook Houses, the fencing and piping around them increasingly elaborate. They appear, for practical intents, permanent. Some blocks away from the housing project, closer to the waterfront where the worst flooding occurred, "interim" flood protection measures—demountable flood walls covered in art-printed tarpaulin—sit along sidewalks and by intersections, to be deployed when the next Sandy-like storm hits (figure 5.2).

In July 2019, during the hottest summer on record in Europe, Rotterdam hosted the 100 Resilient Cities Urban Resilience Summit, during which it was announced that the initiative supported by the Rockefeller Foundation would end that month. The city was both a fitting and ironic location for such an event—maintaining its claims as a center for urban resilience and yet heralding imminent changes. The fervor with which Rotterdam proclaimed its model urban resilience aspirations, so evident five years before, appears to have ebbed somewhat. But the outward momentum of Netherlands climate change response ambitions continues. The Global Commission on Adaptation, established by the Netherlands and launched in October 2018 by former UN secretary general Ban Ki-moon, convenes twenty countries around the world with the objective of spurring investments and political action on climate change adaptation. Secretary General Ban, along with Bill Gates, co-chair of the Bill and Melinda Gates Foundation, and Kristalina Georgieva, International Monetary Fund managing director and former World Bank chief executive officer, lead the commission.⁵

Figure 5.2
Temporary flood protection measures, Red Hook waterfront, Brooklyn, February 2019. Photograph by author.

The Netherlands has also launched the Water as Leverage program, led by Henk Ovink and the Netherlands Enterprise Agency, to leverage investments toward innovative solutions to water problems—echoing some of the ambitions behind Rebuild By Design. Six teams comprising design, international development, engineering, and hydrology firms and institutions are now developing proposals in three cities in Asia: Chennai in India, Khulna in Bangladesh, and Semarang in Indonesia. The program's motivations, according to Ovink, are in part an effort to reinvent our approaches to water, deflecting our future course from the misguided practices of the past and present, and in part a responsibility to the world, a kind of *noblesse oblige*.[6]

Remaking the Spatial Politics of Climate Change

In the face of climate change and uneven social and spatial urban development, how are contesting visions of the future produced and how do they attain power?

A Political Ecology of Design 153

The question that drives this book is framed by a historically specific and geographically generalized context—the environmental threats caused by or linked to climate change and the forms of urban development under globalized capitalism in the early twenty-first century. Within this context, New York, Jakarta, and Rotterdam form a particular set of sites. They are knitted in time and space by historical colonial relationships, present-day diplomatic and economic missions, a set of overlapping actors and institutions, global flows of capital, and environmental and climatic shifts that are globally constituted, but with disparate local impacts.

They are, as well, connected in less tangible ways—through ideas, symbols, and representations. The environmental plans proposed for New York and Jakarta are not simply delineations in space, ideal forms to accomplish stated social, environmental, and economic objectives. They appeal to, and trade on, a set of currencies. When Dutch minister Melanie Schulz refers to the Dutch feeling "very much at home here" (in Indonesia), she means something more than the current efforts at managing water.[7] She alludes to a long background of colonial dependency and postindependence nation building. When Henk Ovink shows a slide with "We All Hate You Sandy" spray-painted on the side of a damaged building, and states, "If you've lost everything you've built up, you want it back, you don't want to look ahead. . . . This fact drives Congress . . . not the science, this emotion,"[8] he invokes a cultural and political familiarity with the United States, and offers a tacit statement that he knows that this is not an engineering problem, even as he brings with him the significant authority of Dutch engineering reputation (figure 5.3).

In this book, I trace across the spectrum of more and less tangible interrelationships. As laid out in the introduction, the question at hand deals in an interrelated manner with politics, environment, space, and design. In engaging this question, the primary and intertwined issues cut across the sites, actors, and institutions, including: *power relationships locally and regionally*, between the processes of urban development and those caught in its path, and often between institutions of the state and on-the-ground communities; *power relationships globally*, across national boundaries, variously between state and nonstate actors; the *interconnected nature* of sociopolitical relationships and spatial-biophysical ecological processes across an urban region; the mechanisms and processes of *urban planning and design*, including the production of plans, and the institutional frameworks through which such plans

Figure 5.3
Henk Ovink at the Deltas in Times of Climate Change II conference, Rotterdam, September 2014. Photograph by author.

are disseminated and implemented; the mechanisms and processes of *policy and idea mobility and adoption* (through what means do ideas actually exist and move?); and the *symbolic nature of ideas and images* (how do visions of the future attain meaning, legitimacy, and power?).

In disentangling these issues, I have focused on questions that can be analyzed in a more direct manner: How is power constituted in these sites (and, alongside, how is marginalization made, enforced, and contested)? How are large-scale environmental plans produced amid the increasing global and urban interconnectedness of policy and planning? And how are specific visions legitimized in the context of contesting visions of urban futures? The key findings to these questions are summarized in the following section.

Nature of Contestation

In chapter 2, I explored the interrelationships between environmental initiatives and sociospatial marginalization in the context of climate change and uneven urban development. Building on theories of urban political ecology, and focused on the intertwined nature of urban socioecological change, I investigated sites and strategies in New York and Jakarta. I looked at high-profile plans produced by city and state agencies and transnational agencies and firms in response to environmental threats, the contestation around their making, and the alternative ideas proposed by marginalized groups on the ground.

In both cities, dominant state-led plans generally conform to and reflect the urban sociospatial systems in which they are embedded. In New York, in the context of reinvigorated attention to urban climate resilience after Hurricane Sandy, Rebuild By Design offered an innovative model of collaboration and financing, and an aspiration to think and plan regionally. At the same time, its implementation structure entailed that the winning concepts negotiate the complexities of local urban politics as they move forward, including decisions about what to build, where and when to build, and how to fully pay for it. In Jakarta, the Dutch-led NCICD Giant Sea Wall masterplan came amid an imperative to mitigate severe flooding. It is posed as a comprehensive solution to flooding, transportation, and city image problems, and yet neglects and exacerbates chronic infrastructural and social problems. By linking its implementation to the fortunes of large-scale privatized real estate development, the masterplan resorts to what is by all counts the "preferred," yet problematic, means of getting things done in the city—a rapid, well-fueled, but haphazard means of urban development.

These are sites of contestation, in which historical trajectories and geographic conditions of urban nature are intertwined with the production of social and spatial marginalization, informing the ways in which marginalized communities were impacted by, and responded to, environmental threats. In many ways, the burdens faced by these communities have simply continued, and have been reproduced through the changing environmental conditions and proposed plans. In other ways, community groups in Red Hook and the Lower East Side in New York, and in the Bukit Duri, Kampung Pulo, and Muara Baru kampungs in Jakarta, have exhibited innovative, grassroots responses to emerging challenges.

Key factors appear in common across the grassroots responses. First, the specific social and spatial condition of marginalization plays a significant role in enabling these groups to organize in the wake of, and in expectation of, disasters. This link between shared struggle and action not only reinforces the relationship between social and environmental resilience but also suggests that community organization and urban spatial form can be harnessed together, something possibly planned and designed. Second, the place of local knowledge remains important. The criticality of such knowledge arises in the most immediate sense, to aid in disaster recovery, as in Red Hook, Brooklyn, directly after Hurricane Sandy. It also arises as a means of organizing toward better responses, as in LES Ready's work to form a coalition in the Lower East Side. In Jakarta, the assertion of local knowledge across urban scales by disenfranchised communities and advocacy groups is a key aspect of resistance in a context in which the dominant plan is visually and technically ambitious, but still operates in a technocratic sphere. And third, broad-based coalition building can have extended impact. In the Lower East Side, coalition building serves as both community-based preparation for future disasters as well as a means of political organizing. In Jakarta, the forming of multilevel coalitions among residents, activists, and allied groups locally and globally is an effective means of local political organizing, and gaining international awareness and support.

Nature of Flows

In chapter 3, I looked at the shifting geographies of climate change governance and planning, in particular the ways in which new global-urban networks enable interrelationships across scales and levels, linking urban-scale environmental planning to national and global policy. Building on theories of relational geographies, the mobility of urban concepts, and the transnationality of climate change governance, I investigated the increasing role of Dutch government agencies, nongovernmental entities, and private firms in the making of urban climate change plans in New York and Jakarta, set in a broader global context.

Probing the actors, networks, and local and global contexts behind the development of these new geographies, I found critical relationships behind a number of concurrent events and policy shifts. First, in recent decades, decentralization of power and decision making on a national level in the Netherlands refocused spatial planning and urban development to the cities. Second, increasing awareness of climate change prompted new research initiatives in 2006–2007 on national and local scales—including a new Delta Commission report and a national research program, Knowledge for Climate. Third, also around that time, specific Dutch national policies and

A Political Ecology of Design

municipal planning programs coalesced with a strategic focus on urban water management and international relationships—including the creation of Deltares as a research institute and the launch of the Rotterdam Climate Proof program. Fourth, internationally focused initiatives such as the independent body NWP and the Netherlands "Top Sectors" provide aligned, cross-sector funding and support. All of this enables a Dutch global strategy that knits firms, scientists and researchers, government policy makers, and aid and investment mechanisms with very specific national priorities.

In tracing these strategies, and the way they land on the ground, embed, and transform themselves in places like Jakarta and New York, I found that, increasingly, global, national, and urban scales are intertwined. These entities and relationships constitute a multiscalar, multilevel network, through which the diffusion of capital, knowledge, and influence takes place (see figure 3.5). Three important factors define the formation of these networks. First, they are motivated by changing economic relationships, particularly new or shifting avenues through which firms, supported by coalitions of national and subnational, public and semipublic entities, find, define, and secure markets for urban environmental plans and projects, often prompted by climate change concerns. Second, they build on situational relationships, historically specific power relationships determined by, for example, colonial and postcolonial institutional links and developing diplomatic arrangements. And third, they are reinforced by specific interface conditions, including the characteristics and dynamics of sites, events, actors, or invocations of cultural appropriateness or environmental urgency.

The relationalities among actors and institutions in the networks span sites and cross geographic scales and institutional levels. Each site takes its place in defining the others. I define the concept of *network formation* to see and understand the interconnected processes, and to categorize relationships among them. The network formation defined among the sites and strategies in this book helps explain the reconfiguring geographies of urban environmental planmaking in the context of climate change and shows how national and corporate strategies can be operationalized through concrete urban policies and projects.

Plans and Counterplans

In chapter 4, I explored the role of design in urban climate change responses. Building on theories of the social production of space, I asked: Why do these projects take on the forms that they do? Design presents visions of alternate futures and brings to the foreground priorities and motivations. Considered simultaneously as process, practice, and outcome, the maneuverings and contestation around design exposes sociopolitical motivations and power relationships in cities. The discourse around design, therefore, offers insight into the making and disseminating of urban climate change responses. A key problem involves the nature of design itself. At its best, design works as informed provocation, able to influence and inspire, but not necessarily to understand and explain. The investigation of urban design and climate change requires a conceptual framework that enables a more reflexive look at design process, practice, and outcome.

Designs in the dominant plans in New York and Jakarta negotiate between the structure of their organizations and the sociopolitical contexts of their localities. For Rebuild By Design in New York, organizers were cognizant from the start that community engagement was necessary—based on the organization's objectives and also to make possible implementation (by local authorities). It made for a context in which the design teams stressed this engagement more than they might have otherwise. However, the conflicts emerging during the early implementation stages put into question the potential of such engagement to change in effective ways power relationships and modes of urban design and development. In Jakarta, the symbolic form of the NCICD Giant Sea Wall masterplan, with its Great Garuda design, had a particular objective. It was meant to resonate with local culture and meaning, and forge a sense of ownership. And in some ways, it has—particularly among those in political power. And yet, there is reticence among local leaders to open a broader engagement with constituents on the ground in Jakarta. Symbol, in this case, may not be enough. Judging by conversations with city officials and kampung organizers alike, Jokowi's *blusukan*, his impromptu walks, proved more compelling, more engaged, than the larger masterplanning efforts.

More generally, design plays multiple roles in the production and legitimization of urban environmental plans. Design connects the pragmatic and the emotional. It bridges the social and spatial aspects of climate change responses, and with it reveals power relationships, and assumes and sometimes amplifies the contestations around those responses. The marshaling of design can be used to connect a more technocratic process of planning with the messier, more unpredictable politics on the ground. This is what the Great Garuda vision attempts in Jakarta; it is what Henk Ovink's appeals to process and emotion are meant to accomplish in New York. But, conversely, design—that is, the practice of the protocols of design, or the production of the documents of design—can give measurable weight to what might be dismissed as emotional appeals. This is what UPC in Muara Baru and Ciliwung Merdeka in Bukit Duri and Kampung Pulo have been able to do. Along with giving form and measure, design is invoked to dispel stereotypes about marginalized residents and strengthen a political campaign. In this way, design can be a mode of political organizing.

Theoretical Reflection and Synthesis
How do these findings reflect on the foundational theories framing the topics in this book? Table 5.1 summarizes the theories, findings, and implications of each chapter. The paragraphs following draw out the primary implications of the findings, and offer a synthesis.

Across the sites and topics, these primary implications emerge. First, historical and systemic urban socioecological marginalization underlies and conditions emerging spaces and modes of urban contestation in the context of climate change impacts and new modes of urban ecological governance facilitated by climate change; the interaction of socioecological and the place-based physical spaces of shared struggle raises the need for attention to sociospatial forms of community-based resilience. Second, a relational analysis is critical to understand the ways in which (1) historical (colonial-postcolonial-geopolitical), cross-scalar, and cross-level power relationships, (2) changing global-local climate-environmental conditions, and, (3) emerging and reconfiguring networks, institutions, and movements in response to new climate conditions, are interrelated; this "network formation" reveals how response strategies emerge and move across scales and levels. And third, design is political, a means of negotiating the power relationships of contested urban sites; the reflexive, political movement-based design discourse and practice in the face of climate change opens up new terrains of contestation and space for alternative, counterhegemonic modes of envisioning urban ecological futures.

Together, the findings and implications illuminate the shifting and contested global and urban spatial politics of climate change. In this new

Table 5.1
Theory, findings, and implications

	Chapter 2 Nature of Contestation	Chapter 3 Nature of Flows	Chapter 4 Plans and Counterplans
Theoretical framework(s)*	Urban as a site of contestation and uneven development socioecological change is codetermined climate plans often for strategic economic security	Relational geographies; concept mobilities "worlding" and urban interreferencing transnational networks in global climate governance	Social production of space; urban design ways of knowing design and climate change design as informed provocation, not a reflexive practice by nature
Research findings	"Top-down" plans tend to reflect economic and sociospatial systems spatial form of marginalization and socioenvironmental resilience linked local knowledge and broad-based coalitions critical to counterplans	Global, national, urban scales intertwined through multiscalar, multilevel networks environmental planning as economic strategy plans embedded in local and global development; climate change facilitates accumulation	Design negotiates between organization and sociopolitical context connects pragmatic to emotional, bridging social and spatial design is not neutral, can be a mode of political organizing
Implications	Systemic urban socioecological marginalization conditions emerging spaces of contestation in the face of climate change need attention to sociospatial forms of resilience	Relational view reveals interconnections among power relationships, emerging conditions, and emerging networks "network formation" reveals how strategies move across scales and levels	Design is political reflexive, political design discourse and practice open new terrains of contestation and possibility of alternative, counterhegemonic urban ecological visions

* See the Introduction for elaboration on these theories.

landscape of climate governance and planning mobilities, urban climate responses, globally constituted, are embedded within and reflect existing urban sociospatial systems. In each of the sites, the dominant, state-led (or state-supported), "top-down" plans are generally produced in negotiation with and conformance to modes of urban development, constitution of market forces, levels of governance, cohesion of climate policies, and patterns of institutionalized community participation. Climate change motivates and enables relationships and plans, but plan objectives often transcend climate-specific goals. Climate change, in fact, exposes and enhances motivations and contradictions in existing global relationships. Alongside the reconfigured spaces and institutions of global and urban environmental planning, it facilitates new avenues for capital exchange and accumulation.

The production of alternative visions of the future opens terrains of contestation, enabling modes of organizing and resistance to dominant plans and hegemonic systems. In responding to the reconfigured global and urban modes of planning, these counterplans are also changing.

Urban Movements for Climate Justice

Dominating visions of urban resilience, too often serving to perpetuate political and economic power and in neglect of social justice, threaten to overrun cities around the world. What if we have found a countermovement against such dominating urban resilience? What if such a movement pays attention to—no, actually is conceived from—lived experiences and struggles on the ground, as well as longstanding views of alternative, more just futures? What if that movement responds to—indeed appropriates and exploits—the reflexive, networked, multiscalar, and multilevel organization of global environmental planning in ways that are situated, radical, and transformative? The prospects are tantalizing. We would then be able to theorize the making of such counterplans, reframe the analysis and understanding of urban climate responses, and conceptualize just visions of urban ecological change.

To return to the research question: *How are contesting visions of the future produced and how do they attain power?* I elaborate on the last point in the synthesis—specifically, how counterplans gain power—by delving further into the issue of contestation in these sites, and the production of the counterplans within their multiscalar contexts.

In the synthesis table (table 5.2), New York and Jakarta—the cities in which I examine dominant strategies, the "big plans," as well as the counterplans, the ground-up alternative visions—flank Rotterdam—the city in which sites and strategies function as a key node in a global network of interactions, as well as a node in the research in this book, a kind of relational pivot. The top section lays out the descriptive context in each site. The main section illustrates the key categories and relationships of the dominant plans (reading top down) and the counterplans (reading bottom up). The middle of this section shows the analytical categories: the structure, organization, and spatial form of both plans and counterplans. The "structure" refers to the institutional, governance, or grassroots formation of the plan. The "organization" refers to the level of institutional cohesion of the primary planmakers, as a singular entity or group. The "spatial form" refers to the level of spatial cohesion of the plan. Together these characteristics point to the ways in which the organizational structures of plans and counterplans form their social and spatial visions.

Counternetworks

The history of urban social and spatial movements is rife with narratives of direct confrontation—the "classic" 1968 urban uprisings in Paris and other cities, for example, with strikes, occupations, and taking to the streets, and the protests against the World Trade Organization in Seattle in 1999. We saw this again in the Arab Spring and Occupy Wall Street movements,[9] and, recently, in the resurgent movement for Black lives in cities in the United States and beyond. The countermovements in this book have exhibited various ways of asserting or wresting agency and power. They do this not necessarily through direct confrontation. They embrace alternative social imaginaries and practices through multiple modes.[10]

In Jakarta, these imaginaries and practices operate at a number of different geographic scales and institutional levels. First, at the scale of the immediate site. The floods—and the normalization plans—threaten kampungs along the Ciliwung, and have been the primary focus of community-designed alternatives, in particular the design and community activism by the Ciliwung Merdeka coalition. This is reflective of the place-based and local nature of many movements against social and environmental injustice. Second, the relationship between normalization projects and broader rules

Table 5.2 Synthesis of plans, counterplans, and connections

	New York	Rotterdam	Jakarta
URBAN REGION			
POLITICAL / ECONOMIC	US "free market"; global economic driver and financial center; stable growth ≈ 2%	NL, corporatist, welfare state; neoliberalizing; economic crisis	Indonesia, postcolonial, postdictatorial; emerging growth economy; 6% economic growth
ENVIRONMENTAL RISKS	Sea-level rise, extreme events, storm surge, floods	Sea-level rise, precipitation	Subsidence, precipitation, sea-level rise
KEY MOTIVATOR	Hurricane Sandy 2012	1953 floods / 2008 climate plan	2007 / 2013 floods
DOMINANT PLAN	Rebuild By Design	Rotterdam Climate Proof	Giant Sea Wall
NATIONAL RELATIONSHIPS	US HUD	Netherlands Gov (Infrastructure & Water)	Indonesia Gov (Public Works Ministry)
GLOBAL / URBAN NETWORKS		Rotterdam Climate Initiative — Connecting Delta Cities / C40	
OBJECTIVE	Regional resilience; economic growth; innovative design	Local climate preparedness, economic growth, "comfortable & attractive," int'l relationships	Flood protection, economic growth, global / national icon
STRUCTURE	NATIONAL / INSTITUTIONAL	MUNICIPAL	INTERNATIONAL
ORGANIZATION	COHESIVE	COHESIVE	COHESIVE
SPATIAL FORM	FRAGMENTED	COHESIVE	COHESIVE
CONTESTATION	*Local alternatives to an innovative framework challenged by market-reliant, fragmented policy; space / design as part of broader transformation*		*Production of direct spatial form alternative to technocratic top-down plan; space / design changes modes of organizing*
	INSTITUTIONAL / GRASSROOTS		GRASSROOTS
	DISPERSE		DISPERSE
	COHESIVE		FRAGMENTED
MODE OF ORGANIZING	Long-term building social relationships; alternative socioecon & tech visions		Building new coalitions; new "tools", alternative sociospatial visions
MODE OF MARGINALIZATION	Systemic oppression, race, class, poverty; public housing		Informality, class, poverty, citizenship; informal kampungs
COUNTERPLAN	*Community Resiliency*		*Kampung Design Activism*

and regulations. Rujak's work to compile, synthesize, and disseminate information on national laws on dredging, reclamation, and landfill, and plans for large-scale projects, is a response to an expanded territory of contestation. While closely in conjunction with place-based activisms, such advocacy research is positioned more on the broader historical and geographic conditions and constraints in which the place-based conflicts are fought. And third, on a regional scale—the Indonesian archipelago and urban Southeast Asia. UPC has shown success in developing a cohesive, networked movement across a number of Indonesian cities confronting a diverse set of threats, from post-tsunami recovery work in Banda Aceh, to ongoing riverside settlement restoration in Surabaya, and to the current struggles over space in Muara Baru and Waduk Pluit.

This reflexivity of movement building across a diversity of scales is important. In chapter 3, I examined the global-urban networks that enabled the production of large-scale, generally top-down urban climate change response plans. Critically, the strategies of counterplans also form and operate through networks—counternetworks—although often somewhat more limited in scope and reach. In the Jakarta example, UPC, on one level, functions as a network of local organizers across a set of Indonesian cities. On another level, it forms networks across disciplines and professions, with community architects such as Arkomjogja, lawyers such as Lembaga Bantuan Hukum (LBH; Legal Aid Institute) Jakarta, and academic researchers. Through its close working relationship with Rujak it links to a broader initiative of urban social justice and sustainability advocacy, and an extensive network of Indonesian and international scholars and activists, as well as media outlets (figure 5.4).[11] Through such multilevel, multiscalar formations, the counternetwork links more specific, place-based harms and actions with more general and broader spatial scale impacts.

Counterplans

Referring back to the synthesis table (table 5.2), note the structure, form, and organization of the counterplans on far left and right columns. As I have explained, urban climate plans are formed differently in order to account not always for environmental risks, but for structures of governance and modes of development. The resistances to those plans—the "counterplans"—also take different forms. In New York, community organizations like RHI and

A Political Ecology of Design

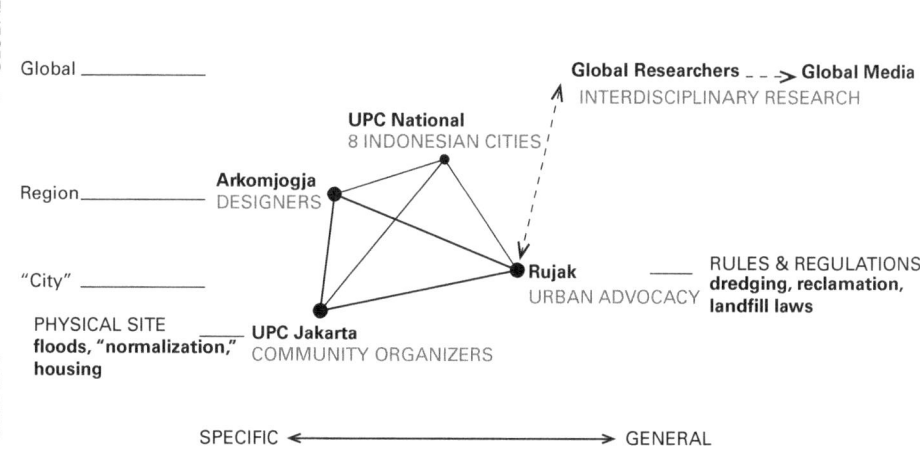

Figure 5.4
Diagram of counternetwork in and beyond Jakarta.

GOLES relied on the long-term building of social relationships, developed in spite of or because of shared social and spatial marginalization. They constitute locally and community-specific approaches to social and environmental resilience. And yet these approaches are socially and spatially cohesive within their place-specific contexts, with well-formed theories of change. Not so much presenting themselves as substitutes for initiatives like Rebuild By Design, they offer ways of conceiving risk and resilience that integrally encompass the agency and voice of their constituents. They continually foreground a different, grounded viewpoint.

In Jakarta, kampung activist groups including UPC and Ciliwung Merdeka confront the imminent, direct threats of flooding and eviction, and the more diffuse threats of a process of city-making often relentless in its pursuit of modernity and global citizenship ("city-zenship"?). In response, they developed broad-based coalitions and new tools to forge negotiations with city officials that are unprecedented in their effectiveness, at least in recent decades. As reactions to both the multiple locations and types of social and environmental threats and the dispersed modes of community building and organizing, these approaches, across the groups and sites, are fragmented. And yet together they pose a resounding, if not always successful, challenge to dominant structures. In Jakarta, as in New York, these approaches center marginalized voices, and do not take their presence or participation as a hurdle to be surpassed.

What about the role of design in the counterplans? In the case of the work of RHI in New York, the design of space functions as part of broader social transformation. Design aids political organizing; it literally provides space for it. In Jakarta, kampung organizers marshaled design to produce social and spatial form alternatives to a top-down, technocratic plan—imaginaries to bring the life of the kampung to the organization of space—in a context in which alternatives have not, as a rule, flourished. In this case, design changes modes of political organizing. The counterplans in New York and Jakarta share an important characteristic. They envision transformative and intertwined social and spatial change as part of environmental resilience.[12]

What we see, then, in the contestation between plans and counterplans is an urban political ecology of design—in that the processes and protocols of design are intertwined with the contested processes of urban socioecological change. And it is a design imaginary of urban spatial politics, in that the evocations and projections of design are invoked in consort with the relationships of power in conflicts over urban space.

Urban Waves
These counternetworks and counterplans present a way of thinking of new, reflexive modes of resistance. They contest dominant plans that are developed through multiscalar, multilevel, relational global-urban networks. It seems only appropriate that the resistance plans reflect and take on, in however limited ways, the reflexive organizational and spatial form of those networks. But plans and counterplans do not emerge only as unequal reflections of each other.

Plans and counterplans take shape in the context of global and local climate change exigencies, as well as the reconfigured global and local spaces and institutions of climate change responses. Indeed, the plans and the counterplans not only form in relation to each other but are *co-constitutive* of each other. That is, in parallel to the ways in which global institutions and networks have been reconfigured in response to global and local climate exigencies, climate change *and* climate changed spaces and institutions have conditioned plans as well as the resistances to those plans. The new wave of globally constituted and urban-refracted big plans emerged

A Political Ecology of Design

out of these new organizational structures of global-urban environmental planning—and could only have emerged from such conditions. But the resistances have emerged too, in ways that not only challenge but also reformat and are reformatted by the plans they challenge. These are new waves—disparate, unequal in scope and power, but nevertheless intertwined in flows and tensions.

So, in the final analysis, a reframing is in order. Throughout this book, I have described and discussed the spatial politics I have observed in somewhat idealized and dichotomous ways. I have posed bottom-up against top-down, grassroots versus state-led, local versus global, community-based against the global corporate and multinational. This is a helpful heuristic. But it is not quite a full picture. In fact, as I have illustrated, plans and counterplans shape each other, in recursive ways. In concrete terms, this shows up in some of the dynamics of the contestation. We have seen that the proponents of the dominant plans have, to some extent, advocated for participation and celebrated the work of grassroots organizations and individuals, and that the counterplans are themselves multiscalar and networked, often through the same organizational formations. But of course, this recursive relationship does not happen over neutral ground. It takes shape over spaces continually formed by and reflecting the unequal impacts of climate change and unjust processes of dominant modes of urban development. This is why partial successes on the part of counterplans, partial accommodations on the part of the dominant plans, incremental repositioning of struggles (such as among the kampung activists in Jakarta), or transformative, smaller-scale, place-based alternative practices (such as modeled by RHI in Brooklyn), should be lauded, critically assessed, understood, and viewed in the context of the continuing movements to envision different urban processes and more just urban climate futures.

The counterplans are urban movements. That is, they are struggles over urban processes and spaces. They are organized in response to powerful new modes of urban development (however globally constituted), and through contests and claims over the production of urban spaces (however locally fought). In the ways in which they respond to climate change impacts and the global and urban reorientations of environmental planning induced by climate change, they represent new, or at least qualitatively reconstituted, urban movements. They are the movements that link and develop the social struggles over the urban with the shifting scales and organizations of a climate-changing world. That is, they situate the urban in the spatially and temporally reflexive globalizing climate justice movement.[13] These are movements for urban climate justice.

Toward Just Urban Climate Futures

The formulation of urban movements for climate justice, particularly the planning of the counterplans, enables urban researchers to "see" specific concerns of urban climate change responses in different ways. Recall the problems with understanding cities and climate change as distinct, bounded places. Or of categorizing climate change responses as social or spatial, siloing our views and thus our solutions. Recall the contested notion of resilience, so easily coopted and invoked to rationalize bouncing back to business-as-usual systems. The formulation we have arrived with enables us to interrogate these problems, and to pose alternatives. I reframe some of the critical issues interrogated in this book.

Reframing 1: A Sociospatial Typology of Adaptation
Urban climate change adaptation measures are typically categorized in ways that are not always suited to understanding the contested and intertwined social and spatial nature of their formation. They are often divided among spatial, physical interventions, social or community-based measures, or governance initiatives. Or they are divided by hard and soft infrastructure. Or low-risk, no-regrets measures versus more ambitious, long-term efforts. A new way to organize these forms of climate responses and movements allows us to learn from dominant plans and counterplans in relationship to their contexts—the social relations and spatial realities of the various sites in which they are formed.

I present a different approach to typology that foregrounds the intertwined nature of social and spatial factors (figure 5.5). This is developed based on the specific sites and strategies in this study and reflects best the measures taken by coastal cities facing water risks—floods, sea-level rise, surges, cloudbursts. However, the ideas about protection measures can be generalized, and appropriately rescaled or reconfigured for a different set of sites and risks. The development of these types is very much reflective of the means and modes of contestation as previously illustrated. The types are categorized according to the organization and form of the strategy (see

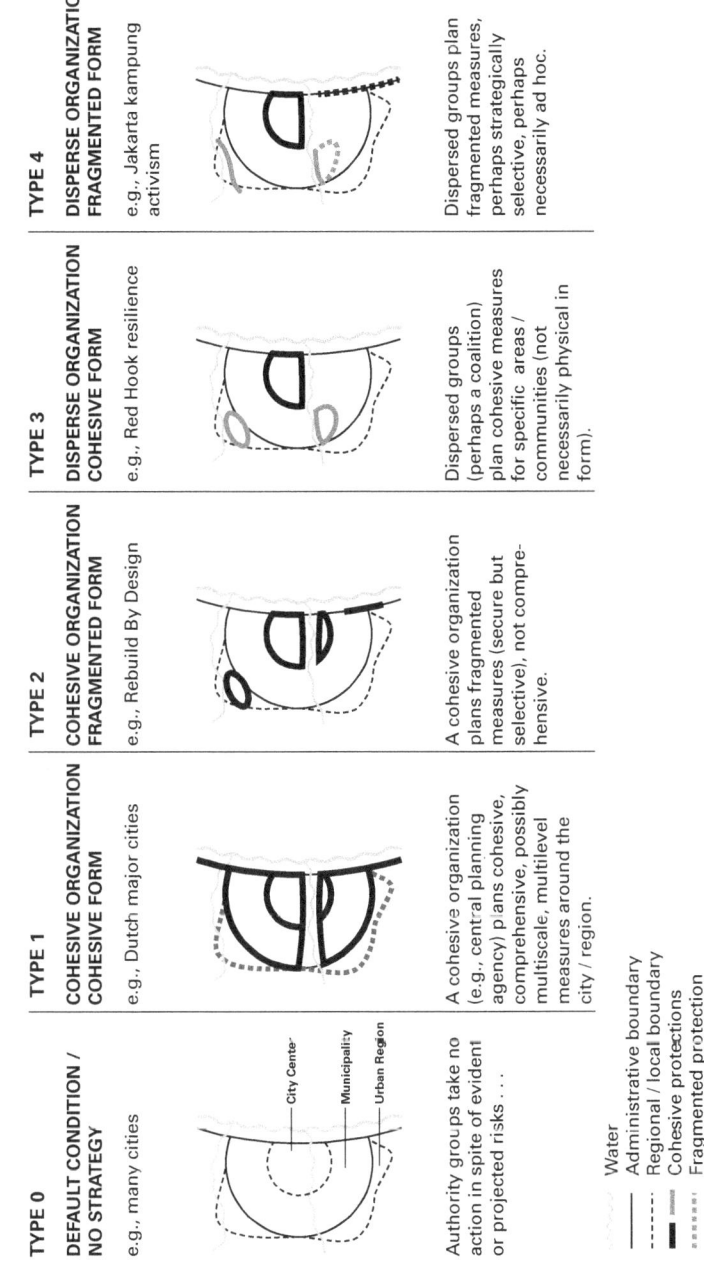

Figure 5.5

A sociospatial typology of coastal urban adaptation strategies.

synthesis table 5.2). A key proposition here is that these strategies are simultaneously social and spatial—in organizational and formal terms.

Type 0 shows the default condition. A city confronts threats from environmental change, and does nothing.

Type 1 shows what is perhaps the preferred option, if one were primarily concerned with protection and safety for all constituents of a city. A cohesive organization (possibly of many scales and levels) plans cohesive, comprehensive protection. We might take, for example, Dutch major cities as epitomizing this type, but only in their idealized form, when in consideration of the extensive multilevel governance, including national government, water boards, and local agencies that must be in sync. As we've seen in this book, the loosening of national support can change the way local agencies choose to act.

Type 2 shows a cohesive organization and fragmented form. Because of urban policies, governance systems, funding structures, or prioritizing of security and protection, an organization chooses or is forced to plan selectively. It is not comprehensive. For example, Rebuild By Design, at least in its competition phase, developed a cohesive organization, but the strategies as such are delimited by locality or municipality. As the projects move into implementation, the strategies are sometimes further fragmented, dissipating into neighborhood or subneighborhood spatial scales.

Type 3 shows a dispersed organization with a cohesive form. Groups with aligned or unaligned motivations (perhaps a coalition) plan cohesive measures for specific areas and/or communities, in response to specific threats. In reference to more classic social movements, the strength of organizing here is critical, such as in the form of a shared political vision that drives social and spatial strategies. Protection might be planned as comprehensive, but it is not necessarily physically so. For example, RHI forms a number of linked, mutually reinforcing initiatives based on a well-formed theory of change, in the process relying on coalitions and partnerships with a variety of groups (technology advocates, designers, neighborhood organizations) with diverse interests. It is not comprehensive by design, but prioritizes select marginalized groups and organizing goals.

Type 4 shows dispersed organization and fragmented form. Dispersed groups plan fragmented measures, possibly in response to direct threats to some constituents, and more diffuse threats to others. Plans might be strategically selective, measures necessarily ad hoc, and experimental. In Jakarta, for example, in confronting a situation that is rife with uncertainty and rapid change, Ciliwung Merdeka, UPC, and allies embark on a suite of initiatives that address multiple sets of risks. Ciliwung Merdeka's humanitarian kampung vision is selective, constrained to a strategically bounded site. UPC, in its Muara Baru organizing, shifts from previous strategies to upgrade protections in place, acknowledging, if not fully accepting, some fairly extensive demolition in return for secure, innovative housing.

This sociospatial typology offers a way to understand and categorize the plans and counterplans investigated in this book in ways true to the sociospatial nature of their formation. It also presents a way to frame the analysis of other climate response strategies in other sites in ways that do not preclude a more reflexive understanding of their making. This is particularly critical when considering the political nature of contested visions and, as recounted in this book, the expanded terrains and institutional contexts through which such contestations are fought.

Reframing 2: A Just Resilience

Resilience is contested. In the introduction, I outlined some of the emerging tensions and conflicts around this concept. Theoretically, the diverse and slightly chaotic treatment of resilience is perhaps to be expected, given the array of disciplines and practices invoking it. A clear danger stemming from this looseness of meaning is that resilience is easily invoked and operationalized to protect political economic systems in cities, driven by a global constellation of powerful actors and institutions, and, along with this, it is used to justify the continued oppression of historically marginalized groups. And yet, as I have observed in the course of this research, resilience can also be developed as a means of countering such oppressive structures and to give form to struggles for change.[14] How do we do this concept justice?

Researchers critical of uninterrogated notions of resilience have demanded a more political analysis, or one more grounded in historical oppressions, lived experience, and community-based knowledges.[15] I share their concerns and critiques. I also think that, as long as organizers and activists are fighting for social and environmental justice around concepts of resilience, critical researchers are compelled to understand why and how such notions might be formulated.[16] I want to contextualize and conceptualize a more just resilience. And I want to extend this, in a way that is observant of the concerns and critiques, and at the same time situates the possibility for transformative social and spatial action. Can we imagine a more just resilience, a "resilience from below?"

Take the example of the Lower East Side of Manhattan and resilience planning after Hurricane Sandy. Resilience plans, as often critiqued, are understood to be protecting and promoting dominant modes of urban development, primarily privatized real estate interests, over the vulnerability of communities. It is possible, in many ways, simply to dismiss the proposal here as catering to such elite political economic interests—a giant landscaped sea wall defending and capturing land values. But there's more to it than that. From the research in this book, we understand that the Lower Manhattan proposal does not only gain traction as a giant real estate plan, it does so as a vision of a future city—opposite the one on the cover of *New York* magazine, shrouded in darkness—that literally includes appeals to all manner of urban residents. And these sites in cities are not only strategic centers to be protected. The areas in Lower Manhattan, including the Lower East Side and the adjacent Financial District, do not preclude the poor. In fact, they are sites of longtime contesting voices and struggles of the poor.

One analytical approach would paint these large-scale resilience projects in one way, as initiatives for "urban ecological security," protecting economic interests and dominant ideas about the present and future of cities. But the recursive nature of plans and counterplans invites a different view, a different analysis of space and justice, specifically one more attuned to the ways in which climate change threats and responses raise and challenge assumptions of vulnerability and shared struggle in particular urban spaces.

Consider the broader context. Funding organizations, sustainability consultants, and development agencies invested in resilience, some aware and wary of the critiques and potential inequities, have been striving for a more comprehensive notion of the term resilience. Among the various concepts of resilience that have gained ground in urban climate governance discussions is the "City Resilience Framework," as proposed by engineering firm Arup and the Rockefeller Foundation and published in 2014. The framework strives for comprehensiveness, proposing twelve indicators in four broad categories—health and wellbeing (people), urban systems and services (place), economy and society (organization), and leadership and strategy (knowledge).[17] The indicators, including livelihoods, social stability, strong finance, mobility and communications, and effective leadership,

A Political Ecology of Design 173

prompt the question, what's the difference between this resilient city and simply a *good* city?

Asked about this, Nancy Kete, then managing partner of the Rockefeller Foundation, agrees that this point bears attention and distinction, and explains the foundation's work on the framework:

> We've really tried to keep sharp on that question. In the resilience framework, there's a version that could be just a description of the functions of any city that works, so we really challenged ourselves: What is it about a city that enables it to deliver so many essential functions? In fact, it is that city's ability or capacity to be resilient. From the research, and lots of case studies, we have been able to systematically define the qualities or characteristics of the city and the systems within the city that allow it to keep delivering all of these functions—no matter what kind of chronic stresses it's facing, or particularly what kinds of shocks it might endure. So, that's the difference.
>
> There's also the matter of sustainability. The way I see it, you want cities to be both resilient and sustainable in the long term, but you can't get anywhere unless you are resilient now, and in the near term. One of the core elements in that process is inclusivity. Look at New York. And all the theory on resilience suggests that a lack of inclusivity or a widening of the gap leaves you not resilient to future shocks and stresses. A resilient city is resilient for everyone—and its people embody that, too.[18]

Kete emphasizes attention to the poor. Indeed, many of the more comprehensive resilience frameworks are explicit in considering the needs of the most vulnerable. But while researchers critical of the concept take issue with apolitical invocations of resilience, Kete downplays politics in the Rockefeller Foundation's resilience framework. She emphasizes that the effort to be comprehensive enables people with different political viewpoints to take part in the process, and make their own decisions about what to prioritize.[19]

This is reflective of broader petitions among scientists and commentators not to "politicize" climate change. And yet, climate change is political. And it is this ambivalence toward questions of power—say, prioritizing community engagement but not political confrontations—that contributes to both the perceived and the actual injustices perpetuated by projects for resilience. The findings throughout this book have emphasized that a critical political analysis is a necessary and core component of any notion of a just urban resilience. Politics is central to the making of plans, the mobilizing and disseminating of ideas about resilience, and the appeals to legitimacy. This is particularly crucial with regard to issues of justice, given the tendency in the dominant mechanics of urban development to ignore existing or projected socioeconomic disparities and unequal environmental impacts.

But an appeal to a politics of resilience is not enough. Critiques, even if accordingly political, need to pay sufficient attention to the voices of the marginalized and to the kind of social imaginaries and practices developed through contestations on the ground. They need also to recognize the embeddedness of urban politics within a broader (social and spatial-physical) terrain of shifting global and urban climate governance. So here, I want to ground a point about a more just resilience—bring it literally down to the ground. Operationalizing a grounded just resilience, via paying attention to and learning lessons from the political agency, voices, social imaginaries, and practices of those historically marginalized, offers a more sustained and potentially transformative path forward.

Recall Jill Eisenhard's explanation about how RHI staff were able to respond so effectively to the chaos of Hurricane Sandy. RHI staff members were part of the community and neighborhood, keenly aware of its struggles, with firsthand experience of working through challenging conditions and sudden emergencies, central figures in maintaining the social relationships among RHI constituents and broader Red Hook Houses residents.[20] Eisenhard describes how the lessons of these social relationships were instilled among its youth constituents, way before the storm hit:

> So, before October 29th, 2012, we talked about resilience every day, and our definition of it was: Life will inevitably knock you down, and you need to be able to get back up again. Resilience is being able to know that you have the strength, or knowledge, or self-belief, or motivation, or confidence within yourself to get up and try again. And that you also have a social support network around you that is going to help you when you can't do that for yourself.[21]

In other words, individual resilience, in the face of systemic challenges, matters. But more importantly, individuals are part of a collective, a community similarly invested in survival and flourishing, developed through a history of shared struggle. This is a political notion of resilience, born of a distinct theory and practice of change.[22]

Eisenhard, in follow-up conversations on this matter, always emphasizes the *place-bound* and *ground-up* nature of such resilience. She explains:

> I think that our work is contingent, and a key piece of it working in the way that we have designed it is because it's place-based. . . . A lot of what we're responding

to is directly related to the systems and forces and circumstances that are true in this neighborhood.

... Here, what is the case is everyone has the same experience with transportation or how long it takes to get somewhere. Everyone has the same experience with the fact that there is no public high school here. Everyone has the same experience that all of that open ball field space is closed so there's nowhere to go.... Or, like, their relationship to the [Red Hook] Farm has to do with what stores are here and what your choices are for produce.[23]

Eisenhard emphasizes the shared social experiences and structural conditions that are linked to a specific geographic boundary. She speaks from the point of view of a community organization working with residents of a public housing project—a format of urban housing that has been thoroughly critiqued in the United States from public policy, urban design, and socioeconomic perspectives—and her words remind us of the importance of recognizing social relationships that form as part of (and in spite of) public, institutional systems and places. This is not to fetishize the struggles of public housing residents or other marginalized urban communities. Or to rose-tint the power of the state. It is to emphasize that a just resilience—in political-economic systems that have generally neglected and harmed poor urban residents, and in climate conditions whose impacts are generalized and highly uneven—requires attention to the possibilities of radical imaginaries and practices of place-based, ground-up community voices as well as public institutions across levels of urban governance to remake places and social relationships across scales.

This aspect of resilience is especially important to recognize at a time when progressive politicians and community organizations alike are looking to large-scale federally coordinated public programs, such as the Green New Deal, to save us from climate catastrophes and to right social wrongs. Powerful ideas of justice are centered on the agency, claims, and rights of local communities. But at a time of increasing appeals to large-scale, top-down, public initiatives commensurate with the exigencies of climate change and social inequality, much more attention ought to be given to the possibilities of just and transformative community social relationships within public places, systems, and institutions.[24]

Resilience, here, is always positional. It is grounded in the historical social relationships emerging from shared struggle against systemic oppression. But it is also grounded in the physical spaces—the grounds—from which such struggle is formed. Such an idea about place-specific, spatially meaningful justice and resilience opens up considerations of how to design for it in social and spatial ways. In this way, a more just resilience broaches new approaches for envisioning alternative urban landscapes.

A More Radical Adaptation?
One thing remains disconcerting. Climate justice is not only about protection from disparate climate change impacts. It is also about a just transition to new, radically decarbonized societies and spaces. The contestations explored and analyzed among the sites and strategies in this book have not included, in substantive ways, pathways toward a low-carbon future. A troubling implication of this is that, as warnings over the climate crisis intensify, those in power will take concrete steps to protect their interests, raising one manner of wall or other against storms and rising seas.[25] Sometimes, this might happen more equitably—due, perhaps, to the kinds of counterplanning investigated here—with more people and places protected, or it might not, leading to exclusionary enclaves and, possibly, social movements rising in protest. Either way, we don't get where we need to go for the future of the planet.

It is unjust and cruel to ask that marginalized groups take responsibility for the carbon accounting of their counteractions when faced with and protesting against dominating and exclusionary resilience plans. But what seems very clear is that just urban climate futures must be about a justly decarbonized society-space. This calls for renewed attention to the transformative aspects of urban climate movements—a more radical adaptation. In social scientific studies of climate change, a high level of consideration is accorded to the specificity of concepts we use. This is necessary for rigorous knowledge production. Mitigation means reducing greenhouse gas emissions. Adaptation means shifting and altering in response to projected impacts. But this moment invites a loosening and merging of concepts, at least toward the reimagining of possibilities. Adaptation, considered in appropriately sociospatial terms, cannot be understood only as a response to increasingly urgent climate change impacts, but as the movement toward and transformation to the necessarily new social and spatial relationships, and new political economies for a climate change–changed world.

This is an incipient notion for now, compelled by the implications of this research and the continued quandaries faced at the end of it. Mitigation, as a means to avoid the catastrophic ends of our own making, is always adaptation—to the new, more sustainable, more just societies and spaces climate change has made imperative.

Insurgent Urban Landscapes

So I end with a discussion of possibilities. A central focus of this research has been the production of, and conflicts over, urban ecologies—the multivalent place of nature in the city. What I can now assert:

1. Urban ecologies are contested, part of social and spatial power relationships in the city.
2. The production of such urban ecologies is interconnected across multiple scales and levels. On the matter of scale: urban ecologies on smaller geographic scales are linked through urban infrastructure and ecological processes to broader urban-regional ecological scales. On the matter of levels, there are two aspects: localized and place-based struggles over urban ecologies are linked—and coproductive, in aligned and contested ways—first, with the shifting and networked organizational formations of institutions of environmental governance *and*, second, across conceptual levels, from concrete places and projects through more abstract processes (at both smaller and larger scales) including historical and embodied social and cultural relationships and the more generalized and globalized processes of political economic change and global climate change.
3. As such, one might consider the envisioning of and interventions in urban ecologies in the face of local and global climate change impacts to be intertwined with, on one hand, local sociocultural practices and political contestation, on the other, global networks of cultural, political, and economic exchange.
4. Understanding the relationship between urban landscapes and these social and cultural practices might produce alternative narratives to—and ways of intervening in—hegemonic processes related to global capitalism and urbanization.

So, consider the urban ecological design project. A critical project of urban ecological research and design in the last fifteen years or so—spearheaded especially by proponents of ecological urbanism and practitioners in the field of landscape architecture—has been to assert the centrality of urban landscapes in the understanding and ordering of urban form. Researchers and practitioners have unearthed and exploited the complex interplay of "built" and "natural," contested the false dichotomies between city and nature, and, importantly, showed us that the operations of urban ecologies transcend boundaries—of the project, also of governance and traditional planning and political institutions—always in relation to, and ideally in tune with, the appropriate ecological systems and scales (the watershed, for example). They have made the case that landscape is the appropriate scale of envisioning urban sustainability.[26]

Now, the critical project might be to extend those frameworks, and to probe the relationships between the making of urban landscapes and two sets of interconnected processes, larger and smaller (figure 5.6). The first is that of the generalized flows of global urban development, at the nexus of urban and national development initiatives and globalized economic development and environmental planning. The second is the grassroots urban movements for climate justice, operating at the level of historically determined, place-particular social relationships, amid unequal and oppressive urban social structures.[27]

How do designers do this? One might observe, in any number of design studios or schools, the approaches that designers bring to their work. Often these include diverse, reflexive sets of tools and ideas, explored in iterative and adaptive ways. In designing an urban ecological project, for example, one might work between physical and parametric modeling—looking at different scales of hydrological interaction—and multiple levels of urban social and spatial networks. Designers are often very good at translating information—environment, to systems, to form. So how do we tune this to engage more deeply with the multiscalar, multilevel processes and interconnections that inform the way that sustained change is made?

Further, how do we do this at a time when designers, in academia and in practice, from humanitarian initiatives to megaprojects, are increasingly working in a global, transnational context, tasked with envisioning projects across the world over relatively short timeframes? Or when designers must take seriously differences in power and privilege born not only from imperialism, globalization, and racism across the far reaches of the planet but from the parallel and overlapping struggles in and around their own cities? There are challenges to understanding problems and solutions in places we do not live in and that are often quite distant, in social and spatial, positional

A Political Ecology of Design   179

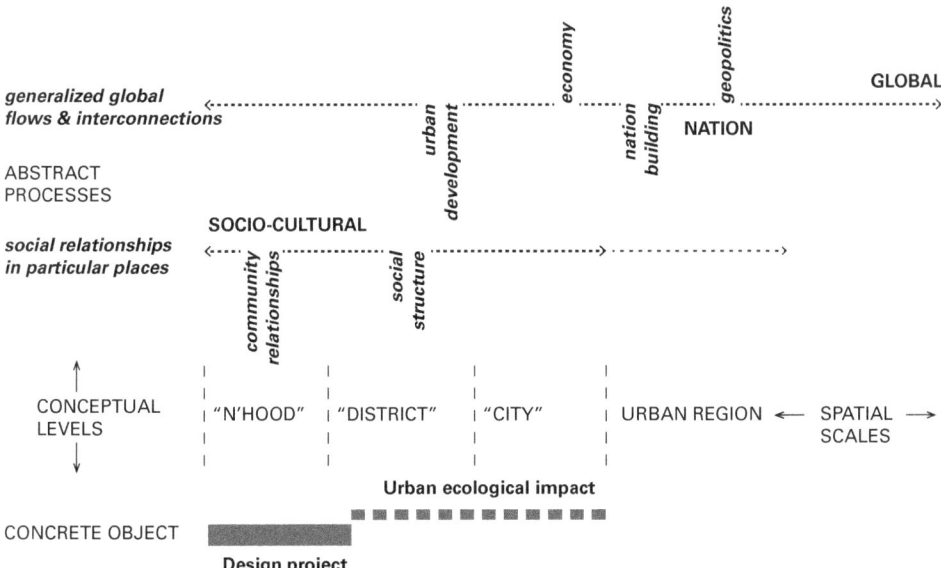

Figure 5.6
Extended scales and levels of urban ecologies, connected to local social relationships and global networks.

and embodied, ways. These challenges are particularly acute when designers are faced with the aspiration to consider sites and points of view in an interrelated manner, as this research explores and espouses. When we cannot know everything, how do we situate learning and doing in a relational sense, to understand the limits of our knowledge and yet have impact? In other words, how do we effectively not know?

These problems intertwine concepts about urban change from lived experience; the relationality of place and power; and the relationship between virtual, abstract, and interconnected flows with grounded, in-place struggles. I am prompted by the intractable problems—or the overwhelming possibilities—raised by researchers and theorists thinking through these concerns. James Holston, in claiming that modernist utopian planning did not reconcile societal contradictions, urged that planners pay attention to "insurgent citizenship," that is, "new kinds of practices and narratives about belonging to and participating in society," outside formal concepts of nation and statehood.[28] He proposes the embracing of ethnographic methods—tracing, decoding, rearticulating—to reenvision the realm of possibilities that might develop from, to riff on a phrase, actually existing social relationships. Ruth Wilson Gilmore, tracing the political geography of race, contextualizes particularly emplaced and embodied struggles within more abstract, structural power relationships within and across multiple geographic scales and political territories. She states, "If justice is embodied, it is then therefore always spatial, which is to say, part of a process of making a place."[29] Far from simply pointing to the problem, she searches out avenues for radical political activism toward more liberatory ends.[30] And, Manuel Castells, investigating new urban social movements in a time of pervasive digital networks, speaks of the "space of autonomy"—the "space of movement" as "an interaction between the space of flows (of digital communications) . . . and the space of places (of occupied sites and protest actions)."[31]

Together, these broad concepts, attuned to place-based and historically determined social relationships as well as the spaces of possibilities in reconstituting global, urban, and virtual worlds, offer the terms for new design practices engaged with questions of urban ecologies, landscapes, and a just resilience. Building on these conceptual provocations, I propose that designers embolden their conceptual array in order to operate across scales and levels. On the one hand, they should engage the multitude of social practices on the ground, cognizant of their own situated limitations in understanding them, and, on the other, they should build hybridized, networked design movements in the manner of Castells's space of autonomy.

The appeal to boldness is important. There has been a move, especially in urban studies and planning research conscious of previous grand errors, either to critique grand, bold design visions or to shy away from them. The tendency, among so many critical researchers, is not to trust big plans, visionary things. And yet, the problems we face are grand, possibly the grandest yet. A retuning of design toward emboldened conceptual engagement and conditional, reflexive, and situated practices offers a way to consider transformative sociospatial change, across scales, in positional, political ways.

First, designers should take seriously political education, including theories of social change, critical world histories, and critical pedagogies, learning how to learn from diverse, global sites. Beyond aspects of participation and engagement, more concerted attention to the places of design within broader and longer-term organizing movements for social change would open opportunities for new practices, where the specific iterative and projective processes and protocols of design might well be part of emerging political movements. It would also help designers to understand better when to step back, listen, and be part of. Second, designers should create new forms of collaborative, networked practices that are globally informed, but situated in (or among particular places). Designers will not be experts everywhere. And yet, as shown across this book, ideas do not always emerge from one specific place. And power—in relationships and movements, but also in ideas and visions—is constituted across space, and is dependent on time.[32]

Consider, then, what we might call practices of insurgent urban landscapes that situate themselves firmly in Holston's "ethnography of the present" while building movements across the global networks in which we are all learning to be effective.

Epilogue

We need new ways of seeing, and new ways of doing. If we know anything, we know that the future will be urbanized and that the urbanized future will be defined by what we have done to climate. No matter what we do now, we will be fighting the mistakes of the past and present for a long time to come.

Most people involved in urban governance who have given these concerns a second look—politicians, city managers, urban researchers, urban practitioners, the informed public—understand and acknowledge that climate change is a critical, and terrifying, problem. In a relatively short time, there has been an explosion of activity among cities to develop initiatives to mitigate and adapt to climate impacts. But, as I've explained in this book, even the more innovative and ambitious initiatives to respond to climate change are, first, embedded in the sociopolitical systems of cities, and often circumscribed by historically determined norms and regulations, and second, a part of the networks in which they are formed, and by design, captive to or at least constrained by the aims and structures of those networks. Through all this, one aspect remains constant among those in power. There is a strong, indeed resilient, belief that there are urban development solutions to climate change problems, if done properly. Many urban climate plans across the world, rich and poor, South and North, are propelled by this dictum. But how can this be the case when it is those same systems of urban development that created, and continue to perpetuate, these problems? This is the key quandary.

When we look at the situation now, in places like New York and Jakarta, there are striking glimmers of hope. The work of the Red Hook Initiative in cultivating a social milieu that enabled a cohesive, collective, and affirming response in the wake of Hurricane Sandy, the clear impact and scalability of a project like Red Hook WiFi, and the widespread acknowledgment of the value of this work on social and environmental resilience all hint at transformative possibilities beyond the immediate constituents and neighborhood. The same can be said of the work of Good Old Lower East Side in tying long-term struggles for housing rights to the issue of climate justice, and in its effectiveness at forging strong coalitions in a very contested urban space. That someone like Henk Ovink cites Damaris Reyes of GOLES as a key motivator to get things done is a marked step in the right direction. Likewise, the work of the Urban Poor Consortium and Ciliwung Merdeka in Jakarta to form innovative, effective resistance in the face of sometimes extreme challenges is unprecedented. Alongside, the evident acknowledgment of the importance of local buy-in on the part of the Dutch consultants in Jakarta hints at the possibility of a different kind of development.

But are any of these efforts about to transform urban development in New York or in Jakarta? The answer is short. No. Not yet. Such initiatives—even in their incipient, intriguing and inspiring networks—have tended to remain locally transformative, effective on a smaller scale. Sometimes their limitations emerge abruptly, and forcefully, as in the evictions and demolitions in Kampung Pulo on August 20, 2015. Often they shift, deform, and reemerge, as when kampung activists in Jakarta formed a pact with gubernatorial candidate Anies Baswedan. Mostly they remain contingent, struggles that are ongoing and provisional.

I have suggested that some of these smaller-scale initiatives are not necessarily posed as substitutes for the big plans. But what if they could be? These grassroots initiatives cannot simply be "scaled up." Consider, for example, the typology of sociospatial adaptation I presented in chapter 5. Some examples of "counterplans," such as Jakarta kampung activism, are organizationally dispersed and fragmented in form. These initiatives are often selective and necessarily ad hoc. Scaling up, in the usual sense, does not make a cohesive whole out of fragmented parts. I have asserted throughout this research that the making of—and contestation over—urban nature is part of urban processes, and have suggested that it is through these processes that social change might be formed. If so, then what needs to happen is that the relevant aspects of these alternative urban processes are rescaled—not always up, but across—and networked out. These aspects might include, for example, centering the agency of marginalized voices or explicitly positioning strategies in opposition to specific hegemonic power structures—in Red Hook, Brooklyn, the reproduction of systemic poverty and racial oppression, in Jakarta the continual delegitimizing of kampung residents as participants in urban society.

Ultimately, this implies that our objective must be a new kind of urban development. It demands a reckoning with and a dismantling of the touchstones we look to, which have underscored urban thinking for the last fifty years, that is, a dominant mode of urban development characterized by, in particularly intertwined ways, the demise of a hegemony of modernist urban planning, the renaissance of privatized urban development (and the rise of financialized urban space), the at-least-momentary triumph of globalization, the institutionalizing of an idealized community engagement that often reproduces the status quo, and the emergency of our climate crisis. As I have suggested here, it will require a more radical adaptation, not only in response to the present and projected impacts of climate change, but in expectation of deeply transformed sociospatial relationships that actually herald and sustain a just and continuing future.

So many researchers and commentators of climate change and societal futures speak of the imperative to change our ways: we ought to do this and that, to have this and that . . . we must decarbonize, and we must have justice. Too few, to date, have offered compelling alternative social and spatial visions of what this might mean.

Here is where insurgent urban landscapes might play a critical role. Exploring design as a terrain of contestation reveals the power relationships and motivations underlying the making of urban ecologies. Marshaling an insurgent urban ecological design as an overt critique of such power relationships exposes and possibly disrupts such systems. Recall the sociospatial typologies of adaptation and the notion of just resilience—positional and grounded, historically and spatially—two reframings developed through the course of this book. An insurgent approach to designing urban landscapes, framed around a more radical adaptation, offers social and spatial imaginaries that might be more or less comprehensive, more or less cohesive. They might even be deliberately distributed and fragmentary, like a million kampung activisms, resituated and repositioned in each instance.

Confronting, at the moment, chaotic concepts of resilience, variable concepts and practices of urban adaptation, and ill-formed assumptions about design theory and practice, we face tremendous challenges simply in deciding why, where, and how to produce climate change response plans, in the context in which long-term implications hinge on these present-day decisions. In this situation, invocations of the threats of climate change and the corresponding necessity to procure "ecological security" and "resilience" often take on an uninterrogated urgency. This needs to change. We need a new urban development; we need a new urban future. Transformative futures demand the production of alternative visions.

Appendix 1: Methodological Excursions

I investigate sites and strategies in three cities. The unit of analysis is the *design strategy*—within and beyond the city. New York and Jakarta are the *primary sites*, in which I focus on contested visions, the plans and counterplans. Rotterdam functions as a *reflexive site*—the site itself, and the relationship between this site and the other two sites, illuminating and sharpening the analysis of strategies in each of the three sites, and the comprehension of the whole.

Methodologically, the work addresses two key problems. First, it investigates intertwined social and spatial change by fusing more traditional qualitative methods, including interviews and observation, with analyses of photographs, drawings, and design documents to take into account existing and projected changes in biophysical conditions. It takes seriously the projective agency of design and the power of visual representations. Second, it develops an approach of urban relational analysis to study disparate yet interconnected sites. I conducted field visits and site and participant observation in Indonesia, the Netherlands, and the United States between January 2013 and March 2019. I conducted approximately fifty-five in-depth semistructured interviews across the sites (appendix 2), and numerous informal interviews, including with residents of informal settlements in Jakarta, public housing residents in New York, participants in and around Rebuild By Design, and designers and water management officials in the Netherlands. I reviewed approximately thirty-five planning and design documents for strategies across the three sites (appendix 3).

In terms of a multisite, multistrategy study, I build on frameworks for a more reflexive approach to case selection and analysis[1] and a relational reading of sites—each understood through the others.[2] This involves, in essence,

(1) sites and strategies observed and analyzed in relation to—and not in comparison with—each other; (2) "cases," as such, considered not as place-bound entities but as a set of sites, documents, actors, and actions that span space and time; and (3) variables explored not as static units, but in terms of how they might be affected by actors and processes in other sites. I also look to methods that relate biophysical materiality and environmental processes with social processes, including Anne Rademacher's work on the ethnographies of waterscapes and cultural change, in pursuing an understanding of what she has termed the "social ideas and practices of urban ecology."[3]

Relational Urban Research and Reflexive Sites
This is, in essence, a multiple case study set within a relational reading of sites. But when we really consider where a relational study takes us, we might make the argument that this is actually a particular snapshot into dynamic global phenomena—a *single case*, perhaps the critical one in a set of many possibilities, or a *single sample* of a *network formation*.

How do we actually *do* relational urban research? Network analysis in planning and economics often refers to the quantitative analysis of flows and large datasets. In sociology, it refers to the study of social structure. Neither of these offers an appropriate approach for this particular urban network condition. Scholars of relational geography have implored researchers, for example, to see cities and regions as "spatial formations . . . summoned up as temporary placements of ever moving material and immanent geographies, as 'hauntings' of things that have moved on but left their mark";[4] or, "to view *all* cities from *this* particular place on the map,"[5] to "[u]se one site to pose questions of another."[6] Concretely, this might imply resituating one's point of view to the global no matter where one may be investigating locally, or interrogating a site not in and of itself but from the point of view of another site.

So, building on these, and considering some empirical findings, I develop a preliminary method of relational urban research. Some guidelines: The unit of analysis is the design strategy, for example, the Giant Sea Wall masterplan in Jakarta, or Rebuild By Design (a strategy that includes multiple substrategies in the various design proposals), or kampung design activism as practiced by Ciliwung Merdeka along the riverbanks of the Ciliwung in Jakarta. The sites are the "spatial formations," the "cities" as such, that serve as the territory of governance and the terrain of contestation. New York and Jakarta function as *primary sites*, Rotterdam as a *reflexive site*—itself and its relationships with the other sites illuminating the whole. Actors and institutions take their place in producing the strategies, with their own relationships to one or more sites. Networks link the strategies across the sites. The networks include the relationships between actors and institutions (illustrated in detail in chapter 3).

The process of relational analysis in this work proceeds in the following manner. First, take a snapshot of the network—the entire network, or a specific sample of it. In this research, it was a preliminary observation of a set of actors and institutions conducting actions for a particular purpose—urban plans to respond to climate change—linked and overlapping in unexpected ways. Second, define the strategies, actors, institutions, and relationships among and between each of them. Third, conduct an initial overview analysis of the similarities and differences across the relationships; map distinct or nominally defined power relationships, and define expectations of what we might observe. In this study, it was clear that Rotterdam was not a parallel site, where comparable observations were happening, but a reflexive site, through which one could gain more acute knowledge of the network. Fourth, disentangle the key topics or issues that animate the relationships that one observes. In this situation, power relationships (due to conflicts over society and nature), the formation of the network, and the legitimization of design strategies appeared to be critical issues. Analyze each issue, with sites viewed relationally. And fifth, synthesize the findings, pulling out key factors that crosscut the issues and sites.

Why do this? What does it get us? I propose that what is observed here cannot be understood without a relational approach. It would not make sense to look at these sites strictly as comparative studies. New York and Jakarta may be comparable based on territorial and population size. But the motivations that drive environmental planning in each city are so different and so much based on their political histories and broader relationships to global economy. Likewise, to look at either of those sites without an analysis of Netherlands spatial politics and political economy, and Rotterdam municipal plans, would be to bracket out an understanding of the Dutch institutions, designers, and planners, and therefore the sites and strategies themselves. Further, I propose that we cannot fully understand even the internal contestations of these sites without a relational analysis. Kampung activism takes on new light when seen in relation to the heightened awareness brought on by transnational activity, particularly in terms of coalition building, and the extended terrain of contestation provoked by large-scale, high-profile projects and the networks through which they are produced.

Cautions and Affirmations

This book attempts a relational analysis of cities, searching out a way to "see" the multilevel and multiscalar relationships between strategies, across the sites. Much like the oft-stated criticisms of small-n case studies, one might assert that this study examines only one specific network formation, one type of reflexive site. Perhaps, if we were to look at a different formation, we would see different dynamics. I think that is true, and explain as much in chapter 3. At the same time, I think that the relational method itself serves as resistance against simple dismissal of its specificity. Its very relationality suggests that we might reformat or reframe this approach to look at shades or articulations of difference, for example, by looking at strategies in Dhaka or Ho Chi Minh City instead of Jakarta, probing whether New York maintains its reconfiguring global city role within other formations, or inquiring whether Hamburg or London or Singapore plays a similar role to Rotterdam.

Relatedly, if you always see something relationally, do you miss the place? In this book, there is symmetry, in a manner of speaking, between the global networks and the local contestation. The narratives, concepts, and categories unearthed in this book affirm the criticality of iterative, multiscalar, and multilevel research. By following global flows and exchanges and dwelling in local, place-based social relationships, the book contests explanations of urban change that overly prioritize generalized global forces, on the one hand, or historically and place-specific local contexts, on the other.

In this study I've largely treated the various kampung activist coalitions in Jakarta similarly in terms of their relationships to power structures. They are not the same. A study focused more specifically on the shades of strategies and organizing, and a more in-depth ethnographic exploration of the activism and coalition building would unearth these differences. In New York, the focus is clearly on the broader Rebuild By Design initiative, and the dynamics around it, and less on the individual team proposals. This is appropriate given the objectives and scope of the research, in particular the emphasis on broader relationships. At the same time, a deeper investigation into the design teams might reveal a lot more about team motivations and community engagement experiences.

Finally, because of the framework of the research, Rotterdam plays a distinct role. On one level, the city (and its country) is prioritized, a key part of the method and analysis. On another level, the local "embedding" and "transformation" of concepts is not necessarily given the same level of analysis as they are in the other sites.

Research Worldview

In proposing the problem and framework for research, I have already determined that the typical ways of looking at these issues and these sites are inadequate. This particular approach led the study to wrestle with method—productively, I think, but also in a manner that led me to disentangle and, perhaps, to reentangle a number of rather complex issues, and to cut through a large swath of theories while doing it. Recall, from the introduction, the caution about privilege and power in knowledge production. The relational analysis in this research is intrinsically multipositional. It is not situated in one place or from one point of view. At the same time, my deliberate centering of the analyses in this book, across the sites and strategies, on contestation against dominant modes of urban development and hegemonic global systems is a way to acknowledge and be accountable to the relationships of power in which the objects of research and the processes—including *my* processes—of knowledge production are embedded.

Further, as a person of Southeast Asian descent who speaks Bahasa Indonesia, and also as one who called New York City home for more than a decade, part of privileged realms of professional practice, and who is conducting research from elite US academic institutions, I bring complex, shifting positionalities to fieldwork and writing, to data collection and analysis, and to the sense-making of lineages of urban, environmental, design, and political theories. In my view, mine is a reflexive, unstable position. And this is something I do not attempt to gloss over or suppress in doing this work. This research is a testament to worldviews that are all of the following, if not always at once: embodied, positional, privileged, empowered, and legitimized. I wield the power of institutionalized, Euro-American, scientific and social scientific modes of knowledge. And I take on the struggle of uneven and unjust systems. With the renewed debates about general theories and positional knowledge in urban research,[7] my position, and my work in this book, reinforces the importance and power of "seeing" across and through multiple modes of knowledge and from multiple viewpoints.

Appendix 2: List of Interviews Conducted by Author

Azwar, Sylvira, researcher, Jakarta Research Council, Jakarta, Indonesia: July 16, 2014

Boer, Florian, De Urbanisten, Rotterdam, Netherlands: June 30, 2014; March 25, 2019

Bons, Kees, Deltares, Jakarta, Indonesia: July 11, 2014

Brown, Anna, senior associate director, Rockefeller Foundation Asia, Bangkok, Thailand: July 3, 2014

Chester, Amy, manager, Rebuild By Design, New York: June 19, 2014; July 18, 2018

Davis, Scott, senior adviser in the Office of the Secretary, US Department of Housing and Urban Development, Washington, DC: October 31, 2014

De Vries, Christopher, Rademacher de Vries Architects, Amsterdam, Netherlands: June 25, 2014 (informal interview)

De Vries, Hugo, project adviser, Partners for Water, Netherlands Enterprise Agency, The Hague: March 26, 2019

Doepel, Duzan, principal, Doepel Strijkers, Rotterdam, Netherlands: September 29, 2014

Eisenhard, Jill, executive director, Red Hook Initiative, Brooklyn, NY: September 13, 2014; July 19, 2018; August 2, 2019

Eng, Fook Chuan, senior water and sanitation specialist, World Bank, Jakarta, Indonesia: July 17, 2014

Gunawan, Iwan, senior disaster risk management specialist, World Bank, Jakarta, Indonesia: July 18, 2013

Gurusamy, Senthil, research fellow, Singapore ETH Centre, Singapore: July 10, 2013

Handhayani, Sarwo, deputy governor for spatial planning and environment, previously chief of BAPPEDA (Department of City Planning), DKI Jakarta, Jakarta, Indonesia: July 18, 2013

Irawaty, Dian Tri, housing activist, Rujak Center for Urban Studies, Jakarta, Indonesia: July 16, 2013; July 10, 2014

Jacobs, John, strategic adviser water, City of Rotterdam, Rotterdam, Netherlands: October 1, 2014

Kete, Nancy, managing director, Rockefeller Foundation, New York: June 16, 2014

Krisbandono, Adji, Ministry of Public Works and Housing, Jakarta, Indonesia: September 26, 2017

Kusumawijaya, Marco, founder and director, Rujak Center for Urban Studies, Jakarta, Indonesia: July 2013, July 2014 (informal interview)

Lee, Ivana, activist, Ciliwung Merdeka, Jakarta, Indonesia: July 17, 2014

Letitre, Peter, senior project manager, Deltares, Jakarta: September 24, 2017; December 11, 2018

Maas, Winy, director, MVRDV, Rotterdam, Netherlands: June 26, 2014

Marrella, Michael, director of waterfront and open space planning, New York City Department of City Planning, New York: May 11, 2015

McFadden, Marion, deputy assistant secretary for grant programs, US Department of Housing and Urban Development, Washington, DC: October 31, 2014

Molenaar, Arnoud, manager, Rotterdam Climate Proof, Rotterdam, Netherlands: October 1, 2014; video call: April 25, 2019

Muhammad, Gugun, Urban Poor Consortium, Jakarta, Indonesia: December 11, 2018

Muhammad, Kamil, coordinator, Architecture Sans Frontierès Indonesia, Jakarta, Indonesia: December 17, 2018

Mungkasa, Oswar, deputy governor for spatial planning and environment, DKI Jakarta, Jakarta, Indonesia: September 24, 2017; December 13, 2018

Nandan, Gita, co-chair, Red Hook NY Rising Community Reconstruction Plan, Brooklyn, NY: August 22, 2014

Niesten, Mark, project manager, Netherlands Water Partnership, The Hague, Netherlands: March 22, 2019

Otter, Henriette, urban water and subsurface management, Deltares, Utrecht, Netherlands: March 21, 2019

Oudkerk Pool, Chantal, senior adviser, Rotterdam Climate Proof, video call, August 7, 2014

Ovink, Henk, principal, Rebuild By Design, video call, November 24, 2014; The Hague, Netherlands: March 25, 2019

Padawangi, Rita, senior research fellow, National University of Singapore, Singapore: July 21, 2014

Appendix 2

Rahman, Arlan, infrastructure specialist, World Bank, Jakarta, Indonesia: July 17, 2014

Reyes, Damaris, executive director, Good Old Lower East Side, New York: December 18, 2014

Saidi, Edi, coordinator, Urban Poor Consortium, Jakarta, Indonesia: July 15, 2014

Sannen, Ad, senior consultant water governance, Royal Haskoning, Rotterdam, Netherlands: September 25, 2014 (informal interview)

Shaikh, Michael, deputy director for external affairs, climate policy and program, New York City Office of the Mayor, New York: July 19, 2018

Shepherd, Ariel, previously fellow at Asian Coalition for Housing Rights, Jakarta, Indonesia: July 17, 2014

Simone, AbdouMaliq, scholar and researcher, Jakarta, Indonesia: July 21, 2013 (informal interview)

Soehodho, Sutanto, deputy governor for industry, trade and transportation, DKI Jakarta, Rotterdam, Netherlands: September 25, 2014 (informal interview)

Sumardi, I. Sandyawan, activist, Ciliwung Merdeka, Jakarta, Indonesia: July 18, 2014; December 10, 2018

Sutanudjaja, Elisa, executive director, Rujak Center for Urban Studies, Jakarta, Indonesia: September 20, 2017; December 13, 2018

Taylor, John, founder, Yayasan Kota Kita, Jakarta, Indonesia: January 27, 2013; July 17, 2013 (informal interviews)

Tijook, Wiwi, landscape architect, City of Rotterdam, Rotterdam, Netherlands: June 30, 2014

Tobing, Aisa, chairman, Climate Change Task Force, DKI Jakarta, Jakarta, Indonesia: July 16, 2014

Uennatornwaranggoon, Praerung, senior program associate, Rockefeller Foundation Asia, Bangkok, Thailand: July 3, 2014

Van den Boomen, Gijs, director, KuiperCompagnons, Rotterdam, Netherlands: October 1, 2014

Van der Linden, Ivo, Netherlands Water Partnership, The Hague, Netherlands: September 30, 2014; July 14, 2016.

Van Woerden, Arend, adviser, regional and urban development, Grontmij (now Sweco), Houten, Netherlands: September 29, 2014; Utrecht, Netherlands: July 18, 2016.

Winayanti, Lana, senior expert, Ministry of Public Works and Housing, Jakarta, Indonesia: July 23, 2013

Appendix 3: List of Planning and Design Documents Analyzed

New York

City of New York. *East Side Coastal Resiliency Project*. New York: City of New York, March 19, 2015. http://www.nyc.gov/html/planyc/downloads/pdf/150319_ESCR_FINAL.pdf.

City of New York, Office of the Mayor. *PlaNYC: A Greener, Greater New York*. New York: Office of the Mayor, 2007. http://www.nyc.gov/html/planyc/downloads/pdf/publications/full_report_2007.pdf.

City of New York, Office of the Mayor. *PlaNYC: A Greener, Greater New York—Update April 2011*. New York: Office of the Mayor, 2011. http://www.nyc.gov/html/planyc/downloads/pdf/publications/planyc_2011_planyc_full_report.pdf.

City of New York, Office of the Mayor. *A Stronger, More Resilient New York*. Report of the Special Initiative for Rebuilding and Resiliency (SIRR). New York: Office of the Mayor, 2013. http://s-media.nyc.gov/agencies/sirr/SIRR_singles_Lo_res.pdf.

Hurricane Sandy Rebuilding Task Force. *Hurricane Sandy Rebuilding Strategy: Stronger Communities, a Resilient Region*. Washington, DC: US Department Housing and Urban Development, August 2013. http://portal.hud.gov/hudportal/documents/huddoc?id=HSRebuildingStrategy.pdf.

LES Ready! *Getting LES Ready: Learning from Hurricane Sandy to Create a Community-Based Disaster Plan for the Future*. New York: Lower East Side Long Term Recovery Group, 2014. https://cdp.urbanjustice.org/sites/default/files/CDP.WEB.doc_Report_LESready_20141117.pdf.

New York City Department of City Planning (NYC DCP). *Vision 2020: The NYC Comprehensive Waterfront Plan*. New York: New York City Department of City Planning, March 2011. https://www1.nyc.gov/assets/planning/download/pdf/plans-studies/vision-2020-cwp/vision2020/vision2020_nyc_cwp.pdf.

New York City Department of City Planning (NYC DCP). "Coastal Climate Resilience: Urban Waterfront Adaptive Strategies." New York, NY, June 2013. https://www.nyc.gov/assets/planning/download/pdf/plans-studies/sustainable-communities/climate-resilience/urban_waterfront.pdf.

Nordenson, Guy, Catherine Seavitt, and Adam Yarinsky. *On the Water | Palisade Bay*. Ostfildern: Hatje Cantz; New York: Museum of Modern Art, 2010.

NY Rising Community Reconstruction Program (NYRCR). *Red Hook: NY Rising Community Reconstruction Plan*. New York: NY Rising Community Reconstruction Program, March 2014. https://stormrecovery.ny.gov/sites/default/files/crp/community/documents/redhook_nyrcr_plan_20mb_0.pdf.

NYS 2100 Commission. *Recommendations to Improve the Strength and Resilience of the Empire State's Infrastructure*. Albany, NY, January 2013. http://www.governor.ny.gov/sites/governor.ny.gov/files/archive/assets/documents/NYS2100.pdf.

Rebuild By Design. "Promoting Resilience Post-Sandy Through Innovative Planning and Design." Design Brief, June 21, 2013. http://portal.hud.gov/hudportal/documents/huddoc?id=REBUILDBYDESIGNBrief.pdf.

Red Hook Initiative. "Recovering from Sandy: RHI WiFi Project." December 2012.

Red Hook Initiative. *Red Hook Initiative: A Community Response to Hurricane Sandy*. Brooklyn, NY: Red Hook Initiative, June 2013. https://rhicenter.org/wp-content/uploads/2019/11/RHI-Hurricane-Report-6_2013.pdf.

New York—Rebuild By Design proposals

BIG Team. "The BIG U." Rebuild By Design, 2014. http://www.rebuildbydesign.org/project/big-team-final-proposal/.

HR&A Advisors, Inc. with Cooper, Robertson & Partners. "The Commercial Corridor Resiliency Project." Rebuild By Design, 2014. http://www.rebuildbydesign.org/project/hra-advisors-inc-with-cooper-robertson-partners-final-proposals/.

Interboro Team. "Living with the Bay." Rebuild By Design, 2014. http://www.rebuildbydesign.org/our-work/all-proposals/winning-projects/ny-living-with-the-bay.

MIT CAU+ZUS+URBANISTEN Team. "New Meadowlands." Rebuild By Design, 2014. http://www.rebuildbydesign.org/our-work/all-proposals/winning-projects/nj-meadowlands.

OMA Team. "Resist, Delay, Store, Discharge: A Comprehensive Strategy for Hoboken." Rebuild By Design, 2014. http://www.rebuildbydesign.org/our-work/all-proposals/winning-projects/nj-hudson-river-project-resist-delay-store-discharge.

PennDesign / OLIN Team. "Hunts Point Lifelines." Rebuild By Design, 2014. http://www.rebuildbydesign.org/our-work/all-proposals/winning-projects/hunts-point-lifelines.

Sasaki/Rutgers/Arup Team. "Resilience+The Beach." Rebuild By Design, 2014. http://www.rebuildbydesign.org/our-work/all-proposals/finalist/resilience--the-beach.

SCAPE / Landscape Architecture Team. "Living Breakwaters." Rebuild By Design, 2014. http://www.rebuildbydesign.org/our-work/all-proposals/winning-projects/ny-living-breakwaters.

WB unabridged with Yale ARCADIS Team. "Resilient Bridgeport." Rebuild By Design, 2014. http://www.rebuildbydesign.org/our-work/all-proposals/winning-projects/ct-resilient-bridgeport.

WXY/West 8 Team. "Blue Dunes: The Future of Coastal Protection." Rebuild By Design, 2014. http://www.rebuildbydesign.org/our-work/all-proposals/finalist/blue-dunes--the-future-of-coastal-protection.

Jakarta

Ciliwung Merdeka. "Kampung Susun Manusiawi Bukit Duri." Microsoft Powerpoint, Jakarta, Indonesia, n.d.

Ciliwung Merdeka. "Process for Creating Solutions by and for People: Humanitarian-Growth Vertical Kampung." Exhibit at the *Jakarta Vertical Kampung* exhibition, Jakarta, Indonesia, 2013.

Government of Indonesia. *Jakarta Coastal Defence Strategy (JCDS)*. Jakarta, Indonesia: Ministry of Public Works, September 30, 2011.

Government of Jakarta. *Ciliwung River Regulations*. Jakarta, Indonesia: Jakarta Regional Development Planning Agency (BAPPEDA), 2012.

Government of Jakarta. *Rencana Tata Ruang Wilayah Jakarta 2030 (Jakarta Region Spatial Plan 2030)*. Jakarta, Indonesia: Jakarta Regional Development Planning Agency (BAPPEDA), 2012.

Indonesia, Coordinating Ministry for Economic Affairs (MENKO). "Master Plan: National Capital Integrated Coastal Development Master Plan." October 1, 2014. Accessed January 1, 2015. http://ncicd.com/wp-content/uploads/2014/10/MP-final-NCICD-LR.pdf (link has since expired).

Urban Poor Consortium (UPC), Jaringan Rakyat Miskin Kota (JRMK), Universitas Indonesia (UI), Arkomjogja, and RCUS. "Proposal of Participatory Design Concept Kebon Tebu Rusunami, Muara Baru, Waduk Pluit." Exhibit at the *Jakarta Vertical Kampung* exhibition, Jakarta, Indonesia, 2013.

Rotterdam/Netherlands

Delta Commission. *Working Together with Water: A Living Land Builds for Its Future— Findings of the Deltacommissie 2008, Summary and Conclusions*. The Hague: Delta Commission, November 2008. http://www.deltacommissie.com/doc/deltareport_full.pdf.

Deltares. *Deltares 2.0: Strategic Plan 2012–2015*. Delft, Netherlands: Deltares, February 2012. https://www.deltares.nl/app/uploads/2015/02/Deltares-Strategic-Plan-Def-ENG.pdf.

Deltares. *Sinking Cities: An Integrated Approach towards Solutions*. Delft, Netherlands: Deltares, 2013. https://www.deltares.nl/app/uploads/2015/09/Sinking-cities.pdf.

Government of the Netherlands, Delta Committee. *Report of the Delta Committee: Final Report*. The Hague, Netherlands: State Printing and Publication Office, 1962. http://publicaties.minienm.nl/download-bijlage/3705/final-report-1-report-of-the-delta-committee.pdf.

Government of the Netherlands. *Summary National Policy Strategy for Infrastructure and Spatial Planning: Making the Netherlands Competitive, Accessible, Liveable and Safe*. The Hague: Ministry of Infrastructure and the Environment, March 2011. www.government.nl/files/documents-and-publications/publications/2013/07/24/summary-national-policy-strategy-for-infrastructure-and-spatial-planning/summary-national-policy-strategy-for-infrastructure-and-spatial-planning.pdf.

Government of the Netherlands. *Building on the Strength of Design: Action Agenda for Architecture and Spatial Design 2013–2016*. The Hague: Ministry of Infrastructure and the Environment; Ministry of Education, Culture and Science; Ministry of the Interior and Kingdom Relations; Ministry of Economic Affairs, Agriculture and Innovation; Ministry of Defence, September 2012. www.government.nl/files/documents-and-publications/reports/2012/09/21/the-action-agenda-for-architecture-and-spatial-design/action-agenda-for-architecture-and-spatial-design-2013–2016-uk.pdf.

Municipality of Rotterdam, Schieland and Krimpenerwaard Water Control Board, Hollandse Delta Water Authority, and Delfland Water Control Board. *Rotterdam Waterplan 2: Working on Water for an Attractive City*. Rotterdam, September 2007. http://www.rotterdamclimateinitiative.nl/documents/Documenten/WATERPLAN_engels.pdf (link has since expired).

Rotterdam Climate Initiative. *Rotterdam Climate Change Adaptation Strategy*. Rotterdam: City of Rotterdam, October 2013. http://www.urbanisten.nl/wp/wp-content/uploads/UB_RAS_EN_lr.pdf (link has since expired).

Notes

Introduction

1. IPCC, *Climate Change 2013: The Physical Science Basis. Contribution of Working Group I to the Fifth Assessment Report of the Intergovernmental Panel on Climate Change*, ed. T. F. Stocker et al. (Cambridge: Cambridge University Press, 2013). http://www.ipcc.ch/report/ar5/wg1/.

2. IPCC, *Global Warming of 1.5°C*, IPCC, 2018. https://www.ipcc.ch/sr15.

3. Sheila Jasanoff, "A New Climate for Society," *Theory, Culture and Society* 27, nos. 2–3 (2010): 236.

4. Dipesh Chakrabarty, "The Climate of History: Four Theses," *Critical Inquiry* 35, no. 2 (2009): 212.

5. See, for example, the European Climate Adaptation Platform: Necessary for "decisions with potentially long term consequences on the basis of incomplete knowledge and uncertain information." Climate-ADAPT: European Climate Adaptation Platform, "What Is Meant by Uncertainty?," accessed December 12, 2020, http://climate-adapt.eea.europa.eu/uncertainty-guidance/topic1.

6. See, for example, John Friedmann, *Planning in the Public Domain: From Knowledge to Action* (Princeton, NJ: Princeton University Press, 1987).

7. Harriet Bulkeley and Michele M. Betsill, "Rethinking Sustainable Cities: Multilevel Governance and the 'Urban' Politics of Climate Change," *Environmental Politics* 14, no. 1 (2005): 42–63, and "Revisiting the Urban Politics of Climate Change," *Environmental Politics* 22, no. 1 (2013): 136–154.

8. World Bank, *Turn down the Heat: Why a 4°C Warmer World Must Be Avoided*, Report for the World Bank by the Potsdam Institute for Climate Impact Research and Climate Analytics (Washington, DC: World Bank, 2012), http://issuu.com/world.bank.publications/docs/turn_down_the_heat.

9. See, for example, Noel Castree, "Neoliberalising Nature: The Logics of Deregulation and Reregulation," *Environment and Planning A* 40, no. 1 (2008): 131–152, and "Neoliberalising Nature: Processes, Effects, and Evaluations," *Environment and Planning A* 40, no. 1 (2008): 153–173; Nik Heynen and Paul Robbins, "The Neoliberalization of Nature: Governance, Privatization, Enclosure and Valuation," *Capitalism Nature Socialism* 16, no. 1 (2005): 5–8; and Karen Bakker, "The Limits of 'Neoliberal Natures': Debating Green Neoliberalism," *Progress in Human Geography* 34, no. 6 (2010): 715–735.

10. Mike Hodson and Simon Marvin, *World Cities and Climate Change: Producing Urban Ecological Security* (Maidenhead, UK: Open University Press, 2010), 125.

11. Hodson and Marvin, *World Cities and Climate Change*, 115.

12. Hannah Reid and David Satterthwaite, "Climate Change and Cities: Why Urban Agendas Are Central to Adaptation and Mitigation," *Sustainable Development Opinion*, December 2007, http://pubs.iied.org/pdfs/17025IIED.pdf; Cynthia Rosenzweig et al., "Cities Lead the Way in Climate-Change Action," *Nature* 467, no. 7318 (2010): 909–911. This assertion is usually couched within the oft-stated statistic that 50 percent of the world's population now lives in cities, is responsible for 70 percent of emissions, and so on.

13. See, for example, Jörn Birkmann et al., "Adaptive Urban Governance: New Challenges for the Second Generation of Urban Adaptation Strategies to Climate Change," *Sustainability Science* 5, no. 2 (2010): 185–206; Saleemul Huq et al., "Editorial: Reducing Risks to Cities from Disasters and Climate Change," *Environment and Urbanization* 19, no. 1 (2007): 3–15; and David Satterthwaite, "The Urban Challenge Revisited," *Environment: Science and Policy for Sustainable Development* 49, no. 9 (2007): 6–17.

14. See, for example, Guy Nordenson, Catherine Seavitt, and Adam Yarinsky, *On the Water: Palisade Bay* (Ostfildern: Hatje Cantz; New York: Museum of Modern Art, 2010).

15. Knowledge for Climate, *Dutch Climate Adaptation Research* (Utrecht, Netherlands: Knowledge for Climate, 2012), https://edepot.wur.nl/342784.

16. Nick Godfrey and Roger Savage, *Future Proofing Cities* (London: Atkins Global, 2012), http://discovery.ucl.ac.uk/1402048/.

17. A long line of studies of the city, from foundational urban sociology to regional urban planning to human geography to studies of global urbanization, reminds us that the urban is a contested process of social, spatial, ecological, and economic change often far outside the city proper. Specific systems, processes, and characteristics that might be seen as "urban" or "city-like" spill over and extend beyond any kind of enforced territorial boundary. In effect, while particular bounded territories may be determined and governed, the factors determining changes and outcomes

within these territories are always dependent on interconnections across space. See, e.g., Louis Wirth, "Urbanism as a Way of Life," *American Journal of Sociology* 44 (1938): 1–24; John Friedmann and John Miller, "The Urban Field," *Journal of the American Institute of Planners* 31, no. 4 (1965): 312–320; and, Jean Gottmann, *Since Megalopolis: The Urban Writings of Jean Gottmann*, ed. Robert Alexander Harper and Jean Gottmann (Baltimore: Johns Hopkins University Press, 1990).

18. See Neil Brenner, "Theses on Urbanization," *Public Culture* 25, no. 1 69 (2013): 85–114, and Neil Brenner and Christian Schmid, "The 'Urban Age' in Question," *International Journal of Urban and Regional Research* 38, no. 3 (2014): 731–755, for critiques of standard accounts of understanding and measuring the urban, and for theoretical excursions on the links between the processes behind the growth of urban agglomerations and the transformation of landscapes on a planetary scale; also, Edward W. Soja and Miguel Kanai, "The Urbanization of the World," in *The Endless City: The Urban Age Project by the London School of Economics and Deutsche Bank's Alfred Herrhausen Society*, ed. Richard Burdett and Deyan Sudjic (London: Phaidon, 2007), 54–69, for a discussion of the expanded worldwide geography of urbanization; and Erle C. Ellis et al., "Anthropogenic Transformation of the Biomes, 1700 to 2000," *Global Ecology and Biogeography* 19, no. 5 (2010): 589–606, for empirical findings of the extent of human-caused changes in the biosphere.

19. See, in particular, work by Ananya Roy on postcolonial urban theory, "The 21st-Century Metropolis: New Geographies of Theory," *Regional Studies* 43, no. 6 (2009): 819–830, and "Who's Afraid of Postcolonial Theory?," *International Journal of Urban and Regional Research* 40, no. 1 (January 1, 2016): 200–209.

20. Henri Lefebvre, *The Urban Revolution*, trans. Robert Bononno (Minneapolis: University of Minnesota Press, 2003), 3.

21. Words by Tracie L. Washington, Louisiana Justice Institute, from artist and activist Candy Chang's blog, http://candychang.com/nola_resilient/.

22. Ideas about resilience have gained traction, particularly after the adoption of the Hyogo Framework for Action in 2005 at the UN World Conference on Disaster Reduction, and through the support and advocacy of the Rockefeller Foundation, which launched the Asian Cities Climate Change Resilience Network (ACCCRN) in 2008, a program to assist ten cities in Vietnam, India, Indonesia, and Thailand to prepare for climate-change threats, and continued to support and promote various resilience initiatives, including Rebuild By Design in New York, see, the Rockefeller Foundation, *Rebound: Building a More Resilient World* (New York: Rockefeller Foundation, 2013), 2, https://www.rockefellerfoundation.org/report/rebound-building-a-more-resilient-world/.

23. See, for a scholarly review, Sara Meerow, Joshua P. Newell, and Melissa Stults, "Defining Urban Resilience: A Review," *Landscape and Urban Planning* 147 (2016): 38–49.

24. Such as ICLEI—Local Governments for Sustainability, the United Kingdom's Department for International Development (DFID), the US Federal Emergency Management Agency (FEMA), and the US Agency for International Development (USAID).

25. The termination of 100 Resilient Cities (100RC), announced in April 2019, took scholars and practitioners by surprise. In July 2019, the month of 100RC's closure, the Rockefeller Foundation announced a new climate resiliency initiative to focus on "market changing opportunities," as well as $8 million in funds to support some of the aspects of 100RC's work, including the "chief resilience officers" installed in member cities of the former network.

26. Including the Clinton Global Initiative, Swiss Re, the World Bank, the American Institute of Architects, Architecture for Humanity, and Palantir (a "big data" technology company partly funded by the CIA).

27. The characteristic of resilience as bouncing back is valued not only as a necessary response to changing conditions, but as an advantage. Indeed it is often framed as a *dividend*—a view held, in various permutations, by the former president of the Rockefeller Foundation, Judith Rodin, *The Resilience Dividend: Being Strong in a World Where Things Go Wrong* (New York: PublicAffairs, 2014); development agencies and lending institutions such as the Overseas Development Institute and the World Bank, Thomas Tanner et al., *The Triple Dividend of Resilience: Realising Development Goals through the Multiple Benefits of Disaster Risk Management* (London: Overseas Development Institute; Washington DC: World Bank, 2015); and academic researchers, Susan L. Cutter et al., "Disaster Resilience: A National Imperative," *Environment: Science and Policy for Sustainable Development* 55, no. 2 (2013): 25–29.

28. See, for example, Andy Pike, Stuart Dawley, and John Tomaney, "Resilience, Adaptation and Adaptability," *Cambridge Journal of Regions, Economy and Society* 3, no. 1 (2010): 1–12; Robin Leichenko, "Climate Change and Urban Resilience," *Current Opinion in Environmental Sustainability* 3, no. 3 (2011): 164–168; Mark Pelling, *Adaptation to Climate Change: From Resilience to Transformation* (Abingdon, UK: Routledge, 2011); Lawrence J. Vale, "The Politics of Resilient Cities: Whose Resilience and Whose City?," *Building Research and Information* 42, no. 2 (2014): 191–201; and Susan Fainstein, "Resilience and Justice," *International Journal of Urban and Regional Research* 39, no. 1 (2015): 157–167.

29. See, for example, Danny MacKinnon and Kate Driscoll Derickson, "From Resilience to Resourcefulness: A Critique of Resilience Policy and Activism," *Progress in Human Geography* 37, no. 2 (2013): 253–270; Kathleen Tierney, "Resilience and the Neoliberal Project: Discourses, Critiques, Practices—and Katrina," *American Behavioral Scientist* 59, no. 10 (2015): 1327–42; Simin Davoudi, Jennifer Lawrence, and Jim Bohland, "Anatomy of the Resilience Machine," in *The Resilience Machine* (Abingdon, UK: Routledge, 2019), 12–28.

Notes to Introduction

30. J. Timmons Roberts and Bradley C. Parks, *A Climate of Injustice: Global Inequality, North-South Politics, and Climate Policy* (Cambridge, MA: MIT Press, 2007).

31. See, e.g., Vanesa Castán Broto, "Urban Governance and the Politics of Climate Change," *World Development* 93 (2017): 1–15.

32. Joshua Long and Jennifer L. Rice, "From Sustainable Urbanism to Climate Urbanism," *Urban Studies* 56, no. 5 (2019): 992–1008; Hodson and Marvin, *World Cities and Climate Change*.

33. Isabelle Anguelovski et al., "Equity Impacts of Urban Land Use Planning for Climate Adaptation: Critical Perspectives from the Global North and South," *Journal of Planning Education and Research* 36, no. 3 (2016): 333–348.

34. See, for example, Linda Shi et al., "Roadmap towards Justice in Urban Climate Adaptation Research," *Nature Climate Change* 6 (February 2016): 131–137.

35. Robert D. Bullard, *Dumping in Dixie: Race, Class, and Environmental Quality* (Boulder, CO: Westview, 1990).

36. For a review, see Paul Mohai, David Pellow, and J. Timmons Roberts, "Environmental Justice," *Annual Review of Environment and Resources* 34 (2009): 405–430. David N. Pellow, "Environmental Inequality Formation: Toward a Theory of Environmental Injustice," *American Behavioral Scientist* 43, no. 4 (2000): 581–601, emphasizes the need to understand the processes behind the formation of inequality. Laura Pulido, "Rethinking Environmental Racism: White Privilege and Urban Development in Southern California," *Annals of the Association of American Geographers* 90, no. 1 (2000): 12–40, and Ryan Holifield, "Defining Environmental Justice and Environmental Racism," *Urban Geography* 22, no. 1 (2001): 78–90, investigate how structural conditions such as systemic racism contribute to the unjust environmental outcomes.

37. David Schlosberg, "Reconceiving Environmental Justice: Global Movements and Political Theories," *Environmental Politics* 13, no. 3 (2004): 517–540; David N. Pellow, *Resisting Global Toxics: Transnational Movements for Environmental Justice* (Cambridge, MA: MIT Press, 2007).

38. Kenneth A. Gould and Tammy L. Lewis, *Green Gentrification: Urban Sustainability and the Struggle for Environmental Justice* (London: Routledge, 2017).

39. These included the antiglobalization activism of the late 1990s (exemplified by the protests against the World Trade Organization [WTO] Ministerial Conference in Seattle in 1999), the work of Global South activists and international environmental and corporate watch organizations during and around multilateral environmental summits. In the period leading up to the Earth Summit in 2002, the International Climate Justice Network was formed and the Bali Principles of Climate Justice were adopted, and indigenous rights movements around the world became increasingly

organized. See International Climate Justice Network (ICJN, made up of organizations including CorpWatch, Third World Network, Oil Watch, and the Indigenous Environmental Network), "Bali Principles of Climate Justice," Corpwatch, August 28, 2002, https://corpwatch.org/article/bali-principles-climate-justice.

40. Paul Chatterton, David Featherstone, and Paul Routledge, "Articulating Climate Justice in Copenhagen: Antagonism, the Commons, and Solidarity," *Antipode* 45, no. 3 (2013): 602–620; Brian Tokar, "Movements for Climate Justice in the US and Worldwide," in *Routledge Handbook of the Climate Change Movement*, ed. Matthias Dietz and Heiko Garrelts (Abingdon, UK: Routledge, 2014), 131–146.

41. Such as the transfer of the use of natural resources from the South to the North, and the shift of manufacturing-based, GHG and other emissions-polluting industries to the countries of the South. See Juan Martínez-Alier, "Environmental Justice (Local and Global)," *Capitalism Nature Socialism* 8, no. 1 (1997): 91–107; see, also, J. Timmons Roberts and Bradley C. Parks, "Ecologically Unequal Exchange, Ecological Debt, and Climate Justice: The History and Implications of Three Related Ideas for a New Social Movement," *International Journal of Comparative Sociology* 50, nos. 3–4 (2009): 385–409.

42. David Schlosberg and Lisette B. Collins, "From Environmental to Climate Justice: Climate Change and the Discourse of Environmental Justice," *Wiley Interdisciplinary Reviews: Climate Change* 5, no. 3 (2014): 359–374.

43. See, for example, ICJN, "Bali Principles of Climate Justice."

44. Elizabeth Yeampierre remarks during a panel discussion at the conference At What Point Managed Retreat? Resilience Building in the Coastal Zone, Opening Panel Event, Earth Institute, Columbia University, New York, June 19, 2019, https://www.earth.columbia.edu/videos/view/at-what-point-managed-retreatquestion.

45. For theoretical elaboration, see Kian Goh, "Urbanising Climate Justice: Constructing Scales and Politicising Difference," *Cambridge Journal of Regions, Economy and Society* 13, no. 3 (2020): 559–574.

46. This description of the conceptual lenses is concentrated, brief, and by nature necessarily incomplete, a conspectus rather than a review.

47. David Harvey, *The Urbanization of Capital: Studies in the History and Theory of Capitalist Urbanization* (Baltimore, MD: Johns Hopkins University Press, 1985); Neil Smith, *Uneven Development: Nature, Capital, and the Production of Space*, 3rd ed. (New York: Blackwell, 2008).

48. See Smith, *Uneven Development*, 71.

49. Raymond Williams, *The Country and the City* (New York: Oxford University Press, 1975), "Ideas of Nature," in *Problems in Materialism and Culture: Selected Essays* (London: Verso, 1980), 67–85; William Cronon, *Nature's Metropolis: Chicago and the Great West* (New York: W. W. Norton, 1991).

50. Nik Heynen, Maria Kaika, and Erik Swyngedouw, "Urban Political Ecology: Politicizing the Production of Urban Natures," in *In the Nature of Cities: Urban Political Ecology and the Politics of Urban Metabolism*, ed. Nik Heynen, Maria Kaika, and Erik Swyngedouw (Abingdon, UK: Routledge, 2006), 8.

51. Erik Swyngedouw, "The City as a Hybrid: On Nature, Society and Cyborg Urbanization," *Capitalism Nature Socialism* 7, no. 2 (1996): 65–80; Matthew Gandy, "Cyborg Urbanization: Complexity and Monstrosity in the Contemporary City," *International Journal of Urban and Regional Research* 29, no. 1 (2005): 26–49.

52. See, in addition to Heynen, Kaika, and Swyngedouw, "Urban Political Ecology," Matthew Gandy, *Concrete and Clay: Reworking Nature in New York City* (Cambridge, MA: MIT Press, 2002); Erik Swyngedouw and Nikolas C. Heynen, "Urban Political Ecology, Justice and the Politics of Scale," *Antipode* 35, no. 5 (2003): 898–918; Roger Keil, "Progress Report: Urban Political Ecology," *Urban Geography* 24, no. 8 (2003): 723–738, and "Progress Report: Urban Political Ecology," *Urban Geography* 26, no. 7 (2005): 640–651; Gene Desfor and Roger Keil, *Nature and the City: Making Environmental Policy in Toronto and Los Angeles* (Tucson: University of Arizona Press, 2004); Maria Kaika, *City of Flows: Modernity, Nature, and the City* (New York: Routledge, 2005); and Nik Heynen, "Urban Political Ecology I: The Urban Century," *Progress in Human Geography* 38, no. 4 (2014): 598–604, "Urban Political Ecology II: The Abolitionist Century," *Progress in Human Geography* 40, no. 6 (2016): 839–845, and "Urban Political Ecology III: The Feminist and Queer Century," *Progress in Human Geography* 42, no. 3 (2018): 446–452.

53. Anne Rademacher, *Reigning the River: Urban Ecologies and Political Transformation in Kathmandu* (Durham, NC: Duke University Press, 2011), 15.

54. In previous writing, I developed Rademacher's ideas in conjunction with concepts and practices of landscape architecture to explain the ways in which worldviews of urban ecologies condition understandings of and solutions for environmental problems in cities, with flooding in Jakarta as an illustrative example. I explained how literal and conceptual shifts in viewpoints—to keep in simultaneous analytical view broader landscape-biophysical and sociopolitical relationships, what I called a "soaking, seeping, spatial politics"—broach new approaches for urban socioecological movements and more just and sustainable urban futures. See Kian Goh, "Urban Waterscapes: The Hydro-Politics of Flooding in a Sinking City," *International Journal of Urban and Regional Research* 43, no. 2 (2019): 250–272.

55. John Friedmann, "The World City Hypothesis," *Development and Change* 17, no. 1 (1986): 69–83, and Saskia Sassen, *The Global City: New York, London, Tokyo* (Princeton, NJ: Princeton University Press, 1991).

56. Manuel Castells, *The Informational City: Information Technology, Economic Restructuring, and the Urban-Regional Process* (Cambridge, MA: Blackwell, 1989), and *The Rise of the Network Society* (Cambridge, MA: Blackwell, 1996).

57. Brenner, "Theses on Urbanization"; Brenner and Schmid, "'Urban Age' in Question"; also, Neil Brenner, "The Urban Question as a Scale Question: Reflections on Henri Lefebvre, Urban Theory and the Politics of Scale," *International Journal of Urban and Regional Research* 24, no. 2 (2000): 361–378.

58. Harriet Bulkeley et al., *Transnational Climate Change Governance* (New York: Cambridge University Press, 2014).

59. Ash Amin, "Regions Unbound: Towards a New Politics of Place," *Geografiska Annaler: Series B, Human Geography* 86, no. 1 (2004): 33–44. See also Jane M. Jacobs, "Urban Geographies I: Still Thinking Cities Relationally," *Progress in Human Geography* 36, no. 3 (2012): 412–422; Doreen Massey, "A Counterhegemonic Relationality of Place," in *Mobile Urbanism: Cities and Policymaking in the Global Age*, ed. Eugene McCann and Kevin Ward (Minneapolis: University of Minnesota Press, 2011), 1–14; and Roy, "21st-Century Metropolis."

60. See, for example, Jennifer Robinson, "Global and World Cities: A View from off the Map," *International Journal of Urban and Regional Research* 26, no. 3 (2002): 531–554; Roy, "21st-Century Metropolis"; and AbdouMaliq Simone, "On the Worlding of African Cities," *African Studies Review* 44, no. 2 (2001): 15–41.

61. Ananya Roy, "Urbanisms, Worlding Practices and the Theory of Planning," *Planning Theory* 10, no. 1 (2011): 6–15.

62. Ananya Roy and Aihwa Ong, eds., *Worlding Cities: Asian Experiments and the Art of Being Global* (Chichester, UK: Wiley-Blackwell, 2011), 3.

63. Jamie Peck, "Geographies of Policy: From Transfer-Diffusion to Mobility-Mutation," *Progress in Human Geography* 35, no. 6 (2011): 773–797. See as well, for example, Allan Cochrane and Kevin Ward, "Guest Editorial: Researching the Geographies of Policy Mobility: Confronting the Methodological Challenges," *Environment and Planning A* 44, no. 1 (2012): 5–12; Eugene McCann and Kevin Ward, "Policy Assemblages, Mobilities and Mutations: Toward a Multidisciplinary Conversation," *Political Studies Review* 10, no. 3 (2012): 325–332; and Jamie Peck and Nikolas Theodore, *Fast Policy: Experimental Statecraft at the Thresholds of Neoliberalism* (Minneapolis: University of Minnesota Press, 2015).

64. For a more "orthodox" discussion of policy transfer, see David P. Dolowitz and David Marsh, "Learning from Abroad: The Role of Policy Transfer in Contemporary Policy-Making," *Governance* 13, no. 1 (2000): 5–23.

65. Peck, "Geographies of Policy," 774.

66. Harriet Bulkeley, "Cities and the Governing of Climate Change" *Annual Review of Environment and Resources* 35 (2010): 229–253; Bulkeley et al., *Transnational Climate Change Governance*.

67. Bulkeley et al., *Transnational Climate Change Governance*, 117–124.

68. This is not the place to undertake an exegesis of urban design. A useful, briefer contextualizing might take on the primary ideas about and lineages of intervention in the modern city: utopian visions emerging in reaction to the deplorable urban conditions of the late 1800s and early 1900s, such as Ebenezer Howard's Garden City (1898) and Tony Garnier's Cité Industrielle (1899–1917); the rise of the functionalist, modernist movement, epitomized by the architects of the Congrès Internationaux d'Architecture Moderne (CIAM), such as Le Corbusier, and the writing of the *Athens Charter* of 1933; the postmodern turn, driven by historicist ideas from Colin Rowe and Aldo Rossi, and accompanied by events like the spectacular demolition of the Pruitt-Igoe public housing complex in St. Louis; and a kind of "social complexity" response to modernist planning, polemicized by journalist and activist Jane Jacobs in her book *The Death and Life of Great American Cities* (New York: Random House, 1961), and given form by Kevin Lynch's ground-up visions of the city, *The Image of the City* (Cambridge, MA, MIT Press, 1960). It would as well touch on, if not fully make sense of, the chaotic and complex terrain of urban design in the late twentieth century and the turn of the millennium, expanded and accelerated by processes of globalization, financialization, and technological permeation, and given urgency by increasingly dire environmental conditions.

69. A number of other urban design researchers have asserted the need to analyze design within broader urban political economic processes. See, for example, Alexander R. Cuthbert, "Urban Design: Requiem for an Era—Review and Critique of the Last 50 Years," *Urban Design International* 12, no. 4 (2007): 177; Anastasia Loukaitou-Sideris, "Addressing the Challenges of Urban Landscapes: Normative Goals for Urban Design," *Journal of Urban Design* 17, no. 4 (2012): 467–484; and Pushpa Arabindoo, "Urban Design in the Realm of Urban Studies," in *Explorations in Urban Design: An Urban Design Research Primer*, ed. Matthew Carmona (Farnham, UK: Ashgate, 2014), 47–58.

70. Henri Lefebvre, *The Production of Space* (Oxford: Blackwell, 1991), 3.

71. Lefebvre, *Production of Space*, 33–40. See also Stuart Elden, "There Is a Politics of Space because Space Is Political," *Radical Philosophy Review* 10, no. 2 (2007): 110.

72. Edward W. Soja, *Postmetropolis: Critical Studies of Cities and Regions* (Oxford: Blackwell, 2000), and *Seeking Spatial Justice* (Minneapolis: University of Minnesota Press, 2010).

73. Lawrence J. Vale, *Architecture, Power, and National Identity* (New Haven, CT: Yale University Press, 1992).

74. For an earlier development of this line of thought, see Kian Goh, "Toward Transformative Urban Spatial Change: Views from Jakarta," in *The New Companion to Urban Design*, ed. Tridib Banerjee and Anastasia Loukaitou-Sideris (Abingdon, UK: Routledge, 2019), 519–532.

75. See, in particular, Katinka Wijsman and Mathieu Feagan, "Rethinking Knowledge Systems for Urban Resilience: Feminist and Decolonial Contributions to Just Transformations," *Environmental Science and Policy* 98 (2019): 70–76; Natalie Osborne, "Intersectionality and Kyriarchy: A Framework for Approaching Power and Social Justice in Planning and Climate Change Adaptation," *Planning Theory* 14, no. 2 (2015): 130–151.

76. James Holston, "Spaces of Insurgent Citizenship," in *Cities and Citizenship*, ed. James Holston (Durham, NC: Duke University Press, 1999), 166.

Chapter 1

1. New York City Department of City Planning (NYC DCP), "Population—Current Population Estimates," accessed May 28, 2015, https://www1.nyc.gov/site/planning/planning-level/nyc-population/current-future-populations.page; US Census Bureau, "Annual Estimates of the Resident Population for Metropolitan Statistical Areas in the United States and Puerto Rico: April 1, 2010 to July 1, 2019," March 2020, https://www2.census.gov/programs-surveys/popest/tables/2010-2019/metro/totals/cbsa-met-est2019-annres.xlsx..

2. Hugh Ferriss, *The Metropolis of Tomorrow* (New York: Ives Washburn, 1929).

3. Robert A. Caro, *The Power Broker: Robert Moses and the Fall of New York* (New York: Vintage, 1975); Anthony Flint, *Wrestling with Moses: How Jane Jacobs Took on New York's Master Builder and Transformed the American City* (New York: Random House, 2009).

4. Larry Zim, Mel Lerner, and Herbert Rolfes, *The World of Tomorrow: The 1939 New York World's Fair* (New York: Harper and Row, 1988); Joseph Tirella, *Tomorrow-Land: The 1964–65 World's Fair and the Transformation of America* (Guilford, CT: Lyons, 2014).

5. Stephen Graham, "Cities and the 'War on Terror,'" in *Indefensible Space: The Architecture of the National Insecurity State*, ed. Michael Sorkin (New York: Routledge, 2008), 1–28; Julie V. Iovine, "The Skyscraper as a Pillar of Confidence," *Wall Street Journal*, September 8, 2011; and Peter Marcuse, "Security or Safety in Cities? The Threat of Terrorism after 9/11," *International Journal of Urban and Regional Research* 30, no. 4 (2006): 919–929.

6. Neil Smith, *The New Urban Frontier: Gentrification and the Revanchist City* (Abingdon, UK: Routledge, 1996), and "Toward a Theory of Gentrification A Back to the City Movement by Capital, Not People," *Journal of the American Planning Association* 45, no. 4 (1979): 538–548.

7. Sharon Zukin, *Loft Living: Culture and Capital in Urban Change* (Baltimore, MD: Johns Hopkins University Press, 1982).

8. See, e.g., Janet L. Abu-Lughod, ed, *From Urban Village to East Village: The Battle for New York's Lower East Side* (Oxford: Blackwell, 1994).

9. Jean Gardner, "Topology of an Island City," in *ECO-TEC: Architecture of the In-Between*, ed. Amerigo Marras (New York: Princeton Architectural Press, 1999), 102.

10. Roy Rosenzweig and Elizabeth Blackmar, *The Park and the People: A History of Central Park* (Ithaca, NY: Cornell University Press, 1992), 64–73, and Diana diZerega Wall, Nan A. Rothschild, and Cynthia Copeland, "Seneca Village and Little Africa: Two African American Communities in Antebellum New York City," *Historical Archaeology* 41, no. 1 (2008): 97–107, provide accounts of the use of eminent domain to evict and demolish existing settlements in the current Central Park area, including Seneca Village, the first African American landowning settlement in New York City, which existed from 1825 to 1857, when it was cleared.

11. Gandy, *Concrete and Clay*.

12. David Harvey, "The Nature of Environment: Dialectics of Social and Environmental Change," *Socialist Register* 29 (1993), 28, italics in the original.

13. See Lisa W. Foderaro, "Law Says Hudson River Park Is Allowed to Sell Air Rights," *New York Times*, November 14, 2013, and New York State Legislature 517 (2013), 2013 Amendment to Hudson River Park Act, Ch. 517 § (2013), for more context around the Hudson River Park air rights legislation efforts; and Kian Goh, "Safe Cities and Queer Spaces: The Urban Politics of Radical LGBT Activism," *Annals of the American Association of Geographers* 108, no. 2 (2018): 463–477, for elaboration on the sociopolitical contestation around the park and adjacent West Village, long a site for queer struggles and activism in the city.

14. Sharon Zukin, "Memo from Manhattan: The High Line at Dusk," OUPblog, September 23, 2010, http://blog.oup.com/2010/09/high-line/.

15. City of New York, Office of the Mayor, *PlaNYC: A Greener, Greater New York* (New York: Office of the Mayor, 2007), http://www.nyc.gov/html/planyc/downloads/pdf/publications/full_report_2007.pdf.

16. The 2011 PlaNYC update substantially increases the focus on climate change. City of New York. "PlaNYC: A Greener, Greater New York—Update April 2011," City of New York, Office of the Mayor, 2011. http://www.nyc.gov/html/planyc/downloads/pdf/publications/planyc_2011_planyc_full_report.pdf.

17. New York City Panel on Climate Change (NPCC), "Climate Change Adaptation in New York City: Building a Risk Management Response," ed. Cynthia Rosenzweig and William Solecki, *Annals of the New York Academy of Sciences* 1196, no. 1 (2010): 22.

18. Cynthia Rosenzweig et al., "Developing Coastal Adaptation to Climate Change in the New York City Infrastructure-Shed: Process, Approach, Tools, and Strategies," *Climatic Change* 106, no. 1 (2011): 93–127.

19. See Sarah Adams-Schoen, "On the Waterfront: New York City's Climate Change Adaptation and Mitigation Challenge (Part 1 of 2)," *Environmental Law in New York* 25, no. 4 (2014): 81–99.

20. New York City Department of City Planning (NYC DCP), "Vision 2020: The NYC Comprehensive Waterfront Plan," New York City Department of City Planning, March 2011, https://www1.nyc.gov/assets/planning/download/pdf/plans-studies/vision-2020-cwp/vision2020/vision2020_nyc_cwp.pdf.

21. Michael Marrella (director of Waterfront and Open Space Planning, New York City Department of City Planning), interview by the author, New York, May 11, 2015.

22. New York City Panel on Climate Change (NPCC), "Building the Knowledge Base for Climate Resiliency: New York City Panel on Climate Change 2015 Report," ed. Cynthia Rosenzweig and William Solecki, *Annals of the New York Academy of Sciences* 1336, no. 1 (2015): 1–150.

23. The photographer recounts furiously chasing down a rental car and helicopter on the Wednesday evening two days after the storm and shooting in the pitch dark out of the open aircraft door in "More Images from New York's Sandy Cover," The Cut, November 5, 2012, https://www.thecut.com/2012/11/more-images-from-new-yorks-sandy-cover.html.

24. See Hurricane Sandy Rebuilding Task Force, *Hurricane Sandy Rebuilding Strategy: Stronger Communities, a Resilient Region* (Washington, DC: US Department Housing and Urban Development, 2013), http://portal.hud.gov/hudportal/documents/huddoc?id=HSRebuildingStrategy.pdf, and NYS 2100 Commission, *Recommendations to Improve the Strength and Resilience of the Empire State's Infrastructure*, Albany, NY: NYS 2100 Commission, January 2013, http://www.governor.ny.gov/sites/governor.ny.gov/files/archive/assets/documents/NYS2100.pdf.

25. Rebuild By Design, "Promoting Resilience Post-Sandy through Innovative Planning and Design," June 21, 2013, http://portal.hud.gov/hudportal/documents/huddoc?id=REBUILDBYDESIGNBrief.pdf.

26. Superstorm Research Lab, "A Tale of Two Sandys," December 21, 2013, http://superstormresearchlab.org/white-paper/.

27. Jill Eisenhard, interview by the author, Brooklyn, NY, September 13, 2014.

28. Based on 2016 data from Badan Pengembangan Infrastruktur Wilayah, Kementerian Pekerjaan Umum dan Perumahan Rakyat [Regional Infrastructure Development Agency, Ministry of Public Works and Housing], "Metropolitan Jakarta, Bogor, Depok, Tangerang, Puncak, Cianjur," PU-Net, accessed September 19, 2020, http://perkotaan.bpiw.pu.go.id/v2/metropolitan/3; Databoks, "Berapa Jumlah Penduduk Jakarta?" [What is the total population of Jakarta?], January 24, 2018, https://databoks.katadata.co.id/datapublish/2018/01/24/berapa-jumlah-penduduk-jakarta.

Notes to Chapter 1   213

29. Jakarta ranks fourth highest in vulnerability to climate change globally, and with ten other Asian cities among the fifteen most vulnerable to sea level rise, according to Verisk Maplecroft, "Environmental Risk Outlook 2020," February 27, 2020, https://www.maplecroft.com/insights/analysis/download-the-environmental-risk-outlook-2020/.

30. Generally, sea-level rise around Southeast Asian oceans appears higher than the global average of 3.0±0.4 mm/year. John T. Fasullo and R. Steven Nerem, "Altimeter-Era Emergence of the Patterns of Forced Sea-Level Rise in Climate Models and Implications for the Future," *Proceedings of the National Academy of Sciences* 115, no. 51 (2018): 12944–12949.

31. Hasanuddin Z. Abidin et al., "Land Subsidence of Jakarta (Indonesia) and Its Relation with Urban Development," *Natural Hazards* 59, no. 3 (2011): 1753–1771; JanJaap Brinkman and Marco Hartman, "Jakarta Flood Hazard Mapping Framework," unpublished Deltares and HKV study, 2009, http://edepot.wur.nl/140833.

32. T. G. McGee, "The Emergence of Desakota Regions in Asia: Expanding a Hypothesis," in *The Extended Metropolis: Settlement Transition in Asia*, ed. Norton Ginsburg, Bruce Koppel, and T. G. McGee (Honolulu: University of Hawai'i Press, 1991), 3–25.

33. See, e.g., Abidin Kusno, Meredith Miller, and Etienne Turpin, "Urban Temporalities: Jakarta after the New Order: Abidin Kusno in Conversation with Meredith Miller and Etienne Turpin," *Scapegoat: Architecture, Landscape, Political Economy* 5 (Summer/Autumn 2013): 180–205; Rita Padawangi, "Climate Change and the North Coast of Jakarta: Environmental Justice and the Social Construction of Space in Urban Poor Communities," in *Urban Areas and Global Climate Change*, ed. William G. Holt (Bingley, UK: Emerald, 2012), 321–340; Pratiwo and Peter J. M. Nas, "Jakarta: Conflicting Directions," in *Directors of Urban Change in Asia*, ed. Peter J. M. Nas (Abingdon, UK: Routledge, 2005), 68–82.

34. See, e.g., Christopher Silver, *Planning the Megacity: Jakarta in the Twentieth Century* (London: Routledge, 2008).

35. Abidin Kusno, *After the New Order: Space, Politics, and Jakarta* (Honolulu: University of Hawai'i Press, 2013).

36. Karen Bakker et al., "Governance Failure: Rethinking the Institutional Dimensions of Urban Water Supply to Poor Households," *World Development* 36, no. 10 (2008): 1891–1915.

37. See, e.g., Mike Douglass, "The Environmental Sustainability of Development: Coordination, Incentives and Political Will in Land Use Planning for the Jakarta Metropolis," *Third World Planning Review* 11, no. 2 (1989): 211; and "Globalization, Mega-Projects and the Environment: Urban Form and Water in Jakarta," *Environment and Urbanization Asia* 1, no. 1 (2010): 45–65; Mark Caljouw, Peter J. M. Nas, and Pratiwo, "Flooding in Jakarta: Towards a Blue City with Improved Water

Management," *Bijdragen Tot de Taal-, Land- en Volkenkunde* 161, no. 4 (2005): 454–484; Wilmar Salim and Tommy Firman, "Governing the Jakarta City-Region: History, Challenges, Risks and Strategies," in *Planning Asian Cities: Risks and Resilience*, ed. Stephen Hamnett and Dean Forbes (Abingdon, UK: Routledge, 2011), 240–263; and Gavin Shatkin, "Planned Grab: Capitalizing on Land Dualism in New Order Jakarta," in *Cities for Profit: The Real Estate Turn in Asia's Urban Politics* (Ithaca, NY: Cornell University Press, 2017), 102–136.

38. See Etienne Turpin, Adam Bobbette, and Meredith Miller, eds. *Jakarta: Architecture + Adaptation*. Depok: Universitas Indonesia Press, 2013.

39. Indonesia, Coordinating Ministry for Economic Affairs (MENKO), "Master Plan: National Capital Integrated Coastal Development," October 1, 2014, accessed January 31, 2015, http://ncicd.com/wp-content/uploads/2014/10/MP-final-NCICD-LR.pdf (site has since been discontinued).

40. For a more detailed account of this, see Goh, "Urban Waterscapes."

41. Rotterdam city and urban region populations in 2013 (CBS Statistics Netherlands, 2014).

42. Netherlands total population in 2009 (CBS Statistics Netherlands, 2013).

43. See, for example, Koolhaas/OMA's work in Rem Koolhaas and Bruce Mau, *Small, Medium, Large, Extra-Large*, ed. Jennifer Sigler (New York: Monacelli, 1995); MVRDV's in Winy Maas, Jacob van Rijs, Richard Koek, and MVRDV, *FARMAX: Excursions on Density* (Rotterdam: 010, 1998); and projects such as West 8's Shouwburgplein, and Lars Spuybroek and Kas Oosterhuis/Ilona Lénárd's Water Pavilion.

44. Ronald Van Kempen and Hugo Priemus, "Undivided Cities in the Netherlands: Present Situation and Political Rhetoric," *Housing Studies* 14, no. 5 (1999): 647.

45. Chantal Oudkerk Pool (senior advisor for Rotterdam Climate Proof), interview by the author, August 7, 2014

46. Rotterdam Climate Initiative, "Rotterdam Climate Change Adaptation Strategy," (Rotterdam: City of Rotterdam, October 2013), 4.

47. Frans R. E. Blom, "Picturing New Netherland and New York: Dutch-Anglo Transfer of New World Information," in *The Dutch Trading Companies as Knowledge Networks*, ed. Siegfried Huigen, Jan L. de Jong, and Elmer Kolfin (Leiden: Brill, 2010), 103–126.

48. Kees Grijns and Peter J. M. Nas, eds., *Jakarta-Batavia: Socio-Cultural Essays* (Leiden: KITLV, 2000).

49. White House, Office of the Press Secretary, "FACT SHEET: National Disaster Resilience Competition," June 14, 2014, http://www.whitehouse.gov/the-press-office/2014/06/14/fact-sheet-national-disaster-resilience-competition.

50. Fred Boltz, "Announcing the Global Resilience Challenge," Rockefeller Foundation, September 19, 2014, http://www.rockefellerfoundation.org/blog/announcing-global-resilience-challenge/.

51. See, for example, Stephane Hallegatte et al., "Future Flood Losses in Major Coastal Cities," *Nature Climate Change* 3, no. 9 (2013): 802–806; and Gordon McGranahan, Deborah Balk, and Bridget Anderson, "The Rising Tide: Assessing the Risks of Climate Change and Human Settlements in Low Elevation Coastal Zones," *Environment and Urbanization* 19, no. 1 (2007): 17–37.

52. Saskia Sassen's classic triplet, in *Global City*.

53. In the development studies formulation—not just about scale, but based on certain often alarmist assumptions about population growth, informality, and deficiencies in governance (see, for example, Roland J. Fuchs et al., eds., *Mega-City Growth and the Future* [Tokyo: United Nations University Press, 1994]).

54. For a more detailed discussion of methods, see appendix 1: Methodological Excursions.

Chapter 2

1. City of New York, Office of the Mayor, *A Stronger, More Resilient New York*, Special Initiative for Rebuilding and Resiliency (SIRR) (New York: Office of the Mayor, 2013), http://s-media.nyc.gov/agencies/sirr/SIRR_singles_Lo_res.pdf; see also Matt Sledge, "Hurricane Sandy Damage In New York by-the-Numbers," *Huffington Post*, December 3, 2012, http://www.huffingtonpost.com/2012/12/03/hurricane-sandy-damage-new-york_n_2234335.html.

2. New York City Mayor's Office of Management and Budget (OMB), "Impact of Hurricane Sandy," accessed February 1, 2021, https://www1.nyc.gov/site/cdbgdr/about/About%20Hurricane%20Sandy.page

3. Sledge, "Hurricane Sandy Damage in New York by-the-Numbers."

4. Superstorm Research Lab, "Tale of Two Sandys"; see also Daniel Aldana Cohen and Max Liboiron, "New York's Two Sandys," *Metropolitics*, October 30, 2014. http://www.metropolitiques.eu/New-York-s-Two-Sandys.html; Sarah Jaffe, "Whose Recovery? A Year after Hurricane Sandy Hit, despite Community Efforts, Marginalized New Yorkers Aren't Back on Their Feet," *In These Times*, October 29, 2013; and Rana Jaleel, "Into the Storm: Occupy Sandy and the New Sociality of Debt," Is This What Democracy Looks Like?, October 8, 2013, https://what-democracy-looks-like.org/into-the-storm-occupy-sandy-and-the-new-sociality-of-debt/.

5. Erin Durkin, "FEMA to Give $3 Billion to NYCHA for Hurricane Sandy Damage," *New York Daily News*, March 31, 2015; City of New York, "Mayor de Blasio, Senator

Schumer Announce $3 Billion in Federal Funds," March 31, 2015, http://www1.nyc.gov/office-of-the-mayor/news/206-15/mayor-de-blasio-senator-schumer-3-billion-federal-funds-repair-protect-33#/0.

6. Sam Bass Warner, *The Urban Wilderness: A History of the American City* (New York: Harper and Row, 1972).

7. Sassen, *Global City*.

8. John H. Mollenkopf and Manuel Castells, eds., *Dual City: Restructuring New York* (New York: Russell Sage Foundation, 1991).

9. See Michael Sorkin, "Too Rich, Too Skinny," *Architectural Record*, May 16, 2015, http://archrecord.construction.com/features/2015/1505-too-rich-too-skinny.asp, for commentary on the "supertalls."

10. Desiree Fields, "Unwilling Subjects of Financialization," *International Journal of Urban and Regional Research* 41, no. 4 (2017): 588–603.

11. For recent statistics and accounts of rising inequality in New York, see New York City Comptroller's Office, *Income Inequality in New York City* (New York: Comptroller of the City of New York, 2012), http://comptroller.nyc.gov/wp-content/uploads/documents/NYC_IncomeInequality_v17.pdf; Sam Pizzigati, "New York, New York, What a Less than Wonderful Town," Inequality.org, June 20, 2018, https://inequality.org/great-divide/new-york-new-york-less-wonderful-town/; and Estelle Sommeiller and Mark Price, *The New Gilded Age: Income Inequality in the U.S. by State, Metropolitan Area, and County* (Washington, DC: Economic Policy Institute, 2018), https://www.epi.org/files/pdf/147963.pdf.

12. Ongoing condominium conversion developments are taking place along the southwest waterfront of the neighborhood. A 2015 proposal for a technology and creative industries center stalled and ended, and, recently, news of a possible UPS logistics hub emerged.

13. Almost the entirety of Red Hook lies within the Category 1 storm-surge zone (http://maps.nyc.gov/hurricane/).

14. I was the architect responsible for designing RHI's space in Red Hook.

15. See the end of chapter 4 for elaboration on this.

16. Red Hook Initiative, *Red Hook Initiative: A Community Response to Hurricane Sandy* (Brooklyn, NY: Red Hook Initiative, 2013); Michael T. Schmeltz et al., "Lessons from Hurricane Sandy: A Community Response in Brooklyn, New York," *Journal of Urban Health* 90, no. 5 (2013): 799–809.

17. Eisenhard interview, September 13, 2014.

18. Eisenhard interview, September 13, 2014.

Notes to Chapter 2

19. Gita Nandan, interview by the author, Brooklyn, NY, August 22, 2014.

20. Eisenhard interview, September 13, 2014.

21. 6,500 residents live in the Red Hook Houses, out of the total 12,400 residents of Red Hook—cited in the "Red Hook—NY Rising Community Reconstruction Plan," based on data from 2010 US Census and NYCHA.

22. See Red Hook—NY Rising Community Reconstruction Program, "Red Hook NY Rising Community Reconstruction Plan," March 2014, https://stormrecovery.ny.gov/sites/default/files/crp/community/documents/redhook_nyrcr_plan_20mb_0.pdf.

23. Eisenhard interview, September 13, 2014.

24. Red Hook Initiative, "Recovering from Sandy: RHI WiFi Project," December 2012; Open Technology Institute (OTI), *Case Study: Red Hook Initiative WiFi and Tidepools* (Washington, DC: New America Foundation, 2013), https://commotionwireless.net/files/rhiwifi_tidepools_casestudy.pdf.

25. OTI, *Case Study*, 10.

26. Christopher Mele, *Selling the Lower East Side: Culture, Real Estate, and Resistance in New York City* (Minneapolis: University of Minnesota Press, 2000); Neil Smith and James DeFilippis, "The Reassertion of Economics: 1990s Gentrification in the Lower East Side," *International Journal of Urban and Regional Research* 23, no. 4 (1999): 638–653; and Two Bridges Neighborhood Council, *Decade After 9/11: A Look at Who We Are Now. How Gentrification Reshaped Manhattan Community Board 3* (New York: Two Bridges Neighborhood Council, 2011), http://www.nyc.gov/html/mancb3/downloads/cb3docs/TwoBridgesDemographicAnalysis.pdf.

27. LES Ready!, *Getting LES Ready: Learning from Hurricane Sandy to Create a Community-Based Disaster Plan for the Future* (New York: Lower East Side Long Term Recovery Group, 2014), https://cdp.urbanjustice.org/sites/default/files/CDP.WEB.doc_Report_LESready_20141117.pdf.

28. Damaris Reyes, interview by the author, New York, December 18, 2014.

29. This project will be discussed in more detail in chapter 4.

30. Reyes interview.

31. Reyes interview.

32. Reyes interview.

33. White House, Office of the Press Secretary, "Executive Order—Establishing the Hurricane Sandy Rebuilding Task Force," December 7, 2012, https://www.whitehouse.gov/the-press-office/2012/12/07/executive-order-establishing-hurricane-sandy-rebuilding-task-force.

34. Rebuild By Design, "Promoting Resilience Post-Sandy Through Innovative Planning and Design," Design Brief, June 21, 2013, http://portal.hud.gov/hudportal/documents/huddoc?id=REBUILDBYDESIGNBrief.pdf.

35. See, as well, Ashley Dawson, *Extreme Cities: The Peril and Promise of Urban Life in the Age of Climate Change* (London: Verso, 2017), for commentary on Rebuild By Design and selected teams' proposals in chap. 4, and the work of Occupy Sandy in chap. 6.

36. US Department of Housing and Urban Development (HUD), "HUD Announces Winning Proposals from the 'Rebuild By Design' Competition," June 2, 2014, HUD Archives. https://archives.hud.gov/news/2014/pr14-063.cfm.

37. Scott Davis, interview by the author, Washington, DC, October 31, 2014.

38. The American COMPETES Act, reauthorized by Congress in 2010.

39. Nancy Kete, interview by the author, New York, June 16, 2014.

40. Kete interview.

41. Kete interview.

42. Marion McFadden, interview by the author, Washington DC, October 31, 2014.

43. US Department of Housing and Urban Development (HUD), "Community Development Block Grant Disaster Recovery Program," HUD Exchange, accessed December 12, 2020, https://www.hudexchange.info/programs/cdbg-dr/.

44. Amy Chester, interview by the author, New York, June 19, 2014.

45. Chester interview, June 19, 2014.

46. Silver, *Planning the Megacity*, 61. See also Michael Leaf, "Land Rights for Residential Development in Jakarta, Indonesia: The Colonial Roots of Contemporary Urban Dualism," *International Journal of Urban and Regional Research* 17, no. 4 (1993): 477–491, for an in-depth discussion of the development of colonial and postcolonial land rights in Jakarta, including layers of conflicting, dichotomous land rights inherited through the colonial period, subsequent attempts at land reform, and privatized real estate development.

47. Paul McCarthy, "The Case of Jakarta, Indonesia," Understanding Slums: Case Studies for the Global Report on Human Settlements 2003, UN-Habitat, 2003, https://www.ucl.ac.uk/dpu-projects/Global_Report/cities/jakarta.htm.

48. This sentiment was conveyed to me by various officials in the DKI Jakarta government, in response to questions about alternatives to relocation.

49. I. Sandyawan Sumardi (activist, Ciliwung Merdeka), interview by the author, Jakarta, July 18, 2014.

50. Human Rights Watch, "Condemned Communities: Forced Evictions in Jakarta, Indonesia," Human Rights Watch, September 5, 2006, https://www.hrw.org/report/2006/09/05/condemned-communities/forced-evictions-jakarta#; Raquel Rolnik and United Nations Human Rights Council (UN HRC), "Report of the Special Rapporteur on Adequate Housing as a Component of the Right to an Adequate Standard of Living, and on the Right to Non-Discrimination in This Context on Her Mission to Indonesia," United Nations Human Rights Council, December 26, 2013, https://www.ohchr.org/EN/HRBodies/HRC/RegularSessions/Session25/Documents/A-HRC-25-54-Add1_en.doc.

51. Aga Khan Development Network, "Kampung Improvement Programme: Aga Khan Award for Architecture," https://www.akdn.org/architecture/project/kampung-improvement-programme.

52. UN-Habitat, *The Challenge of Slums: Global Report on Human Settlements 2003* (London: Earthscan, 2003).

53. See elaboration of these plans in chapter 4.

54. Based on informal conversations with kampung residents in Muara Baru area, North Jakarta, in July 2014.

55. Local news articles by Andreas D. Arditya, "South Korea to Help in Restoring Ciliwung River," *Jakarta Post*, January 5, 2013; Sita W. Dewi, "Jokowi to Launch Pluit Dam City Park," *Jakarta Post*, August 16, 2013; and Indah Setiawati, "Jokowi Inspires Urban Poor to See Light at the End of the Tunnel," *Jakarta Post*, February 18, 2013, among others, describe Jokowi's proposals and relationship with community activists.

56. Aisa Tobing, interview by the author, Jakarta, July 16, 2014.

57. Sylvira Azwar, interview by the author, Jakarta, July 16, 2014. Also, Sita W. Dewi, "'Blusukan' Essential to Jokowi's Bid," *Jakarta Post*, March 23, 2014; Wijayanto Samirin, "Blusukan," *Kompas*, January 12, 2013, http://nasional.kompas.com/read/2013/01/12/11232457/.Blusukan, for news accounts of Jokowi and *blusukan*. The governor brought Facebook founder Mark Zuckerberg on one of these famous impromptu walks when the latter visited Jakarta.

58. Sadly, Edi Saidi passed away in November 2020 after an illness.

59. Edi Saidi, interview (translated from Bahasa Indonesia) by the author, Jakarta, July 15, 2014.

60. Saidi interview.

61. Saidi interview.

62. Basuki Tjahaja Purnama, nicknamed Ahok, served as Jokowi's deputy governor, and was confirmed as governor of Jakarta on November 14, 2014, following Jokowi's win in the Indonesian presidential elections in July 2014.

63. Sumardi interview, July 18, 2014; also, Ariel Shepherd (community architect, Asian Coalition for Housing Rights), interview by the author, Jakarta, July 17, 2014.

64. Sumardi interview, July 18, 2014.

65. See, e.g., Grijns and Nas, *Jakarta-Batavia*; Abidin Kusno, *Behind the Postcolonial: Architecture, Urban Space, and Political Cultures in Indonesia* (London: Routledge, 2000), and Kusno, *After the New Order*; and Silver, *Planning the Megacity*, chaps. 2 and 3.

66. Brinkman and Hartman, "Jakarta Flood Hazard Mapping Framework." Also recounted by Kees Bons, director of Deltares Jakarta, interview by the author, Jakarta, July 11, 2014.

67. Indonesian Ministry of Public Works, *Jakarta Coastal Defence Strategy (JCDS)* (Jakarta: Indonesia, Ministry of Public Works, 2011).

68. MENKO, "Master Plan."

69. Bons interview.

70. This is certainly not the first time that national politics intervened in the trajectory of urban policy in Jakarta—see, for example, Silver, *Planning the Megacity*, 92–103; and Tim Bunnell and Michelle Ann Miller, "Jakarta in Post-Suharto Indonesia: Decentralisation, Neo-Liberalism and Global City Aspiration," *Space and Polity* 15, no. 1 (2011): 35–48.

71. See further discussion about the specifics of the hydrological design in chapter 4.

72. Arend van Woerden (adviser, Regional and Urban Development, Grontmij, now Sweco), interview by the author, Houten, Netherlands, September 29, 2014.

73. Fook Chuan Eng, interview by the author, Jakarta, July 27, 2014.

74. David Harvey, "Neo-Liberalism as Creative Destruction," *Geografiska Annaler: Series B, Human Geography* 88, no. 2 (2006): 145–158.

75. For other scholarly analysis critical of the NCICD Giant Sea Wall masterplan see Emma Colven, "Understanding the Allure of Big Infrastructure: Jakarta's Great Garuda Sea Wall Project," *Water Alternatives* 10, no. 2 (2017): 250–264; Helga Leitner, Emma Colven, and Eric Sheppard, "Ecological Security for Whom? The Politics of Flood Alleviation and Urban Environmental Justice in Jakarta, Indonesia," in *The Routledge Companion to the Environmental Humanities*, ed. Ursula K. Heise, Jon Christensen, and Michelle Niemann (Abingdon, UK: Routledge, 2017), 194–205; and Matt Wade, "Hyper-Planning Jakarta: The Great Garuda and Planning the Global Spectacle," *Singapore Journal of Tropical Geography* 40, no. 1 (2019): 158–172.

76. Dian Tri Irawaty (Rujak Center for Urban Studies), interview by the author, Jakarta, July 10, 2014.

77. These issues of design and visualization will be addressed further in chapter 4.

78. Brinkman and Hartman, "Jakarta Flood Hazard Mapping Framework." See also Deltares, *Sinking Cities: An Integrated Approach towards Solutions* (Delft, Netherlands: Deltares, 2013), https://www.deltares.nl/app/uploads/2015/09/Sinking-cities.pdf.

79. Kees Bons, email discussion with the author, February 4, 2015.

80. See, for studies of subsidence and causes, Makoto Kagabu et al., "Groundwater Age Rejuvenation Caused by Excessive Urban Pumping in Jakarta Area, Indonesia," *Hydrological Processes* 27, no. 18 (2013): 2591–2604; and Estelle Chaussard et al., "Sinking Cities in Indonesia: ALOS PALSAR Detects Rapid Subsidence Due to Groundwater and Gas Extraction," *Remote Sensing of Environment* 128 (2013): 150–161.

81. Bons, interview by the author, Jakarta, July 11, 2014.

82. Hurricane Sandy Rebuilding Task Force, *Hurricane Sandy Rebuilding Strategy*.

83. Eisenhard, interviews, September 13, 2014, and August 2, 2019.

84. Jasanoff, "New Climate for Society." See also further discussion in the introductory chapter.

Chapter 3

1. Connecting Delta Cities, "Indonesian Officials Meet Experts on US East Coast," Newsletter—Connecting Delta Cities, September 2, 2014, http://deltacitiesofthefuture.nl/newsletter/indonesian-officials-meet-experts-on-us-east-coast?news_id=65.

2. Hans van der Cammen et al., *The Selfmade Land: Culture and Evolution of Urban and Regional Planning in the Netherlands* (Houten, Netherlands: Spectrum, 2012).

3. Simon Schama, relating the tale of a "drowning cell"—prisoners forced to pump to avoid a watery death—to a Dutch identity of struggle against water, in *The Embarrassment of Riches: An Interpretation of Dutch Culture in the Golden Age* (New York: Knopf, 1987), 24.

4. Discourses of "survival" dominate Dutch public agendas (see Van der Cammen et al., *Selfmade Land*).

5. Ashok K. Dutt and Frank J. Costa, eds, *Public Planning in the Netherlands: Perspectives and Change since the Second World War* (New York: Oxford University Press, 1985), cited in Van der Cammen et al., *Selfmade Land*.

6. See, for more detailed accounts of the historical and present-day transformations of the Dutch landscape, Mark Van Koningsveld et al., "Living with Sea-Level Rise and Climate Change: A Case Study of the Netherlands," *Journal of Coastal Research* 242 (2008): 367–379; Victor N. de Jonge, "From a Defensive to an Integrated Approach," in *Water Policy in the Netherlands: Integrated Management in a Densely Populated Delta*, ed. Stijn Reinhard and Henk Folmer (Washington, DC: Resources for the Future, 2009), 17–46; Stefan M. M. Kuks, "Institutional Evolution of the Dutch Water Board

Model," in *Water Policy in the Netherlands*, ed. Reinhard and Folmer, 155–170; Marcel Stive and Han Vrijling, "Draining, Dredging, Reclaiming: The Technology of Making a Dry, Safe, and Sustainable Delta Landscape," in *Delta Urbanism: The Netherlands*, ed. Han Meyer, Inge Bobbink, and Steffen Nijhuis (Chicago: American Planning Association, 2010), 20–43; and Wil Zonneveld, "Governing a Complex Delta," in *Delta Urbanism*, ed. Meyer, Bobbink, and Nijhuis, 101–13.

7. Herman Gerritsen, "What Happened in 1953? The Big Flood in the Netherlands in Retrospect," *Philosophical Transactions of the Royal Society A: Mathematical, Physical and Engineering Sciences* 363, no. 1831 (2005): 1271–1291.

8. Netherlands, Delta Commission, *Final Report; Delivered by the Advisory Committee to Provide an Answer to the Question of What Waterways-Technical Provisions Must Be Made for the Areas Devastated by the Storm Flood of February 1, 1953, (Delta Committee) Instituted by Decree of the Minister of Transport and Waterways of February 18, 1953* (The Hague: State Printing and Publication Office, 1962).

9. The Delta Works presents a compelling model for adaptation in that it relied not on historical flood information, but a conceptual framework based on investment costs and modeled risks.

10. Netherlands Delta Commission, *Working Together with Water: A Living Land Builds for Its Future—Findings of the Deltacommissie 2008, Summary and Conclusions* (The Hague: Delta Commission, 2008); Herman Van Der Most and Mark Wehrung, "Dealing with Uncertainty in Flood Risk Assessment of Dike Rings in the Netherlands," *Natural Hazards* 36, nos. 1–2 (2005): 191–206.

11. Johan Van Veen, *Dredge Drain Reclaim: The Art of a Nation* (The Hague: Martinus Nijhoff, 1962), 29.

12. See Kuks, "Institutional Evolution of the Dutch Water Board Model"; Wim van Leussen and Kris Lulofs, "Governance of Water Resources," in *Water Policy in the Netherlands*, ed. Reinhard and Folmer, 171–84; and Zonneveld, "Governing a Complex Delta."

13. Stive and Vrijling, "Draining, Dredging, Reclaiming"; Van Veen, *Dredge Drain Reclaim*.

14. Lasse Gerrits, Ward Rauws, and Gert de Roo, "Dutch Spatial Planning Policies in Transition," *Planning Theory and Practice* 13, no. 2 (2012): 336–341; Tim Marshall, "Infrastructure Futures and Spatial Planning: Lessons from France, the Netherlands, Spain and the UK," *Progress in Planning* 89 (2014): 1–38.

15. Netherlands, Ministry of Infrastructure and the Environment, *Summary National Policy Strategy for Infrastructure and Spatial Planning: Making the Netherlands Competitive, Accessible, Liveable and Safe* (The Hague: Ministry of Infrastructure and the Environment, 2011), 4. This is a significant change on the part of the Dutch

government. The "Action Agenda for Architecture and Spatial Design 2013–2016," jointly authored by five national ministries, states, "The national government is using the basic cultural infrastructure and specific programmes to reinforce initiatives by designers, authorities, private companies and private individuals who display their own ambitions for the quality and innovative strength of design." Netherlands, Ministry of Infrastructure and the Environment, Ministry of Education, Culture and Science, Ministry of the Interior and Kingdom Relations, Ministry of Economic Affairs, Agriculture and Innovation, and Ministry of Defence, *Building on the Strength of Design: Action Agenda for Architecture and Spatial Design, 2013–2016* (The Hague, September 2012), 5.

16. Recounted in Luuk Boelens and Elien Wierenga, "Editorial," in *Compacte stad extended: Agenda voor toekomstig beleid, onderzoek en ontwerp*, ed. Luuk Boelens, Henk Ovink, Hanna Lára Pálsdóttir, and Elien Wierenga (Rotterdam: 010, 2010), 10.

17. It is still very much on their minds, and was almost always brought up in my informal conversations with Dutch architects and urban designers in 2014.

18. Jeroen Rijke et al., "Room for the River: Delivering Integrated River Basin Management in the Netherlands," *International Journal of River Basin Management* 10, no. 4 (2012): 369–382; Maarten Wolsink, "River Basin Approach and Integrated Water Management: Governance Pitfalls for the Dutch Space-Water-Adjustment Management Principle," *Geoforum* 37, no. 4 (2006): 473–487.

19. "Room for the River Waal," Ruimte voor de Waal Nijmegen, accessed December 12, 2020, http://www.ruimtevoordewaal.nl/en/room-for-the-river-waal/.

20. Huib De Vriend and Mark Van Koningsveld, *Building with Nature: Thinking, Acting and Interacting Differently* (Dordrecht: Ecoshape, Building with Nature, 2012); Van Koningsveld et al., "Living with Sea-Level Rise and Climate Change."

21. Rotterdam Climate Initiative, *Rotterdam Climate Change Adaptation Strategy* (Rotterdam: City of Rotterdam, October 2013), 3.

22. Rotterdam was among the first set of cities selected by the Rockefeller Foundation for its 100 Resilient Cities initiative. As part of this selection, the foundation financially supported the position of chief resilience officer, tasked as a city point-person for resilience, coordinating across government departments and other stakeholders, and leading city resiliency strategies.

23. I interviewed Arnoud Molenaar and John Jacobs together.

24. Arnoud Molenaar, interview by the author, Rotterdam, October 1, 2014.

25. Municipality of Rotterdam, Schieland and Krimpenerwaard Water Control Board, Hollandse Delta Water Authority, and Delfland Water Control Board, "Rotterdam Waterplan 2: Working on Water for an Attractive City," Rotterdam, September 2007.

26. http://www.rotterdamclimateinitiative.nl/.

27. International Advisory Board (IAB) Rotterdam, *New Energy for Rotterdam—IAB Conference 2006* (Rotterdam: Economic Development Board Rotterdam, 2006).

28. Knowledge for Climate, *Dutch Climate Adaptation Research* (Utrecht, Netherlands: Knowledge for Climate, 2012), https://edepot.wur.nl/342784.

29. Molenaar interview, October 1, 2014.

30. John Jacobs, interview by the author, Rotterdam, October 1, 2014.

31. Molenaar interview, October 1, 2014.

32. Chantal Oudkerk Pool, confirmed via email communications, August 19, 2015.

33. Oudkerk Pool interview (italics added).

34. Molenaar interview, October 1, 2014.

35. Florian Boer, interview by the author, Rotterdam, June 30, 2014.

36. Boer interview, June 30, 2014.

37. Boer interview, June 30, 2014.

38. In 2013, the CDC network included Ho Chi Minh City, Hong Kong, Jakarta, London, Melbourne, New Orleans, New York, Rotterdam, Copenhagen, and Tokyo. The C40 Cities Climate Leadership group, started in 2005, is a global network of seventy-five cities (as of mid-2015) formed to cooperate on reducing greenhouse gas emissions. The network's partners include the Clinton Climate Initiative, Bloomberg Philanthropies, ICLEI, World Resources Institute, the World Bank, Siemens, Citibank, and the Ford Foundation.

39. Jeroen Aerts et al., *Connecting Delta Cities: Coastal Cities, Flood Risk Management and Adaptation to Climate Change* (Rotterdam: VU University Press, 2009); Piet Dircke, Jeroen Aerts, and Arnoud Molenaar, *Connecting Delta Cities 2: Sharing Knowledge and Working on Adaptation to Climate Change* (Rotterdam: Connecting Delta Cities, 2010); and Arnoud Molenaar et al., *Connecting Delta Cities 3: Resilient Cities and Climate Adaptation Strategies* (Rotterdam: Connecting Delta Cities, 2013).

40. Oudkerk Pool interview.

41. Oudkerk Pool, confirmed via email communication, August 19, 2015.

42. Deltares, *Deltares 2.0: Strategic Plan 2012–2015* (Delft, Netherlands: Deltares, 2012), 13.

43. Deltares, *Deltares 2.0*.

44. Bons interview.

Notes to Chapter 3 225

45. Netherlands Water Partnership. "About NWP." Netherlands Water Partnership. Accessed February 1, 2021. https://www.netherlandswaterpartnership.com/about-nwp.

46. NWP's focus is thus guided by the priorities of national government agencies. Mark Niesten (project manager, NWP), interview by the author, The Hague, Netherlands, March 22, 2019.

47. The full list of Partners for Water target countries in the 2010–2015 period comprises delta areas countries including Bangladesh, Egypt, Indonesia, Mozambique, Vietnam, Colombia, and Myanmar, and other countries including Angola, China, Ethiopia, Estonia, Georgia, Ghana, Hungary, India, Kazakhstan, Kenya, Mali, Malaysia, Mexico, Ukraine, Poland, Russia, Romania, Slovakia, Thailand, Turkey, and South Africa. See Netherlands Enterprise Agency (RVO), Ministry of Economic Affairs and Climate. "Evaluatie Partners voor Water 3 (2010–2015)," May 2016. https://www.rvo.nl/sites/default/files/2020/05/Evaluatie Partners voor Water 3 2016.pdf.

48. Session titled "Indonesia: NCICD, from planning to implementation," at the Deltas in Times of Climate Change 2014 conference in Rotterdam, Netherlands, on September 25, 2014.

49. Interestingly, the founding of modern Singapore as a British colony in 1819, by Stamford Raffles, had the primary intention of breaking the Dutch monopoly in southeast Asia. Discourses of "survival" also dominate historical, public discourse in the island-city-state, mirroring Dutch public agendas.

50. US Department of Housing and Urban Development (HUD) and Netherlands, Ministry of Infrastructure and the Environment. "Memorandum of Understanding between the Department of Housing and Urban Development of the United States of America and the Ministry of Infrastructure and the Environment of the Kingdom of the Netherlands in the Fields of Sustainable Urban Development, Water Management, and Integrated Planning and Cross Sector Collaboration." Washington, DC, March 4, 2013. http://portal.hud.gov/hudportal/documents/huddoc?id=OPA3-4-13DOC.PDF.

51. Dutch Water Sector, "Details Dutch Seawall and Development Plan for Jakarta Bay Well Received by Indonesian Authorities," April 3, 2014, http://www.dutchwatersector.com/news-events/news/10020-details-dutch-seawall-and-development-plan-for-jakarta-bay-well-received-by-indonesian-authorities.html.

52. The Netherlands has signed MOUs with Mexico, Egypt, Bangladesh, Colombia, Indonesia, and the United States on water management and climate change adaptation. There are numerous subnational MOUs between Dutch entities and municipalities and agencies in countries such as Singapore, Vietnam, South Africa, and India. See https://www.netherlandswaterpartnership.com/ and https://www.dutchwatersector.com/.

53. See, for example, Rudolf Mrázek, *Engineers of Happy Land: Technology and Nationalism in a Colony* (Princeton, NJ: Princeton University Press, 2002), 67.

54. McFadden interview.

55. Kete interview.

56. Reyes interview. This point is explored further in chapter 5.

57. Brinkman and Hartman, "Jakarta Flood Hazard Mapping Framework"; see also Abidin et al., "Land Subsidence of Jakarta (Indonesia)."

58. Indonesia, Ministry of Public Works, *Jakarta Coastal Defence Strategy*.

59. Indonesia, Coordinating Ministry for Economic Affairs (MENKO), "National Capital Integrated Coastal Development Master Plan."

60. See Prathiwi W. Putri and Aryani Sari Rahmanti, "Jakarta Waterscape," *Nakhara: Journal of Environmental Design and Planning* 6 (2010): 59–76.

61. Irawaty interview, July 10, 2014, and informal conversations with Etienne Turpin (PetaJakarta). See also Philip Sherwell, "$40bn to Save Jakarta: The Story of the Great Garuda," *The Guardian*, November 22, 2016.

62. Netherlands, Ministry of Economic Affairs and Climate Policy, "Top Sectors in the Netherlands," March 16, 2016, https://www.topsectoren.nl/publicaties/brochures/2016/03/16/hoe-en-waarom-topsector-engels.

63. Ivo van der Linden (Netherlands Water Partnership), interview by the author, The Hague, September 30, 2014.

64. Boer interview, June 30, 2014. In subsequent interviews, Boer has expressed ambivalence about the new opportunities that emerged after the firm's participation in Rebuild By Design, noting the challenges of working transnationally. He affirmed the importance of sustained regional relationships, and noted that most of the firm's work is now in Europe. Interview, March 25, 2019.

65. Government of the Netherlands, "Speech by Melanie Schultz, at the Round Table on Coastal Development, Borobodur Hotel, Jakarta," Government of the Netherlands—Documents and publications—Speeches, April 2, 2014, accessed February 7, 2015, http://www.rijksoverheid.nl/documenten-en-publicaties/toespraken/2014/04/02/speech-for-melanie-schultz-at-the-round-table-on-coastal-development-borobodur-hotel-jakarta.html (link has since expired).

66. Naomi Klein, *The Shock Doctrine: The Rise of Disaster Capitalism* (Toronto: Alfred A. Knopf Canada, 2007).

67. Ann Laura Stoler, "IMPERIAL DEBRIS: Reflections on Ruins and Ruination," *Cultural Anthropology* 23, no. 2 (2008): 191–219.

68. Dutch Water Sector, "South Korea Joins Giant Sea Wall Project to Protect Jakarta, Indonesia," September 4, 2015, https://www.dutchwatersector.com/news-events/news/15268-south-korea-joins-giant-sea-wall-project-to-protect-jakarta-indonesia.html.

Notes to Chapter 4   227

69. Van der Linden interview, July 14, 2016.

70. Peter Letitre (Deltares Jakarta), presentation at Tarumanagara University, Jakarta, May 22, 2017, reiterated in email correspondence, July 18, 2017.

71. See Agnes Anya and Callistasia Anggun Wijaya, "Govt Cancels Great Garuda Seawall," *Jakarta Post*, December 11, 2017.

72. See Russell Shorto, "How to Think Like the Dutch in a Post-Sandy World," *New York Times*, April 9, 2014.

73. Henk Ovink, interview by the author, November 24, 2014.

74. Session titled "Managing urban water under changing climate conditions," at the Deltas in Times of Climate Change II conference, Rotterdam, September 26, 2014.

75. Ovink interview, November 24, 2014.

76. Urban Institute, *Evaluation: Rebuild by Design Phase I* (New York: Rockefeller Foundation, 2014), http://www.urban.org/sites/default/files/alfresco/publication-pdfs/413256-Evaluation-Rebuild-by-Design-Phase-I.PDF.

77. Bons interview.

78. Also conveyed by NCICD designer Gijs van den Boomen (KuiperCompagnon), interview by the author, Rotterdam, October 1, 2014.

79. Tobing interview.

80. Kasia Paprocki, "Threatening Dystopias: Development and Adaptation Regimes in Bangladesh," *Annals of the American Association of Geographers* 108, no. 4 (July 4, 2018): 955–973.

81. Davoudi, Lawrence, and Bohland, "Anatomy of the Resilience Machine."

82. See, for example, Richard Burdett and Deyan Sudjic, eds., *The Endless City: The Urban Age Project by the London School of Economics and Deutsche Bank's Alfred Herrhausen Society* (London: Phaidon, 2007).

83. Castells, *The Rise of the Network Society*.

Chapter 4

1. A book by Elizabeth Wilson and Jake Piper, looking largely at cases and sites in the United Kingdom and the Netherlands, says nothing about design save a handful of peripheral sentences, *Spatial Planning and Climate Change* (Abingdon, UK: Routledge, 2010), 15. Another volume on the same topic, edited by Simin Davoudi, Jenny Crawford, and Abid Mehmood, does better, integrating discussion of urban design into topics including urban form, climate, and building standards: *Planning for Climate Change: Strategies for Mitigation and Adaptation for Spatial Planners* (London: Earthscan, 2009).

2. Alisdair McGregor, Cole Roberts, and Fiona Cousins, *Two Degrees: The Built Environment and Our Changing Climate* (Abingdon, UK: Routledge, 2013).

3. McGregor, Roberts, and Cousins, *Two Degrees*, 115. The firm Arup, with the Rockefeller Foundation, has also developed a "City Resilience Framework," an initiative that builds on and links to two of the foundation's initiatives, the Asian Cities Climate Change Resilience Network (ACCCRN) and the more recent 100 Resilient Cities. The framework consists of twelve indicators in four categories, covering urban systems and services (including mobility, communications, critical services), economy and society (finance and stability), leadership and strategy (matters of governance and development), and health and wellbeing (including livelihoods and vulnerabilities). It strives to be comprehensive—"holistic." See Arup, "City Resilience Framework," Rockefeller Foundation, April 2014 (updated December 2015), https://www.rockefellerfoundation.org/wp-content/uploads/City-Resilience-Framework-2015.pdf; see also Jo da Silva, Sam Kernaghan, and Andrés Luque, "A Systems Approach to Meeting the Challenges of Urban Climate Change," *International Journal of Urban Sustainable Development* 4, no. 2 (2012): 125–145.

4. Nordenson, Seavitt, and Yarinsky, *On the Water*.

5. The MoMA exhibition brought five interdisciplinary teams, led by architects and landscape architects, to reenvision ways to "occupy the harbor itself" with adaptive infrastructure. See Catherine Seavitt, "Rising Currents: High Stakes," MoMA Inside / Out, January 26, 2010, http://www.moma.org/explore/inside_out/2010/01/26/rising-currents-high-stakes. The exhibition, cosponsored by the Rockefeller Foundation, later served as part of the context and knowledge base for Rebuild By Design. One can trace ideas through these initiatives. Landscape architecture firm SCAPE's "oyster-tecture" concept, now in the construction phase as a winning Rebuild By Design project, was first presented at *Rising Currents*.

6. See, for example, an exhibition and book project to revisit Ian McHarg's contributions fifty years after his seminal *Design with Nature* (Garden City, NY: Published for the American Museum of Natural History by the Natural History Press, 1969) in the context of contemporary social and environmental challenges, conducted by designers and researchers at the University of Pennsylvania: Frederick Steiner et al., *Design with Nature Now* (Cambridge, MA: Lincoln Institute of Land Policy, 2019). See, as well, the 2015 Living with Water competition in Boston, jointly coordinated by the city government, a nonprofit organization, and the professional architecture body, and, less specifically embedded in city government, the 2017 Resilient by Design Bay Area Challenge, a design competition for the San Francisco Bay Area modeled after Rebuild By Design, launched by the Rockefeller Foundation and involving a number of city government leaders and social and environmental nonprofit organizations in the region.

7. There are some key exceptions. See, for example, work by Kristina Hill, a landscape architect trained in geology, whose work combines assessments of design, climate

Notes to Chapter 4

change, and social justice with design proposals for ecological adaptation strategies: "Climate Change: Implications for the Assumptions, Goals and Methods of Urban Environmental Planning." *Urban Planning* 1, no. 4 (2016): 103–113, and "Coastal Infrastructure: A Typology for the Next Century of Adaptation to Sea-Level Rise," *Frontiers in Ecology and the Environment* 13, no. 9 (2015): 468–476. See, as well, an essay by Billy Fleming interrogating the political and ecological promises of landscape architecture practice in times of climate crisis: "Design and the Green New Deal," *Places Journal*, April 2019, https://placesjournal.org/article/design-and-the-green-new-deal/.

8. Ovink interview, November 24, 2014.

9. Reyes interview.

10. Chester interview, June 19, 2014.

11. Chester, interview, July 18, 2018.

12. Marrella interview.

13. Boer interview, June 30, 2014.

14. Anna Brown, interview by the author, Bangkok, Thailand, July 3, 2014.

15. Lefebvre, *Production of Space*.

16. See, as well, Andrew Sayer, "Defining the Urban," *GeoJournal* 9, no. 3 (1984): 279–284.

17. MENKO, "Master Plan," 50.

18. All projections for NCICD plan from MENKO, "Master Plan"; Hudson River discharge data from United States Geological Survey (USGS), "Hudson River Freshwater Discharge at New York, NY (Mouth)," accessed December 12, 2020, http://ny.water.usgs.gov/projects/dialer_plots/Hudson_R_at_NYC_Freshwater_Discharge.htm.

19. Deltares, "Jakarta Sinking City," shown at the International Architecture Biennale Rotterdam 2014—Urban By Nature, 2014, YouTube video, 5:41, https://www.youtube.com/watch?v=Amkyt1SMKPc.

20. Presentation at Deltas in Times of Climate Change II conference, Rotterdam, September 2014.

21. Van den Boomen interview.

22. Van den Boomen interview.

23. Holston, "Spaces of Insurgent Citizenship."

24. Le Corbusier, *The Radiant City: Elements of a Doctrine of Urbanism to Be Used as the Basis of Our Machine-Age Civilization*, trans. Pamela Knight, Eleanor Levieux, and Derek Coltman (New York: Orion, 1967), 181.

25. Bons interview.

26. Bons interview, italics added.

27. See Introduction for more elaboration on Lefebvre's concepts.

28. For a discussion on causes of flooding in Jakarta by Marco Kusumawijaya, director of Rujak, an urban research and advocacy organization, see Grace Susetyo, "Once Upon a Sinking City: The Perpetual Floods of Jakarta," Indonesia Expat, February 25, 2013, https://indonesiaexpat.biz/travel/history-culture/once-upon-a-sinking-city-the-perpetual-floods-of-jakarta/.

29. Jakarta, Regional Development Planning Agency (BAPPEDA), "Ciliwung River Regulations," 2012.

30. For more information on rebuilding in Banda Aceh, ten years after the tsunami, including the work of Uplink, see Lawrence J. Vale, Shomon Shamsuddin, and Kian Goh, "Tsunami + 10: Housing Banda Aceh after Disaster," *Places Journal*, December 2014, https://placesjournal.org/article/tsunami-housing-banda-aceh-after-disaster/; and Ade Syukrizal, Wardah Hafidz, and Gabriela Sauter, "Reconstructing Life after the Tsunami: The Work of Uplink Banda Aceh in Indonesia," International Institute for Environment and Development London, UK, August 2009.

31. See Wawan Some, Wardah Hafidz, and Gabriela Sauter, "Renovation Not Relocation: The Work of Paguyuban Warga Strenkali (PWS) in Indonesia," *Environment and Urbanization* 21, no. 2 (October 1, 2009): 463–475. UPC organizers replicated the Strenkali model in Kampung Tongkol, North Jakarta, in 2015 and 2016, working with kampung residents to voluntarily demolish parts of the kampung and reorient the settlement toward the river, including a model house designed by community architects Architecture Sans Frontierès Indonesia. Gugun Muhammad (Urban Poor Consortium), interview by the author, Jakarta, Indonesia, December 11, 2018; Kamil Muhammad (Architecture Sans Frontierès Indonesia), interview by the author, Jakarta, Indonesia, December 17, 2018.

32. Ciliwung Merdeka, "Kampung Susun Manusiawi Bukit Duri," digital presentation, Jakarta, Indonesia, n.d.

33. Architecture for Humanity, *Design like You Give a Damn: Architectural Responses to Humanitarian Crisis* (New York: Metropolis, 2006).

34. Hernando De Soto, *The Mystery of Capital: Why Capitalism Triumphs in the West and Fails Everywhere Else* (New York: Basic Books, 2000); see, also, Colin McFarlane, "The Entrepreneurial Slum: Civil Society, Mobility and the Co-Production of Urban Development," *Urban Studies* 49, no. 13 (2012): 2795–2816.

35. Sumardi interview, July 18, 2014.

36. Shepherd interview. See also Ariel Shepherd, "Jakarta, Indonesia," In *Grounding Knowledge: Reflections on Community-Driven Urban Practices in South-East Asia*, by Johanna Brugman et al. (London, Bangkok: Bartlett Development Planning Unit [DPU], Community Architects Network [CAN], Asian Coalition for Housing Rights [ACHR], 2013), 50–81, https://issuu.com/dpu-ucl/docs/grounding_knowledge_24.2.14_new.

37. Kete interview.

38. Kete interview.

39. Ovink interview, November 24, 2014.

40. The discussion that follows focuses on the six winning proposals originally announced by Rebuild By Design. Another finalist proposal, "Resilient Bridgeport" by the WB unabridged with Yale ARCADIS team, was later also funded by HUD and awarded $10 million in implementation funds.

41. This amount, like the other winning team awards, is less than necessary to complete the designs as proposed. The BIG U proposal, according to the design team, is projected to cost $1.09 billion.

42. Ovink interview, November 24, 2014.

43. HUD, "Community Development Block Grant Disaster Recovery Program."

44. Reyes interview.

45. Kevin Fox Gotham and Miriam Greenberg, "From 9/11 to 8/29: Post-Disaster Recovery and Rebuilding in New York and New Orleans," *Social Forces* 87, no. 2 (2008): 1039–1062.

46. Asian American Federation of New York, *Chinatown after September 11th: An Economic Impact Study* (New York: Asian American Federation of New York, April 4, 2002), http://www.aafny.org/doc/ChinatownAfter911.pdf.

47. Reyes interview.

48. Chester interview, June 19, 2014.

49. The BIG team's BIG U project is arguably the highest-profile of the Rebuild By Design proposals, and LES Ready's experiences during the competition phase and beyond present an important assessment of community engagement.

50. Rebuild By Design, "Projects Are Moving Forward," June 3, 2015, http://www.rebuildbydesign.org/news-and-events/updates/projects-are-moving-forward.

51. Marrella interview.

52. HUD, "HUD Announces Winning Proposals."

53. Dusica Sue Malesevic, "2 Years after Sandy, Who Will Get Shelter from the Storm? Only Some Downtown," *Downtown Express*, October 29, 2014. This was

before the start of the city's own community engagement process, in December 2014. See City of New York (SIRR), *East Side Coastal Resiliency Project*, New York: City of New York, March 19, 2015, http://www.nyc.gov/html/planyc/downloads/pdf/150319_ESCR_FINAL.pdf. Of note: if the community members' contentions of unfair implementation and phasing of the BIG U play out as they claim, it would not be the first time in recent history in the Lower East Side that postdisaster recovery planning has been manipulated against the interests of low-income communities. In their study of disaster recovery in New York after 9/11 and New Orleans after Hurricane Katrina, Kevin Fox Gotham and Miriam Greenberg found that the Lower Manhattan Development Corporation, tasked with planning and coordinating the rebuilding and revitalization of Lower Manhattan after the attacks, sought waivers for the income requirements and "public benefit standards" for the CDBG funds then allocated to the city. They also found that capital grants favored the Financial District and Tribeca over the Lower East Side and Chinatown; Gotham and Greenberg, "From 9/11 to 8/29," 1047.

54. See Joseph Hanania, "To Save East River Park, the City Intends to Bury It," *New York Times*, January 18, 2019.

55. Chester interview, July 18, 2018.

56. Henk Ovink, interview by the author, The Hague, March 25, 2019.

57. Ovink interview, November 24, 2014.

58. With full acknowledgment that it is problematic to summarize complex design projects so reductively.

59. See, for example, the framing of what it means to be an accomplice, by Indigenous Action, "Accomplices Not Allies: Abolishing the Ally Industrial Complex," Indigenous Action (blog), May 4, 2014. http://www.indigenousaction.org/accomplices-not-allies-abolishing-the-ally-industrial-complex/.

60. See Michael Kimmelman, "Next Time, Libraries Could Be Our Shelters from the Storm," *New York Times*, October 2, 2013.

61. Eisenhard interview, September 13, 2014.

Chapter 5

1. See Roanne van Voorst and Rita Padawangi, "Floods and Forced Evictions in Jakarta," *New Mandala*, August 21, 2015, https://www.newmandala.org/floods-and-forced-evictions-in-jakarta/, for detailed commentary on the events leading up to and including the evictions; Corry Elyda, "Kampung Pulo Residents to Get Apartments on Their Land," *Jakarta Post*, July 25, 2015, for a news account of Ahok's initial decision; and Prathiwi Widyatmi Putri, "Insurgent Planner: Transgressing the Technocratic State of Postcolonial Jakarta," *Urban Studies* 57, no. 9 (2019): 1845–1865, for a more theoretical reflection on the evictions.

2. See, for more on the making of the contract, Amalinda Savirani and Edward Aspinall, "Adversarial Linkages: The Urban Poor and Electoral Politics in Jakarta," *Journal of Current Southeast Asian Affairs* 36, no. 3 (2017): 3–34.

3. This decision is not entirely unrealistic. Many nations have moved and rebuilt their capitals, often in the same kind of "greenfield" or tabula rasa conditions likely envisioned here. A striking example is Brasília in Brazil. A parallel but not identical, recent and neighboring example is Putrajaya in Malaysia, a new city now serving as the seat of the federal government, although the capital remains Kuala Lumpur. Jokowi's decision was almost certainly not made only because of environmental challenges. Moving the capital away from Jakarta, and away from Java, the most populous and economically productive island in the archipelago, may help secure political control of the country and open new avenues and sites for investments and development.

4. The ESCR project ran into further conflicts in 2019 as the planning team proposed a revised design to raise the East River Park, a move that some community members say will destroy mature trees, raze historical buildings and longstanding institutions, and close a much-used park for years. See Hanania, "To Save East River Park, the City Intends to Bury It."

5. The Global Commission on Adaptation released its first report in September 2019: *Adapt Now: A Global Call for Leadership on Climate Resilience* (Rotterdam: Global Center on Adaptation; Washington, DC: World Resources Institute, 2019), https://cdn.gca.org/assets/2019-09/GlobalCommission_Report_FINAL.pdf.

6. Ovink interview, March 25, 2019.

7. In Minister Schulz's speech at a roundtable on coastal development in Jakarta on April 2, 2014, in conjunction with her announcement of the NCICD masterplan, she said, "We Dutch feel very much at home here. We feel *senang* [at ease]. The reason is related to today's theme: the battle against water."

8. From Ovink's presentation, titled "Rebuild by Design: Recovering New York after Sandy," at the Deltas in Times of Climate Change II conference in Rotterdam, Netherlands, on September 25, 2014.

9. Yet, it is not solely about direct contestation for digitally networked urban movements, as has been pointed out about by, among others, Manuel Castells, *Networks of Outrage and Hope: Social Movements in the Internet Age* (Cambridge: Polity, 2012), and Bill Wasik, "#Riot: Self-Organized, Hyper-Networked Revolts—Coming to a City Near You," *Wired*, January 16, 2012, http://www.wired.com/magazine/2011/12/ff-riots/.

10. Geographers Helga Leitner, Eric Sheppard, Kristin Sziarto, and Anant Maringanti, in searching out forms of resistance to the hegemony of neoliberal urban governance, propose a means of unconventional urban resistance—beyond direct response. The authors map the recursive relationships between "imaginaries" (including ideals, norms, discourses, and ethics) and "practice," and between forms of capitalism and contestations of capitalism. These "alternative social imaginaries" might include

opposition to specific outcomes instead of the larger system, nonaligned yet collaborative movements against a common target, a more diffuse contestation against a more immediately evident source of oppression or threat, or in contestation against each other. See their "Contesting Urban Futures: Decentering Neoliberalism," in *Contesting Neoliberalism: Urban Frontiers*, ed. Helga Leitner, Jamie Peck, and Eric S. Sheppard (New York: Guilford, 2007), 9.

11. This network is the means of my own introduction to the kampung activism, established quickly through connections with John Taylor of Yayasan Kota Kita, Dian Tri Irawaty and Marco Kusumawijaya of Rujak, and researcher AbdouMaliq Simone, each of whom introduced me to individuals and aspects of the organizing.

12. By "transformative," I mean for systemic change in socioecological and, here as well, sociospatial relationships. See Patricia Romero-Lankao et al., "Urban Transformative Potential in a Changing Climate," *Nature Climate Change* 8, no. 9 (2018): 754.

13. As delineated in the Introduction ("For Climate Justice"). See, as well, for more elaboration on the urban theoretical debates engaged, Goh, "Urbanising Climate Justice."

14. Especially in the account of the RHI's work before, during, and after Hurricane Sandy, described in chapter 2.

15. Susan Fainstein critiques the depoliticizing tendency of ecological analyses in resiliency studies, and suggests that a more just approach to resilience would involve prioritizing the lives of the most vulnerable when making planning decisions: "Resilience and Justice," 165. Malini Ranganathan and Eve Bratman challenge the future-oriented nature of resilience planning and its neglect of rooted experiences and grounded knowledge, proposing that a climate justice framing offers a more historical and political view of intersectional struggles including and beyond climate: "From Urban Resilience to Abolitionist Climate Justice in Washington, DC," *Antipode*, June 28, 2019, https://doi.org/10.1111/anti.12555.

16. In agreement, here, with Ranganathan and Bratman, "From Urban Resilience to Abolitionist Climate Justice."

17. Arup, "City Resilience Framework."

18. Kete interview.

19. Kete interview.

20. This assessment aligns well with other studies of the importance of social relationships during disasters. See, in particular, Eric Klinenberg, *Heat Wave: A Social Autopsy of Disaster in Chicago* (Chicago: University of Chicago Press, 2002).

21. Eisenhard interview, September 13, 2014.

22. These practices resonate with ideas about mutual aid, a form of social and political participation, often by and for those most vulnerable and in need, to survive and

challenge unjust and violent systems. Mutual aid gained popular attention during the 2020 coronavirus pandemic, as governments at all levels in the US by and large failed to provide a coordinated response. It is not surprising that organizations like RHI and GOLES turned their attention to practices of mutual aid as the pandemic spread in New York in the spring.

23. Eisenhard interview, August 2, 2019.

24. See, for discussion on these issues, Kian Goh, "Planning the Green New Deal: Climate Justice and the Politics of Sites and Scales," *Journal of the American Planning Association* 86, no. 2 (2020): 188–195.

25. For example, Daniel Aldana Cohen, analyzing one of the sites and events in this book, argues that weather does not do the work of climate politics, and that the plans and mobilizations in response to severe events does not necessarily lead to decarbonization policies, in "New York City as 'Fortress of Solitude' after Hurricane Sandy: A Relational Sociology of Extreme Weather's Relationship to Climate Politics," *Environmental Politics* (2020): 1–21, https://doi.org/10.1080/09644016.2020.1816380.

26. See, for example, Charles Waldheim, "Landscape as Urbanism," in *The Landscape Urbanism Reader*, ed. Charles Waldheim (New York: Princeton Architectural Press, 2006), 36–53; Pierre Bélanger, "Landscape as Infrastructure," *Landscape Journal* 28, no. 1 (2009): 79–95; Kate Orff, *Toward an Urban Ecology* (New York: Monacelli, 2016); and, for more foundational concepts, Richard T. T Forman, "Ecologically Sustainable Landscapes: The Role of Spatial Configuration," in *Changing Landscapes: An Ecological Perspective*, ed. Isaak S. Zonneveld and Richard T. T. Forman (New York: Springer-Verlag, 1990), 261–278.

27. In an article on the politics of urban flooding in Jakarta, I show one conceptual development of this, explaining how a theoretical shift in explanatory worldviews and a shift in literal points of view inspired by design practice—from top-down to lateral—enable reconceptualized urban ecological design and movement building practices: Goh, "Urban Waterscapes." The article includes an earlier iteration of this diagram.

28. Holston, "Spaces of Insurgent Citizenship."

29. Ruth Wilson Gilmore, "Fatal Couplings of Power and Difference: Notes on Racism and Geography," *Professional Geographer* 54, no. 1 (2002): 16.

30. See also Ruth Wilson Gilmore, "Abolition Geography and the Problem of Innocence," in *Futures of Black Radicalism*, ed. Gaye Theresa Johnson and Alex Lubin (London: Verso, 2017), 225–240; and Katherine McKittrick, "On Plantations, Prisons, and a Black Sense of Place," *Social and Cultural Geography* 12, no. 8 (2011): 947–963.

31. Castells, *Networks of Outrage and Hope*, 222.

32. See, as well, my essay on how design takes seriously social marginalization and large-scale, transformative change: Kian Goh, "Architecture and Global

Ethnographies," *Dimensions of Citizenship*, a Collaboration between *e-Flux Architecture* and the United States Pavilion of the 16th International Architecture Exhibition at La Biennale di Venezia, August 15, 2018, https://www.e-flux.com/architecture/dimensions-of-citizenship/178295/architecture-and-global-ethnographies/.

Appendix 1

1. Primarily Michael Burawoy's extended case method: "The Extended Case Method," *Sociological Theory* 16, no. 1 (1998): 5; and Philip McMichael's notion of incorporated comparison: "World-Systems Analysis, Globalization, and Incorporated Comparison," *Journal of World-Systems Research* 6, no. 3 (2000): 671.

2. Amin, "Regions Unbound"; Massey, "Counterhegemonic Relationality of Place"; Roy, "21st-Century Metropolis."

3. Rademacher, *Reigning the River*, 15.

4. Amin, "Regions Unbound," 34.

5. Roy, "21st-Century Metropolis," 822 (italics in original).

6. Ananya Roy, "Paradigms of Propertied Citizenship: Transnational Techniques of Analysis," *Urban Affairs Review* 38, no. 4 (2003): 466.

7. See, for example, the debates on generalized urban research and historical difference between Allen J. Scott and Michael Storper, "The Nature of Cities: The Scope and Limits of Urban Theory," *International Journal of Urban and Regional Research* 39, no. 1 (2015): 1–15, and Roy, "Who's Afraid of Postcolonial Theory?"; and those on planetary-scale processes of urbanization, Linda Peake et al., "Placing Planetary Urbanization in Other Fields of Vision," *Environment and Planning D: Society and Space* 36, no. 3 (2018): 374–386; Neil Brenner, "Debating Planetary Urbanization: For an Engaged Pluralism." *Environment and Planning D: Society and Space* 36, no. 3 (2018): 570–590; with review and analysis in Hillary Angelo and Kian Goh, "Out in Space: Difference and Abstraction in Planetary Urbanization," *International Journal of Urban and Regional Research* (2020), https://doi.org/10.1111/1468-2427.12911; Goh, "Urbanising Climate Justice."

Selected Bibliography

Abidin, Hasanuddin Z., Heri Andreas, Irwan Gumilar, Yoichi Fukuda, Yusuf E. Pohan, and T. Deguchi. "Land Subsidence of Jakarta (Indonesia) and Its Relation with Urban Development." *Natural Hazards* 59, no. 3 (2011): 1753–1771.

Abu-Lughod, Janet L., ed. *From Urban Village to East Village: The Battle for New York's Lower East Side*. Oxford: Blackwell, 1994.

Adams-Schoen, Sarah. "On the Waterfront: New York City's Climate Change Adaptation and Mitigation Challenge (Part 1 of 2)." *Environmental Law in New York* 25, no. 4 (2014): 81–99.

Aerts, Jeroen, David C. Major, Malcolm J. Bowman, Piet Dircke, and Muh Aris Marfai. *Connecting Delta Cities: Coastal Cities, Flood Risk Management and Adaptation to Climate Change*. Rotterdam: VU University Press, 2009. http://www.deltacityofthefuture.nl/documents/ConnectingDeltaCities.pdf.

Aga Khan Development Network. "Kampung Improvement Programme: Aga Khan Award for Architecture." https://www.akdn.org/architecture/project/kampung-improvement-programme.

Amin, Ash. "Regions Unbound: Towards a New Politics of Place." *Geografiska Annaler: Series B, Human Geography* 86, no. 1 (2004): 33–44.

Angelo, Hillary, and Kian Goh. 2020. "Out in Space: Difference and Abstraction in Planetary Urbanization." *International Journal of Urban and Regional Research* (2020). https://doi.org/10.1111/1468-2427.12911.

Anguelovski, Isabelle, Linda Shi, Eric Chu, Daniel Gallagher, Kian Goh, Zachary Lamb, Kara Reeve, and Hannah Teicher. "Equity Impacts of Urban Land Use Planning for Climate Adaptation: Critical Perspectives from the Global North and South." *Journal of Planning Education and Research* 36, no. 3 (2016): 333–348.

Anya, Agnes, and Callistasia Anggun Wijaya. "Govt Cancels Great Garuda Seawall." *Jakarta Post*, December 11, 2017.

Arabindoo, Pushpa. "Urban Design in the Realm of Urban Studies." In *Explorations in Urban Design: An Urban Design Research Primer*, edited by Matthew Carmona, 47–58. Farnham, UK: Ashgate, 2014.

Architecture for Humanity. *Design like You Give a Damn: Architectural Responses to Humanitarian Crisis*. New York: Metropolis, 2006.

Arditya, Andreas D. "South Korea to Help in Restoring Ciliwung River." *Jakarta Post*, January 5, 2013.

Arup. "City Resilience Framework." Rockefeller Foundation, April 2014 (updated December 2015). https://www.rockefellerfoundation.org/wp-content/uploads/City-Resilience-Framework-2015.pdf.

Asian American Federation of New York. *Chinatown after September 11th: An Economic Impact Study*. New York: Asian American Federation of New York, April 4, 2002. www.aafny.org/doc/ChinatownAfter911.pdf.

Bakker, Karen. "The Limits of 'Neoliberal Natures': Debating Green Neoliberalism." *Progress in Human Geography* 34, no. 6 (2010): 715–735.

Bakker, Karen, Michelle Kooy, Nur Endah Shofiani, and Ernst-Jan Martijn. "Governance Failure: Rethinking the Institutional Dimensions of Urban Water Supply to Poor Households." *World Development* 36, no. 10 (2008): 1891–1915.

Bélanger, Pierre. "Landscape as Infrastructure." *Landscape Journal* 28, no. 1 (2009): 79–95.

Birkmann, Jörn, Matthias Garschagen, Frauke Kraas, and Nguyen Quang. "Adaptive Urban Governance: New Challenges for the Second Generation of Urban Adaptation Strategies to Climate Change." *Sustainability Science* 5, no. 2 (2010): 185–206.

Blom, Frans R. E. "Picturing New Netherland and New York: Dutch-Anglo Transfer of New World Information." In *The Dutch Trading Companies as Knowledge Networks*, edited by Siegfried Huigen, Jan L. de Jong, and Elmer Kolfin, 103–126. Leiden: Brill, 2010.

Boelens, Luuk, and Elien Wierenga. "Editorial." In *Compacte stad extended: Agenda voor toekomstig beleid, onderzoek en ontwerp*, edited by Luuk Boelens, Henk Ovink, Hanna Lára Pálsdóttir, and Elien Wierenga, 10–23. Design and politics, #4. Rotterdam: 010, 2010.

Boltz, Fred. "Announcing the Global Resilience Challenge." Rockefeller Foundation, September 19, 2014. http://www.rockefellerfoundation.org/blog/announcing-global-resilience-challenge/.

Brenner, Neil. "Debating Planetary Urbanization: For an Engaged Pluralism." *Environment and Planning D: Society and Space* 36, no. 3 (2018): 570–590.

Brenner, Neil. "Theses on Urbanization." *Public Culture* 25, no. 1 69 (2013): 85–114.

Selected Bibliography

Brenner, Neil. "The Urban Question as a Scale Question: Reflections on Henri Lefebvre, Urban Theory and the Politics of Scale." *International Journal of Urban and Regional Research* 24, no. 2 (2000): 361–378.

Brenner, Neil, and Christian Schmid. "The 'Urban Age' in Question." *International Journal of Urban and Regional Research* 38, no. 3 (2014): 731–755.

Brinkman, JanJaap, and Marco Hartman. "Jakarta Flood Hazard Mapping Framework." Unpublished Deltares and HKV study, 2009. http://edepot.wur.nl/140833.

Bulkeley, Harriet. "Cities and the Governing of Climate Change." *Annual Review of Environment and Resources* 35 (2010): 229–253.

Bulkeley, Harriet, Liliana B. Andonova, Michele M. Betsill, Daniel Compagnon, Thomas Hale, Matthew J. Hoffman, Peter Newell, Matthew Paterson, Charles Roger, and Stacy D. Vandeveer. *Transnational Climate Change Governance*. New York: Cambridge University Press, 2014.

Bulkeley, Harriet, and Michele M. Betsill. "Rethinking Sustainable Cities: Multilevel Governance and the 'Urban' Politics of Climate Change." *Environmental Politics* 14, no. 1 (2005): 42–63.

Bulkeley, Harriet, and Michele M. Betsill. "Revisiting the Urban Politics of Climate Change." *Environmental Politics* 22, no. 1 (2013): 136–154.

Bulkeley, Harriet, Gareth A. S. Edwards, and Sara Fuller. "Contesting Climate Justice in the City: Examining Politics and Practice in Urban Climate Change Experiments." *Global Environmental Change* 25 (2014): 31–40.

Bullard, Robert D. *Dumping in Dixie: Race, Class, and Environmental Quality*. Boulder, CO: Westview, 1990.

Bunnell, Tim, and Michelle Ann Miller. "Jakarta in Post-Suharto Indonesia: Decentralisation, Neo-Liberalism and Global City Aspiration." *Space and Polity* 15, no. 1 (2011): 35–48.

Burawoy, Michael. "The Extended Case Method." *Sociological Theory* 16, no. 1 (1998): 4–33.

Burdett, Richard, and Deyan Sudjic, eds. *The Endless City: The Urban Age Project by the London School of Economics and Deutsche Bank's Alfred Herrhausen Society*. London: Phaidon, 2007.

Caljouw, Mark, Peter J. M. Nas, and Pratiwo. "Flooding in Jakarta: Towards a Blue City with Improved Water Management." *Bijdragen Tot de Taal-, Land- en Volkenkunde* 161, no. 4 (2005): 454–484.

Cammen, Hans van der, Len de Klerk, Gerhard Dekker, and Peter Paul Witsen. *The Selfmade Land: Culture and Evolution of Urban and Regional Planning in the Netherlands*. Houten, Netherlands: Spectrum, 2012.

Caro, Robert A. *The Power Broker: Robert Moses and the Fall of New York*. New York: Vintage, 1975.

Castán Broto, Vanesa. "Urban Governance and the Politics of Climate Change." *World Development* 93 (2017): 1–15.

Castells, Manuel. *The Informational City: Information Technology, Economic Restructuring, and the Urban-Regional Process*. Cambridge, MA: Blackwell, 1989.

Castells, Manuel. *Networks of Outrage and Hope: Social Movements in the Internet Age*. Cambridge: Polity, 2012.

Castells, Manuel. *The Rise of the Network Society*. Cambridge, MA: Blackwell, 1996.

Castree, Noel. "Neoliberalising Nature: The Logics of Deregulation and Reregulation." *Environment and Planning A* 40, no. 1 (2008): 131–152.

Castree, Noel. "Neoliberalising Nature: Processes, Effects, and Evaluations." *Environment and Planning A* 40, no. 1 (2008): 153–173.

Chakrabarty, Dipesh. "The Climate of History: Four Theses." *Critical Inquiry* 35, no. 2 (2009): 197–222.

Chatterton, Paul, David Featherstone, and Paul Routledge. "Articulating Climate Justice in Copenhagen: Antagonism, the Commons, and Solidarity." *Antipode* 45, no. 3 (2013): 602–620.

Chaussard, Estelle, Falk Amelung, Hasanudin Abidin, and Sang-Hoon Hong. "Sinking Cities in Indonesia: ALOS PALSAR Detects Rapid Subsidence Due to Groundwater and Gas Extraction." *Remote Sensing of Environment* 128 (2013): 150–161.

City of New York. "Mayor de Blasio, Senator Schumer Announce $3 Billion in Federal Funds." NYC, March 31, 2015. https://www1.nyc.gov/office-of-the-mayor/news/206-15/mayor-de-blasio-senator-schumer-3-billion-federal-funds-repair-protect-33#/0.

City of New York, Office of the Mayor. *PlaNYC: A Greener, Greater New York*. New York: Office of the Mayor, 2007. http://www.nyc.gov/html/planyc/downloads/pdf/publications/full_report_2007.pdf.

City of New York, Office of the Mayor. *PlaNYC: A Greener, Greater New York—Update April 2011*. New York: Office of the Mayor, 2011. http://www.nyc.gov/html/planyc/downloads/pdf/publications/planyc_2011_planyc_full_report.pdf.

City of New York, Office of the Mayor. *A Stronger, More Resilient New York*. Report of the Special Initiative for Rebuilding and Resiliency (SIRR). New York: Office of the Mayor, 2013. http://s-media.nyc.gov/agencies/sirr/SIRR_singles_Lo_res.pdf.

Climate-ADAPT: European Climate Adaptation Platform. "What Is Meant by Uncertainty?" Accessed December 12, 2020. http://climate-adapt.eea.europa.eu/uncertainty-guidance/topic1.

Cochrane, Allan, and Kevin Ward. "Guest Editorial: Researching the Geographies of Policy Mobility: Confronting the Methodological Challenges." *Environment and Planning A* 44, no. 1 (2012): 5–12.

Cohen, Daniel Aldana. "New York City as 'Fortress of Solitude' after Hurricane Sandy: A Relational Sociology of Extreme Weather's Relationship to Climate Politics." *Environmental Politics* (2020): 1–21. https://doi.org/10.1080/09644016.2020.1816380.

Cohen, Daniel Aldana, and Max Liboiron. "New York's Two Sandys." *Metropolitics*, October 30, 2014. http://www.metropolitiques.eu/New-York-s-Two-Sandys.html.

Colven, Emma. "Understanding the Allure of Big Infrastructure: Jakarta's Great Garuda Sea Wall Project." *Water Alternatives* 10, no. 2 (2017): 250–264.

Congrès Internationaux d'Architecture Moderne (CIAM). *La Charte d'Athenes, 1933*. Paris: 1943. Translated by Jaqueline Tyrwhitt as *The Athens Charter, 1933*. Paris: Library of the Graduate School of Design, Harvard University, 1946. http://www.getty.edu/conservation/publications_resources/research_resources/charters/charter04.html.

Connecting Delta Cities. "Indonesian Officials Meet Experts on US East Coast." Newsletter—Connecting Delta Cities, September 2, 2014. http://deltacitiesofthefuture.nl/newsletter/indonesian-officials-meet-experts-on-us-east-coast?news_id=65.

Cronon, William. *Nature's Metropolis: Chicago and the Great West*. New York: W. W. Norton, 1991.

Crutzen, Paul J., and Eugene F. Stoermer. "The Anthropocene." *Global Change Newsletter* 41, no. 1 (2000): 17–18.

Cuthbert, Alexander R. "Urban Design: Requiem for an Era—Review and Critique of the Last 50 Years." *Urban Design International* 12, no. 4 (2007): 177.

Cutter, Susan L., Joseph A. Ahearn, Bernard Amadei, Patrick Crawford, Elizabeth A. Eide, Gerald E. Galloway, Michael F. Goodchild, Howard C. Kunreuther, Meredith Li-Vollmer, and Monica Schoch-Spana. "Disaster Resilience: A National Imperative." *Environment: Science and Policy for Sustainable Development* 55, no. 2 (2013): 25–29.

da Silva, Jo, Sam Kernaghan, and Andrés Luque. "A Systems Approach to Meeting the Challenges of Urban Climate Change." *International Journal of Urban Sustainable Development* 4, no. 2 (2012): 125–145.

Davoudi, Simin, Jennifer Lawrence, and Jim Bohland. "Anatomy of the Resilience Machine." In *The Resilience Machine*, edited by Jim Bohland, Simin Davoudi, and Jennifer Lawrence, 12–28. Abingdon, UK: Routledge, 2019.

Davoudi, Simin, Jenny Crawford, and Abid Mehmood, eds. *Planning for Climate Change: Strategies for Mitigation and Adaptation for Spatial Planners*. London: Earthscan, 2009.

Dawson, Ashley. *Extreme Cities: The Peril and Promise of Urban Life in the Age of Climate Change*. London: Verso, 2017.

Deltares, "Sinking Cities: An Integrated Approach towards Solutions," Delft, The Netherlands: Deltares, October 2013. https://www.deltares.nl/app/uploads/2015/09/Sinking-cities.pdf.

Desfor, Gene, and Roger Keil. *Nature and the City: Making Environmental Policy in Toronto and Los Angeles*. Tucson: University of Arizona Press, 2004.

De Soto, Hernando. *The Mystery of Capital: Why Capitalism Triumphs in the West and Fails Everywhere Else*. New York: Basic Books, 2000.

De Vriend, Huib, and Mark Van Koningsveld. *Building with Nature: Thinking, Acting and Interacting Differently*. Dordrecht: Ecoshape, Building with Nature, 2012.

Dewi, Sita W. "'Blusukan' Essential to Jokowi's Bid." *Jakarta Post*, March 23, 2014.

Dewi, Sita W. "Jokowi to Launch Pluit Dam City Park." *Jakarta Post*, August 16, 2013.

Dircke, Piet, Jeroen Aerts, and Arnoud Molenaar. *Connecting Delta Cities: Sharing Knowledge and Working on Adaptation to Climate Change*. Rotterdam: Connecting Delta Cities, 2010. http://www.deltacityofthefuture.nl/documents/CDC_Boek_II.pdf.

Dolowitz, David P., and David Marsh. "Learning from Abroad: The Role of Policy Transfer in Contemporary Policy-Making." *Governance* 13, no. 1 (2000): 5–23.

Douglass, Mike. "The Environmental Sustainability of Development: Coordination, Incentives and Political Will in Land Use Planning for the Jakarta Metropolis." *Third World Planning Review* 11, no. 2 (1989): 211.

Douglass, Mike "Globalization, Mega-Projects and the Environment: Urban Form and Water in Jakarta." *Environment and Urbanization Asia* 1, no. 1 (2010): 45–65.

Durkin, Erin. "FEMA to Give $3 Billion to NYCHA for Hurricane Sandy Damage." *New York Daily News*, March 31, 2015.

Dutch Water Sector. "Details Dutch Seawall and Development Plan for Jakarta Bay Well Received by Indonesian Authorities." April 3, 2014. http://www.dutchwatersector.com/news-events/news/10020-details-dutch-seawall-and-development-plan-for-jakarta-bay-well-received-by-indonesian-authorities.html.

Dutch Water Sector. "South Korea Joins Giant Sea Wall Project to Protect Jakarta, Indonesia." September 4, 2015. https://www.dutchwatersector.com/news-events/news/15268-south-korea-joins-giant-sea-wall-project-to-protect-jakarta-indonesia.html.

Dutt, Ashok K., and Frank J. Costa, eds. *Public Planning in the Netherlands: Perspectives and Change since the Second World War*. New York: Oxford University Press, 1985.

Elden, Stuart. "There Is a Politics of Space because Space Is Political." *Radical Philosophy Review* 10, no. 2 (2007): 101–116.

Ellis, Erle C., Kees Klein Goldewijk, Stefan Siebert, Deborah Lightman, and Navin Ramankutty. "Anthropogenic Transformation of the Biomes, 1700 to 2000." *Global Ecology and Biogeography* 19, no. 5 (2010): 589–606.

Elyda, Corry. "Kampung Pulo Residents to Get Apartments on Their Land." *Jakarta Post*, July 25, 2015.

Fainstein, Susan. "Resilience and Justice." *International Journal of Urban and Regional Research* 39, no. 1 (2015): 157–167.

Fasullo, John T., and R. Steven Nerem. "Altimeter-Era Emergence of the Patterns of Forced Sea-Level Rise in Climate Models and Implications for the Future." *Proceedings of the National Academy of Sciences* 115, no. 51 (2018): 12944–12949.

Ferriss, Hugh. *The Metropolis of Tomorrow*. New York: Ives Washburn, 1929.

Fields, Desiree. "Unwilling Subjects of Financialization." *International Journal of Urban and Regional Research* 41, no. 4 (2017): 588–603.

Fleming, Billy. "Design and the Green New Deal." *Places Journal*, April 2019. https://placesjournal.org/article/design-and-the-green-new-deal/.

Flint, Anthony. *Wrestling with Moses: How Jane Jacobs Took on New York's Master Builder and Transformed the American City*. New York: Random House, 2009.

Foderaro, Lisa W. "Law Says Hudson River Park Is Allowed to Sell Air Rights." *New York Times*, November 14, 2013.

Forman, Richard T. T. "Ecologically Sustainable Landscapes: The Role of Spatial Configuration." In *Changing Landscapes: An Ecological Perspective*, edited by Isaak S. Zonneveld and Richard T. T. Forman, 261–278. New York: Springer-Verlag, 1990.

Friedmann, John. *Planning in the Public Domain: From Knowledge to Action*. Princeton, NJ: Princeton University Press, 1987.

Friedmann, John. "The World City Hypothesis." *Development and Change* 17, no. 1 (1986): 69–83.

Friedmann, John, and John Miller. "The Urban Field." *Journal of the American Institute of Planners* 31, no. 4 (1965): 312–320.

Fuchs, Roland J., Ellen Brennan, Joseph Chamie, Fu-chen Lo, and Juha I. Uitto, eds. *Mega-City Growth and the Future*. Tokyo: United Nations University Press, 1994.

Gandy, Matthew. *Concrete and Clay: Reworking Nature in New York City*. Cambridge, MA: MIT Press, 2002.

Gandy, Matthew. "Cyborg Urbanization: Complexity and Monstrosity in the Contemporary City." *International Journal of Urban and Regional Research* 29, no. 1 (2005): 26–49.

Gardner, Jean. "Topology of an Island City." In *ECO-TEC: Architecture of the In-Between*, edited by Amerigo Marras, 100–107. New York: Princeton Architectural Press, 1999.

Gerrits, Lasse, Ward Rauws, and Gert de Roo. "Dutch Spatial Planning Policies in Transition." *Planning Theory and Practice* 13, no. 2 (2012): 336–341.

Gerritsen, Herman. "What Happened in 1953? The Big Flood in the Netherlands in Retrospect." *Philosophical Transactions of the Royal Society A: Mathematical, Physical and Engineering Sciences* 363, no. 1831 (2005): 1271–1291.

Gilmore, Ruth Wilson. "Abolition Geography and the Problem of Innocence." In *Futures of Black Radicalism*, edited by Gaye Theresa Johnson and Alex Lubin, 225–240. London: Verso, 2017.

Gilmore, Ruth Wilson. "Fatal Couplings of Power and Difference: Notes on Racism and Geography." *Professional Geographer* 54, no. 1 (2002): 15–24.

Global Commission on Adaptation. *Adapt Now: A Global Call for Leadership on Climate Resilience*. Rotterdam: Global Center on Adaptation; Washington, DC: World Resources Institute, 2019. https://cdn.gca.org/assets/2019-09/GlobalCommission_Report_FINAL.pdf.

Godfrey, Nick, and Roger Savage. *Future Proofing Cities*. London: Atkins Global, 2012. http://discovery.ucl.ac.uk/1402048/.

Goh, Kian. "Architecture and Global Ethnographies." *Dimensions of Citizenship*, a collaboration between *e-Flux Architecture* and the United States Pavilion of the 16th International Architecture Exhibition at La Biennale di Venezia, August 15, 2018. https://www.e-flux.com/architecture/dimensions-of-citizenship/178295/architecture-and-global-ethnographies/.

Goh, Kian. "Flows in Formation: The Global-Urban Networks of Climate Change Adaptation." *Urban Studies* 57, no. 11 (2020): 2222–2240.

Goh, Kian. "Planning the Green New Deal: Climate Justice and the Politics of Sites and Scales." *Journal of the American Planning Association* 86, no. 2 (2020): 188–195.

Goh, Kian. "Safe Cities and Queer Spaces: The Urban Politics of Radical LGBT Activism." *Annals of the American Association of Geographers* 108, no. 2 (2018): 463–477.

Goh, Kian. "Toward Transformative Urban Spatial Change: Views from Jakarta." In *The New Companion to Urban Design*, edited by Tridib Banerjee and Anastasia Loukaitou-Sideris, 519–532. Abingdon, UK: Routledge, 2019.

Goh, Kian. "Urbanising Climate Justice: Constructing Scales and Politicising Difference." *Cambridge Journal of Regions, Economy and Society* 13, no. 3 (2020): 559–74.

Goh, Kian. "Urban Waterscapes: The Hydro-Politics of Flooding in a Sinking City." *International Journal of Urban and Regional Research* 43, no. 2 (2019): 250–272.

Gotham, Kevin Fox, and Miriam Greenberg. "From 9/11 to 8/29: Post-Disaster Recovery and Rebuilding in New York and New Orleans." *Social Forces* 87, no. 2 (2008): 1039–1062.

Gottmann, Jean. *Since Megalopolis: The Urban Writings of Jean Gottmann*. Edited by Robert Alexander Harper and Jean Gottmann. Baltimore, MD: Johns Hopkins University Press, 1990.

Gould, Kenneth A., and Tammy L. Lewis. *Green Gentrification: Urban Sustainability and the Struggle for Environmental Justice*. London: Routledge, 2017.

Graham, Stephen. "Cities and the 'War on Terror.'" In *Indefensible Space: The Architecture of the National Insecurity State*, edited by Michael Sorkin, 1–28. New York: Routledge, 2008.

Grijns, Kees, and Peter J. M. Nas, eds. *Jakarta-Batavia: Socio-Cultural Essays*. Leiden: KITLV, 2000.

Hallegatte, Stephane, Colin Green, Robert J. Nicholls, and Jan Corfee-Morlot. "Future Flood Losses in Major Coastal Cities." *Nature Climate Change* 3, no. 9 (2013): 802–806.

Hanania, Joseph. "To Save East River Park, the City Intends to Bury It." *New York Times*, January 18, 2019.

Harvey, David. "The Nature of Environment: Dialectics of Social and Environmental Change." *Socialist Register* 29, no. 29 (1993).

Harvey, David. "Neo-Liberalism as Creative Destruction." *Geografiska Annaler: Series B, Human Geography* 88, no. 2 (2006): 145–158.

Harvey, David. *The Urbanization of Capital: Studies in the History and Theory of Capitalist Urbanization*. Baltimore, MD: Johns Hopkins University Press, 1985.

Heynen, Nik. "Urban Political Ecology I: The Urban Century." *Progress in Human Geography* 38, no. 4 (2014): 598–604.

Heynen, Nik. "Urban Political Ecology II: The Abolitionist Century." *Progress in Human Geography* 40, no. 6 (2016): 839–845.

Heynen, Nik. "Urban Political Ecology III: The Feminist and Queer Century." *Progress in Human Geography* 42, no. 3 (2018): 446–452.

Heynen, Nik, Maria Kaika, and Erik Swyngedouw. "Urban Political Ecology: Politicizing the Production of Urban Natures." In *In the Nature of Cities: Urban Political Ecology and the Politics of Urban Metabolism*, edited by Nik Heynen, Maria Kaika, and Erik Swyngedouw, 1–20. Abingdon, UK: Routledge, 2006.

Heynen, Nik, and Paul Robbins. "The Neoliberalization of Nature: Governance, Privatization, Enclosure and Valuation." *Capitalism Nature Socialism* 16, no. 1 (2005): 5–8.

Hill, Kristina. "Climate Change: Implications for the Assumptions, Goals and Methods of Urban Environmental Planning." *Urban Planning* 1, no. 4 (2016): 103–113.

Hill, Kristina. "Coastal Infrastructure: A Typology for the Next Century of Adaptation to Sea-Level Rise." *Frontiers in Ecology and the Environment* 13, no. 9 (2015): 468–476.

Hodson, Mike, and Simon Marvin. *World Cities and Climate Change: Producing Urban Ecological Security*. Maidenhead, UK: Open University Press, 2010.

Holifield, Ryan. "Defining Environmental Justice and Environmental Racism." *Urban Geography* 22, no. 1 (2001): 78–90.

Holston, James. "Spaces of Insurgent Citizenship." In *Cities and Citizenship*, edited by James Holston, 155–174. Durham, NC: Duke University Press, 1999.

Human Rights Watch. "Condemned Communities: Forced Evictions in Jakarta, Indonesia." Human Rights Watch, September 5, 2006. https://www.hrw.org/report/2006/09/05/condemned-communities/forced-evictions-jakarta#.

Huq, Saleemul, Sari Kovats, Hannah Reid, and David Satterthwaite. "Editorial: Reducing Risks to Cities from Disasters and Climate Change." *Environment and Urbanization* 19, no. 1 (2007): 3–15.

Hurricane Sandy Rebuilding Task Force. *Hurricane Sandy Rebuilding Strategy: Stronger Communities, a Resilient Region*. Washington, DC: US Department Housing and Urban Development, 2013. http://portal.hud.gov/hudportal/documents/huddoc?id=HSRebuildingStrategy.pdf.

Indigenous Action. "Accomplices Not Allies: Abolishing the Ally Industrial Complex." Indigenous Action (blog), May 4, 2014. http://www.indigenousaction.org/accomplices-not-allies-abolishing-the-ally-industrial-complex/.

Indonesia, Coordinating Ministry for Economic Affairs (MENKO), "Master Plan: National Capital Integrated Coastal Development." October 1, 2014, accessed January 31, 2015. http://ncicd.com/wp-content/uploads/2014/10/MP-final-NCICD-LR.pdf (site has since been discontinued).

Indonesian Ministry of Public Works. *Jakarta Coastal Defence Strategy (JCDS)*. Jakarta: Indonesia, Ministry of Public Works, 2011.

Intergovernmental Panel on Climate Change (IPCC). *Global Warming of 1.5°C*. IPCC, 2018. https://www.ipcc.ch/sr15/.

Intergovernmental Panel on Climate Change (IPCC). *Climate Change 2013: The Physical Science Basis. Contribution of Working Group I to the Fifth Assessment Report of the Intergovernmental Panel on Climate Change*. Edited by T. F. Stocker, D. Qin, G.-K.

Plattner, M. Tignor, S. K. Allen, J. Boschung, A. Nauels, Y. Xia, V. Bex and P.M. Midgley. Cambridge: Cambridge University Press, 2013. http://www.ipcc.ch/report/ar5/wg1/.

International Advisory Board Rotterdam (IAB Rotterdam). *New Energy for Rotterdam—IAB Conference 2006*. Rotterdam: Economic Development Board Rotterdam, 2006. https://en.rotterdampartners.nl/app/uploads//2019/03/IAB-2006-report.pdf.

International Climate Justice Network. "Bali Principles of Climate Justice." Corpwatch, August 28, 2002. https://corpwatch.org/article/bali-principles-climate-justice.

Iovine, Julie V. "The Skyscraper as a Pillar of Confidence." *Wall Street Journal*, September 8, 2011.

Jacobs, Jane M. *The Death and Life of Great American Cities*. New York: Random House, 1961.

Jacobs, Jane M. "Urban Geographies I: Still Thinking Cities Relationally." *Progress in Human Geography* 36, no. 3 (2012): 412–422.

Jaffe, Sarah. "Whose Recovery? A Year after Hurricane Sandy Hit, despite Community Efforts, Marginalized New Yorkers Aren't Back on Their Feet." *In These Times*, October 29, 2013.

Jaleel, Rana. "Into the Storm: Occupy Sandy and the New Sociality of Debt." Is This What Democracy Looks Like?, October 8, 2013. https://what-democracy-looks-like.org/into-the-storm-occupy-sandy-and-the-new-sociality-of-debt/.

Jasanoff, Sheila. "A New Climate for Society." *Theory, Culture and Society* 27, nos. 2–3 (2010): 233–253.

Jonge, Victor N. de. "From a Defensive to an Integrated Approach." In *Water Policy in the Netherlands: Integrated Management in a Densely Populated Delta*, edited by Stijn Reinhard and Henk Folmer, 17–46. Washington, DC: Resources for the Future, 2009.

Kagabu, Makoto, Jun Shimada, Robert Delinom, Toshio Nakamura, and Makoto Taniguchi. "Groundwater Age Rejuvenation Caused by Excessive Urban Pumping in Jakarta Area, Indonesia." *Hydrological Processes* 27, no. 18 (2013): 2591–2604.

Kaika, Maria. *City of Flows: Modernity, Nature, and the City*. New York: Routledge, 2005.

Kaika, Maria. "'Don't Call Me Resilient Again!': The New Urban Agenda as Immunology . . . Or . . . What Happens When Communities Refuse to Be Vaccinated with 'Smart Cities' and Indicators." *Environment and Urbanization* 29, no. 1 (2017): 89–102.

Keil, Roger. "Progress Report: Urban Political Ecology." *Urban Geography* 24, no. 8 (2003): 723–738.

Keil, Roger. "Progress Report: Urban Political Ecology." *Urban Geography* 26, no. 7 (2005): 640–651.

Khan, Mizan R., and J. Timmons Roberts. "Adaptation and International Climate Policy." *Wiley Interdisciplinary Reviews: Climate Change* 4, no. 3 (2013): 171–189.

Kimmelman, Michael. "Next Time, Libraries Could Be Our Shelters from the Storm." *New York Times*, October 2, 2013.

Klein, Naomi. *The Shock Doctrine: The Rise of Disaster Capitalism*. Toronto: Alfred A. Knopf Canada, 2007.

Klinenberg, Eric. *Heat Wave: A Social Autopsy of Disaster in Chicago*. Chicago: University of Chicago Press, 2002.

Knowledge for Climate. *Dutch Climate Adaptation Research*. Utrecht, Netherlands: Knowledge for Climate, 2012. https://edepot.wur.nl/342784.

Koolhaas, Rem, and Bruce Mau. *Small, Medium, Large, Extra-Large*. Edited by Jennifer Sigler. Rotterdam: 010; New York: Monacelli, 1995.

Kuks, Stefan M. M. "Institutional Evolution of the Dutch Water Board Model." In *Water Policy in the Netherlands: Integrated Management in a Densely Populated Delta*, edited by Stijn Reinhard and Henk Folmer, 155–170. Washington, DC: Resources for the Future, 2009.

Kusno, Abidin. *After the New Order: Space, Politics, and Jakarta*. Honolulu: University of Hawai'i Press, 2013.

Kusno, Abidin. *Behind the Postcolonial: Architecture, Urban Space, and Political Cultures in Indonesia*. London: Routledge, 2000.

Kusno, Abidin, Meredith Miller, and Etienne Turpin. "Urban Temporalities: Jakarta after the New Order: Abidin Kusno in Conversation with Meredith Miller and Etienne Turpin." *Scapegoat: Architecture, Landscape, Political Economy* 5 (Summer/Autumn 2013): 180–205.

Leaf, Michael. "Land Rights for Residential Development in Jakarta, Indonesia: The Colonial Roots of Contemporary Urban Dualism." *International Journal of Urban and Regional Research* 17, no. 4 (1993): 477–491.

Le Corbusier. *The Radiant City: Elements of a Doctrine of Urbanism to Be Used as the Basis of Our Machine-Age Civilization*. Translated by Pamela Knight, Eleanor Levieux, and Derek Coltman. New York: Orion, 1967.

Lefebvre, Henri. *The Production of Space*. Oxford: Blackwell, 1991.

Lefebvre, Henri. *The Urban Revolution*. Translated by Robert Bononno. Minneapolis: University of Minnesota Press, 2003.

Leichenko, Robin. "Climate Change and Urban Resilience." *Current Opinion in Environmental Sustainability* 3, no. 3 (2011): 164–168.

Leitner, Helga, Emma Colven, and Eric Sheppard. "Ecological Security for Whom? The Politics of Flood Alleviation and Urban Environmental Justice in Jakarta, Indonesia." In *The Routledge Companion to the Environmental Humanities*, edited by Ursula K. Heise, Jon Christensen, and Michelle Niemann, 194–205. Abingdon, UK: Routledge, 2017.

Leitner, Helga, Eric S. Sheppard, Kristin Sziarto, and Anant Maringanti. "Contesting Urban Futures: Decentering Neoliberalism." In *Contesting Neoliberalism: Urban Frontiers*, edited by Helga Leitner, Jamie Peck, and Eric S. Sheppard, 1–25. New York: Guilford, 2007.

LES Ready! *Getting LES Ready: Learning from Hurricane Sandy to Create a Community-Based Disaster Plan for the Future*. New York: Lower East Side Long Term Recovery Group, 2014. https://cdp.urbanjustice.org/sites/default/files/CDP.WEB.doc_Report_LESready_20141117.pdf.

Leussen, Wim van, and Kris Lulofs. "Governance of Water Resources." In *Water Policy in the Netherlands: Integrated Management in a Densely Populated Delta*, edited by Stijn Reinhard and Henk Folmer, 171–184. Washington, DC: Resources for the Future, 2009.

Long, Joshua, and Jennifer L. Rice. "From Sustainable Urbanism to Climate Urbanism." *Urban Studies* 56, no. 5 (2019): 992–1008.

Loukaitou-Sideris, Anastasia. "Addressing the Challenges of Urban Landscapes: Normative Goals for Urban Design." *Journal of Urban Design* 17, no. 4 (2012): 467–484.

Lynch, Kevin. *The Image of the City*. Cambridge, MA: MIT Press, 1960.

Maas, Winy, Jacob van Rijs, Richard Koek, and MVRDV. *FARMAX: Excursions on Density*. Rotterdam: 010, 1998.

MacKinnon, Danny, and Kate Driscoll Derickson. "From Resilience to Resourcefulness: A Critique of Resilience Policy and Activism." *Progress in Human Geography* 37, no. 2 (2013): 253–270.

Malesevic, Dusica Sue. "2 Years after Sandy, Who Will Get Shelter from the Storm? Only Some Downtown." *Downtown Express*, October 29, 2014.

Marcuse, Peter. "Security or Safety in Cities? The Threat of Terrorism after 9/11." *International Journal of Urban and Regional Research* 30, no. 4 (2006): 919–929.

Marshall, Tim. "Infrastructure Futures and Spatial Planning: Lessons from France, the Netherlands, Spain and the UK." *Progress in Planning* 89 (2014): 1–38.

Martínez-Alier, Juan. "Environmental Justice (Local and Global)." *Capitalism Nature Socialism* 8, no. 1 (1997): 91–107.

Massey, Doreen. "A Counterhegemonic Relationality of Place." In *Mobile Urbanism: Cities and Policymaking in the Global Age*, edited by Eugene McCann and Kevin Ward, 1–14. Minneapolis: University of Minnesota Press, 2011.

McCann, Eugene, and Kevin Ward. "Policy Assemblages, Mobilities and Mutations: Toward a Multidisciplinary Conversation." *Political Studies Review* 10, no. 3 (2012): 325–332.

McCarthy, Paul. "The Case of Jakarta, Indonesia." Understanding Slums: Case Studies for the Global Report on Human Settlements 2003. UN-Habitat, 2003. https://www.ucl.ac.uk/dpu-projects/Global_Report/cities/jakarta.htm.

McFarlane, Colin. "The Entrepreneurial Slum: Civil Society, Mobility and the Co-Production of Urban Development." *Urban Studies* 49, no. 13 (2012): 2795–2816.

McGee, T. G. "The Emergence of Desakota Regions in Asia: Expanding a Hypothesis." In *The Extended Metropolis: Settlement Transition in Asia*, edited by Norton Ginsburg, Bruce Koppel, and T. G. McGee, 3–25. Honolulu: University of Hawai'i Press, 1991.

McGranahan, Gordon, Deborah Balk, and Bridget Anderson. "The Rising Tide: Assessing the Risks of Climate Change and Human Settlements in Low Elevation Coastal Zones." *Environment and Urbanization* 19, no. 1 (2007): 17–37.

McGregor, Alisdair, Cole Roberts, and Fiona Cousins. *Two Degrees: The Built Environment and Our Changing Climate*. Abingdon, UK: Routledge, 2013.

McHarg, Ian L. *Design with Nature*. Garden City, NY: Published for the American Museum of Natural History by the Natural History Press, 1969.

McKittrick, Katherine. "On Plantations, Prisons, and a Black Sense of Place." *Social and Cultural Geography* 12, no. 8 (2011): 947–963.

McMichael, Philip. "World-Systems Analysis, Globalization, and Incorporated Comparison." *Journal of World-Systems Research* 6, no. 3 (2000): 668–689.

Meerow, Sara, Joshua P. Newell, and Melissa Stults. "Defining Urban Resilience: A Review." *Landscape and Urban Planning* 147 (2016): 38–49.

Mele, Christopher. *Selling the Lower East Side: Culture, Real Estate, and Resistance in New York City*. Minneapolis: University of Minnesota Press, 2000.

Mohai, Paul, David Pellow, and J. Timmons Roberts. "Environmental Justice." *Annual Review of Environment and Resources* 34 (2009): 405–430.

Molenaar, Arnoud, Jeroen Aerts, Piet Dircke, and Mandy Ikert. *Connecting Delta Cities 3: Resilient Cities and Climate Adaptation Strategies*. Rotterdam: Connecting Delta Cities, 2013. http://www.deltacityofthefuture.nl/documents/CDC_volume_3_Resilient_Cities_and_Climate_Adaptation_Strategies.pdf.

Mollenkopf, John H., and Manuel Castells, eds. *Dual City: Restructuring New York*. New York: Russell Sage Foundation, 1991.

Mrázek, Rudolf. *Engineers of Happy Land: Technology and Nationalism in a Colony*. Princeton, NJ: Princeton University Press, 2002.

Mumford, Eric Paul. *Defining Urban Design: CIAM Architects and the Formation of a Discipline, 1937–69*. New Haven, CT: Yale University Press, 2009.

Netherlands, Government of. "Speech by Melanie Schultz, at the Round Table on Coastal Development, Borobodur Hotel, Jakarta." Government of the Netherlands—Documents and publications—Speeches, April 2, 2014. http://www.rijksoverheid.nl/documenten-en-publicaties/toespraken/2014/04/02/speech-for-melanie-schultz-at-the-round-table-on-coastal-development-borobodur-hotel-jakarta.html (link has since expired).

Netherlands, Ministry of Economic Affairs and Climate Policy. "Top Sectors in the Netherlands." Ministerie van Economische Zaken en Klimaat, March 16, 2016. https://www.topsectoren.nl/publicaties/brochures/2016/03/16/hoe-en-waarom-topsector-engels.

Netherlands Enterprise Agency (RVO), Ministry of Economic Affairs and Climate. "Evaluatie Partners voor Water 3 (2010–2015)," May 2016. https://www.rvo.nl/sites/default/files/2020/05/Evaluatie Partners voor Water 3 2016.pdf.

Netherlands Water Partnership. "About NWP." Netherlands Water Partnership. Accessed February 1, 2021. https://www.netherlandswaterpartnership.com/about-nwp.

New York City Comptroller's Office. *Income Inequality in New York City*. New York: Comptroller of the City of New York, 2012. http://comptroller.nyc.gov/wp-content/uploads/documents/NYC_IncomeInequality_v17.pdf.

New York City Mayor's Office of Management and Budget (OMB). "Impact of Hurricane Sandy." Accessed February 1, 2021. https://www1.nyc.gov/site/cdbgdr/about/About Hurricane Sandy.page.

New York City Panel on Climate Change (NPCC). "Building the Knowledge Base for Climate Resiliency: New York City Panel on Climate Change 2015 Report." Edited by Cynthia Rosenzweig and William Solecki. *Annals of the New York Academy of Sciences* 1336, no. 1 (2015): 1–150.

New York City Panel on Climate Change (NPCC). "Climate Change Adaptation in New York City: Building a Risk Management Response." Edited by Cynthia Rosenzweig and William Solecki. *Annals of the New York Academy of Sciences* 1196, no. 1 (2010): 1–354.

New York State Legislature 517 (2013). 2013 Amendment to Hudson River Park Act, Ch. 517 § (2013).

Nordenson, Guy, Catherine Seavitt, and Adam Yarinsky. *On the Water | Palisade Bay*. Ostfildern: Hatje Cantz; New York: Museum of Modern Art, 2010.

NYS 2100 Commission. *Recommendations to Improve the Strength and Resilience of the Empire State's Infrastructure*. Albany, NY: NYS 2100 Commission, January 2013. http://www.governor.ny.gov/sites/governor.ny.gov/files/archive/assets/documents/NYS2100.pdf.

Open Technology Institute (OTI). *Case Study: Red Hook Initiative WiFi and Tidepools*. Washington, DC: New America Foundation, 2013. https://commotionwireless.net/files/rhiwifi_tidepools_casestudy.pdf.

Orff, Kate. *Toward an Urban Ecology*. New York: Monacelli, 2016.

Osborne, Natalie. "Intersectionality and Kyriarchy: A Framework for Approaching Power and Social Justice in Planning and Climate Change Adaptation." *Planning Theory* 14, no. 2 (2015): 130–151.

Padawangi, Rita. "Climate Change and the North Coast of Jakarta: Environmental Justice and the Social Construction of Space in Urban Poor Communities." In *Urban Areas and Global Climate Change*, edited by William G. Holt, 321–340. Bingley, UK: Emerald, 2012.

Paprocki, Kasia. "Threatening Dystopias: Development and Adaptation Regimes in Bangladesh." *Annals of the American Association of Geographers* 108, no. 4 (2018): 955–973.

Peake, Linda, Darren Patrick, Rajyashree N. Reddy, Gökbörü Sarp Tanyildiz, Sue Ruddick, and Roza Tchoukaleyska. "Placing Planetary Urbanization in Other Fields of Vision." *Environment and Planning D: Society and Space* 36, no. 3 (2018): 374–386.

Peck, Jamie. "Geographies of Policy: From Transfer-Diffusion to Mobility-Mutation." *Progress in Human Geography* 35, no. 6 (2011): 773–797.

Peck, Jamie, and Nikolas Theodore. *Fast Policy: Experimental Statecraft at the Thresholds of Neoliberalism*. Minneapolis: University of Minnesota Press, 2015.

Pelling, Mark. *Adaptation to Climate Change: From Resilience to Transformation*. Abingdon, UK: Routledge, 2011.

Pelling, Mark, Karen O'Brien, and David Matyas. "Adaptation and Transformation." *Climatic Change* 133, no. 1 (2015): 113–127.

Pellow, David N. "Environmental Inequality Formation: Toward a Theory of Environmental Injustice." *American Behavioral Scientist* 43, no. 4 (2000): 581–601.

Pellow, David N. *Resisting Global Toxics: Transnational Movements for Environmental Justice*. Cambridge, MA: MIT Press, 2007.

Pike, Andy, Stuart Dawley, and John Tomaney. "Resilience, Adaptation and Adaptability." *Cambridge Journal of Regions, Economy and Society* 3, no. 1 (2010): 1–12.

Pizzigati, Sam. "New York, New York, What a Less than Wonderful Town." Inequality.org, June 20, 2018. https://inequality.org/great-divide/new-york-new-york-less-wonderful-town/.

Pratiwo, and Peter J. M. Nas. "Jakarta: Conflicting Directions." In *Directors of Urban Change in Asia*, edited by Peter J. M. Nas, 68–82. Abingdon, UK: Routledge, 2005.

Pulido, Laura. "Rethinking Environmental Racism: White Privilege and Urban Development in Southern California." *Annals of the Association of American Geographers* 90, no. 1 (2000): 12–40.

Putri, Prathiwi Widyatmi. "Insurgent Planner: Transgressing the Technocratic State of Postcolonial Jakarta." *Urban Studies* 57, no. 9 (2019): 1845–1865.

Putri, Prathiwi Widyatmi, and Aryani Sari Rahmanti. "Jakarta Waterscape." *Nakhara: Journal of Environmental Design and Planning* 6 (2010): 59–76.

Rademacher, Anne. *Reigning the River: Urban Ecologies and Political Transformation in Kathmandu.* Durham, NC: Duke University Press, 2011.

Ranganathan, Malini, and Eve Bratman. "From Urban Resilience to Abolitionist Climate Justice in Washington, DC." *Antipode*, June 28, 2019. https://doi.org/10.1111/anti.12555.

Rebuild By Design. "Projects Are Moving Forward," June 3, 2015. http://www.rebuildbydesign.org/news-and-events/updates/projects-are-moving-forward.

Rebuild By Design, "Promoting Resilience Post-Sandy Through Innovative Planning and Design." Design Brief, June 21, 2013, http://portal.hud.gov/hudportal/documents/huddoc?id=REBUILDBYDESIGNBrief.pdf.

Red Hook Initiative. *Red Hook Initiative: A Community Response to Hurricane Sandy.* Brooklyn, NY: Red Hook Initiative, 2013.

Reid, Hannah, and David Satterthwaite. "Climate Change and Cities: Why Urban Agendas Are Central to Adaptation and Mitigation." *Sustainable Development Opinion*, December 2007. http://pubs.iied.org/pdfs/17025IIED.pdf.

Rijke, Jeroen, Sebastiaan van Herk, Chris Zevenbergen, and Richard Ashley. "Room for the River: Delivering Integrated River Basin Management in the Netherlands." *International Journal of River Basin Management* 10, no. 4 (2012): 369–382.

Roberts, J. Timmons, and Bradley C. Parks. *A Climate of Injustice: Global Inequality, North-South Politics, and Climate Policy.* Cambridge, MA: MIT Press, 2007.

Roberts, J. Timmons, and Bradley C. Parks. "Ecologically Unequal Exchange, Ecological Debt, and Climate Justice: The History and Implications of Three Related Ideas for a New Social Movement." *International Journal of Comparative Sociology* 50, nos. 3–4 (2009): 385–409.

Robinson, Jennifer. "Global and World Cities: A View from off the Map." *International Journal of Urban and Regional Research* 26, no. 3 (2002): 531–554.

Rockefeller Foundation. *Rebound: Building a More Resilient World*. New York: Rockefeller Foundation, 2013. https://www.rockefellerfoundation.org/report/rebound-building-a-more-resilient-world/.

Rodin, Judith. *The Resilience Dividend: Being Strong in a World Where Things Go Wrong*. New York: PublicAffairs, 2014.

Rolnik, Raquel, and United Nations Human Rights Council (UN HRC). "Report of the Special Rapporteur on Adequate Housing as a Component of the Right to an Adequate Standard of Living, and on the Right to Non-Discrimination in This Context on Her Mission to Indonesia." United Nations Human Rights Council, December 26, 2013. https://www.ohchr.org/EN/HRBodies/HRC/RegularSessions/Session25/Documents/A-HRC-25-54-Add1_en.doc.

Romero-Lankao, Patricia, Harriet Bulkeley, Mark Pelling, Sarah Burch, David J. Gordon, Joyeeta Gupta, Craig Johnson, Priya Kurian, Emma Lecavalier, and David Simon. "Urban Transformative Potential in a Changing Climate." *Nature Climate Change* 8, no. 9 (2018): 754.

Rosenzweig, Cynthia, William D. Solecki, Reginald Blake, Malcolm Bowman, Craig Faris, Vivien Gornitz, Radley Horton, et al. "Developing Coastal Adaptation to Climate Change in the New York City Infrastructure-Shed: Process, Approach, Tools, and Strategies." *Climatic Change* 106, no. 1 (2011): 93–127.

Rosenzweig, Cynthia, William Solecki, Stephen A. Hammer, and Shagun Mehrotra. "Cities Lead the Way in Climate-Change Action." *Nature* 467, no. 7318 (2010): 909–911.

Rosenzweig, Roy, and Elizabeth Blackmar. *The Park and the People: A History of Central Park*. Ithaca, NY: Cornell University Press, 1992.

Rotterdam Climate Initiative. Rotterdam Climate Change Adaptation Strategy. Rotterdam: City of Rotterdam, October 2013. http://www.urbanisten.nl/wp/wp-content/uploads/UB_RAS_EN_lr.pdf.

Roy, Ananya. "Paradigms of Propertied Citizenship: Transnational Techniques of Analysis." *Urban Affairs Review* 38, no. 4 (2003): 463–491.

Roy, Ananya. "The 21st-Century Metropolis: New Geographies of Theory." *Regional Studies* 43, no. 6 (2009): 819–830.

Roy, Ananya. "Urbanisms, Worlding Practices and the Theory of Planning." *Planning Theory* 10, no. 1 (2011): 6–15.

Roy, Ananya. "Who's Afraid of Postcolonial Theory?" *International Journal of Urban and Regional Research* 40, no. 1 (January 1, 2016): 200–209.

Roy, Ananya, and Aihwa Ong, eds. *Worlding Cities: Asian Experiments and the Art of Being Global*. Chichester, UK: Wiley-Blackwell, 2011.

Salim, Wilmar, and Tommy Firman. "Governing the Jakarta City-Region: History, Challenges, Risks and Strategies." In *Planning Asian Cities: Risks and Resilience*, edited by Stephen Hamnett and Dean Forbes, 240–263. Abingdon, UK: Routledge, 2011.

Samirin, Wijayanto. "Blusukan." *Kompas*, January 12, 2013. http://nasional.kompas.com/read/2013/01/12/11232457/.Blusukan.

Sassen, Saskia. *The Global City: New York, London, Tokyo*. Princeton, NJ: Princeton University Press, 1991.

Satterthwaite, David. "The Urban Challenge Revisited." *Environment: Science and Policy for Sustainable Development* 49, no. 9 (2007): 6–17.

Savirani, Amalinda, and Edward Aspinall. "Adversarial Linkages: The Urban Poor and Electoral Politics in Jakarta." *Journal of Current Southeast Asian Affairs* 36, no. 3 (2017): 3–34.

Sayer, Andrew. "Defining the Urban." *GeoJournal* 9, no. 3 (1984): 279–284.

Schama, Simon. *The Embarrassment of Riches: An Interpretation of Dutch Culture in the Golden Age*. New York: Knopf, 1987.

Schlosberg, David. "Reconceiving Environmental Justice: Global Movements and Political Theories." *Environmental Politics* 13, no. 3 (2004): 517–540.

Schlosberg, David, and Lisette B. Collins. "From Environmental to Climate Justice: Climate Change and the Discourse of Environmental Justice." *Wiley Interdisciplinary Reviews: Climate Change* 5, no. 3 (2014): 359–374.

Schmeltz, Michael T., Sonia K. González, Liza Fuentes, Amy Kwan, Anna Ortega-Williams, and Lisa Pilar Cowan. "Lessons from Hurricane Sandy: A Community Response in Brooklyn, New York." *Journal of Urban Health* 90, no. 5 (2013): 799–809.

Scott, Allen J., and Michael Storper. "The Nature of Cities: The Scope and Limits of Urban Theory." *International Journal of Urban and Regional Research* 39, no. 1 (2015): 1–15.

Seavitt, Catherine. "Rising Currents: High Stakes." MoMA Inside / Out, January 26, 2010, http://www.moma.org/explore/inside_out/2010/01/26/rising-currents-high-stakes.

Setiawati, Indah. "Jokowi Inspires Urban Poor to See Light at the End of the Tunnel." *Jakarta Post*, February 18, 2013.

Shatkin, Gavin, "Planned Grab: Capitalizing on Land Dualism in New Order Jakarta." In *Cities for Profit: The Real Estate Turn in Asia's Urban Politics*, 102–136. Ithaca, NY: Cornell University Press, 2017.

Shepherd, Ariel. "Jakarta, Indonesia." In *Grounding Knowledge: Reflections on Community-Driven Urban Practices in South-East Asia*, by Johanna Brugman, Barbara Dovarch, Zahra Kassam, Francesco Pasta, and Ariel Shepherd, 50–81. London, Bangkok: Bartlett Development Planning Unit (DPU), Community Architects Network (CAN), Asian Coalition for Housing Rights (ACHR), 2013. https://issuu.com/dpu-ucl/docs/grounding_knowledge_24.2.14_new.

Shi, Linda, Eric Chu, Isabelle Anguelovski, Alexander Aylett, Jessica Debats, Kian Goh, Todd Schenk, et al. "Roadmap towards Justice in Urban Climate Adaptation Research." *Nature Climate Change* 6 (February 2016): 131–137.

Sherwell, Philip. "$40bn to Save Jakarta: The Story of the Great Garuda." *The Guardian*, November 22, 2016.

Shorto, Russell. "How to Think Like the Dutch in a Post-Sandy World." *New York Times*, April 9, 2014.

Silver, Christopher. *Planning the Megacity: Jakarta in the Twentieth Century*. Abingdon, UK: Routledge, 2008.

Simone, AbdouMaliq. *Jakarta: Drawing the City Near*. Minneapolis: University of Minnesota Press, 2014.

Simone, AbdouMaliq. "On the Worlding of African Cities." *African Studies Review* 44, no. 2 (2001): 15–41.

Sledge, Matt. "Hurricane Sandy Damage in New York by-the-Numbers." *Huffington Post*, December 3, 2012. http://www.huffingtonpost.com/2012/12/03/hurricane-sandy-damage-new-york_n_2234335.html.

Smith, Neil. *The New Urban Frontier: Gentrification and the Revanchist City*. Abingdon, UK: Routledge, 1996.

Smith, Neil. "Toward a Theory of Gentrification: A Back to the City Movement by Capital, Not People." *Journal of the American Planning Association* 45, no. 4 (1979): 538–548.

Smith, Neil. *Uneven Development: Nature, Capital, and the Production of Space*. 3rd ed. New York: Blackwell, 2008.

Smith, Neil, and James DeFilippis. "The Reassertion of Economics: 1990s Gentrification in the Lower East Side." *International Journal of Urban and Regional Research* 23, no. 4 (1999): 638–653.

Soja, Edward W. *Postmetropolis: Critical Studies of Cities and Regions*. Oxford: Blackwell, 2000.

Soja, Edward W. *Seeking Spatial Justice*. Minneapolis: University of Minnesota Press, 2010.

Soja, Edward W., and Miguel Kanai. "The Urbanization of the World." In *The Endless City: The Urban Age Project by the London School of Economics and Deutsche*

Bank's Alfred Herrhausen Society, edited by Richard Burdett and Deyan Sudjic, 54–69. London: Phaidon, 2007.

Some, Wawan, Wardah Hafidz, and Gabriela Sauter. "Renovation Not Relocation: The Work of Paguyuban Warga Strenkali (PWS) in Indonesia." *Environment and Urbanization* 21, no. 2 (October 1, 2009): 463–475.

Sommeiller, Estelle, and Mark Price. *The New Gilded Age: Income Inequality in the U.S. by State, Metropolitan Area, and County*. Washington, DC: Economic Policy Institute, 2018. https://www.epi.org/files/pdf/147963.pdf.

Sorkin, Michael. "Too Rich, Too Skinny." *Architectural Record*, May 16, 2015. http://archrecord.construction.com/features/2015/1505-too-rich-too-skinny.asp.

Spirn, Anne Whiston. *The Granite Garden: Urban Nature and Human Design*. New York: Basic Books, 1984.

Steiner, Frederick, Richard Weller, Karen M'Closkey, and Billy Fleming. *Design with Nature Now*. Cambridge, MA: Lincoln Institute of Land Policy, 2019.

Stive, Marcel, and Han Vrijling. "Draining, Dredging, Reclaiming: The Technology of Making a Dry, Safe, and Sustainable Delta Landscape." In *Delta Urbanism: The Netherlands*, edited by Han Meyer, Inge Bobbink, and Steffen Nijhuis, 20–43. Chicago: American Planning Association, 2010.

Stoler, Ann Laura. "IMPERIAL DEBRIS: Reflections on Ruins and Ruination." *Cultural Anthropology* 23, no. 2 (2008): 191–219.

Superstorm Research Lab. "A Tale of Two Sandys," December 21, 2013. http://superstormresearchlab.org/white-paper/.

Susetyo, Grace. "Once Upon a Sinking City: The Perpetual Floods of Jakarta." Indonesia Expat, February 25, 2013. https://indonesiaexpat.biz/travel/history-culture/once-upon-a-sinking-city-the-perpetual-floods-of-jakarta/.

Swyngedouw, Erik. "The City as a Hybrid: On Nature, Society and Cyborg Urbanization." *Capitalism Nature Socialism* 7, no. 2 (1996): 65–80.

Swyngedouw, Erik, and Nikolas C. Heynen. "Urban Political Ecology, Justice and the Politics of Scale." *Antipode* 35, no. 5 (2003): 898–918.

Syukrizal, Ade, Wardah Hafidz, and Gabriela Sauter. "Reconstructing Life after the Tsunami: The Work of Uplink Banda Aceh in Indonesia." International Institute for Environment and Development. London, UK, August 2009.

Tanner, Thomas, Swenja Surminski, Emily Wilkinson, Robert Reid, Jun Rentschler, and Sumati Rajput. *The Triple Dividend of Resilience: Realising Development Goals through the Multiple Benefits of Disaster Risk Management*. London: Overseas Development Institute; Washington DC: World Bank, 2015.

Tierney, Kathleen. "Resilience and the Neoliberal Project: Discourses, Critiques, Practices—and Katrina." *American Behavioral Scientist* 59, no. 10 (2015): 1327–1342.

Tirella, Joseph. *Tomorrow-Land: The 1964–65 World's Fair and the Transformation of America.* Guilford, CT: Lyons, 2014.

Tokar, Brian. "Movements for Climate Justice in the US and Worldwide." In *Routledge Handbook of the Climate Change Movement*, edited by Matthias Dietz and Heiko Garrelts, 131–146. Abingdon, UK: Routledge, 2014.

Turpin, Etienne, Adam Bobbette, and Meredith Miller, eds. *Jakarta: Architecture + Adaptation.* Depok: Universitas Indonesia Press, 2013.

Two Bridges Neighborhood Council. *Decade After 9/11: A Look at Who We Are Now. How Gentrification Reshaped Manhattan Community Board 3.* New York: Two Bridges Neighborhood Council, 2011. http://www.nyc.gov/html/mancb3/downloads/cb3docs/TwoBridgesDemographicAnalysis.pdf.

UN-Habitat. *The Challenge of Slums: Global Report on Human Settlements 2003.* London: Earthscan, 2003.

United Nations Conference on Housing and Sustainable Urban Development (Habitat III). *New Urban Agenda.* Quito, Ecuador: United Nations, 2017. https://habitat3.org/the-new-urban-agenda/.

United States Geological Survey (USGS). "Hudson River Freshwater Discharge at New York, NY (Mouth)." Accessed December 12, 2020. http://ny.water.usgs.gov/projects/dialer_plots/Hudson_R_at_NYC_Freshwater_Discharge.htm.

Urban Institute. *Evaluation: Rebuild by Design Phase I.* New York: Rockefeller Foundation, 2014. http://www.urban.org/sites/default/files/alfresco/publication-pdfs/413256-Evaluation-Rebuild-by-Design-Phase-I.PDF.

US Department of Housing and Urban Development (HUD). "Community Development Block Grant Disaster Recovery Program." HUD Exchange. Accessed December 12, 2020. https://www.hudexchange.info/programs/cdbg-dr/.

US Department of Housing and Urban Development (HUD). "HUD Announces Winning Proposals from the 'Rebuild By Design' Competition." June 2, 2014. HUD Archives. https://archives.hud.gov/news/2014/pr14-063.cfm.

US Department of Housing and Urban Development (HUD) and Netherlands, Ministry of Infrastructure and the Environment. "Memorandum of Understanding between the Department of Housing and Urban Development of the United States of America and the Ministry of Infrastructure and the Environment of the Kingdom of the Netherlands in the Fields of Sustainable Urban Development, Water Management, and Integrated Planning and Cross Sector Collaboration." Washington, DC, March 4, 2013. http://portal.hud.gov/hudportal/documents/huddoc?id=OPA3-4-13DOC.PDF.

Vale, Lawrence J. *Architecture, Power, and National Identity*. New Haven, CT: Yale University Press, 1992.

Vale, Lawrence J. "The Politics of Resilient Cities: Whose Resilience and Whose City?" *Building Research and Information* 42, no. 2 (2014): 191–201.

Vale, Lawrence J., Shomon Shamsuddin, and Kian Goh. "Tsunami+10: Housing Banda Aceh after Disaster." *Places Journal*, December 2014. https://placesjournal.org/article/tsunami-housing-banda-aceh-after-disaster/.

Van Der Most, Herman, and Mark Wehrung. "Dealing with Uncertainty in Flood Risk Assessment of Dike Rings in the Netherlands." *Natural Hazards* 36, nos. 1–2 (2005): 191–206.

Van Kempen, Ronald, and Hugo Priemus. "Undivided Cities in the Netherlands: Present Situation and Political Rhetoric." *Housing Studies* 14, no. 5 (1999): 641–657.

Van Koningsveld, Mark, Jan P. M. Mulder, Marcel J. F. Stive, L. Van Der Valk, and A. W. Van Der Weck. "Living with Sea-Level Rise and Climate Change: A Case Study of the Netherlands." *Journal of Coastal Research* 242 (2008): 367–379.

Van Veen, Johan. *Dredge Drain Reclaim: The Art of a Nation*. The Hague: Martinus Nijhoff, 1962.

Van Voorst, Roanne, and Rita Padawangi. "Floods and Forced Evictions in Jakarta." *New Mandala*, August 21, 2015. https://www.newmandala.org/floods-and-forced-evictions-in-jakarta/.

Verisk Maplecroft. "Environmental Risk Outlook 2020," February 27, 2020. https://www.maplecroft.com/insights/analysis/download-the-environmental-risk-outlook-2020/.

Wachsmuth, David, Daniel Aldana Cohen, and Hillary Angelo. "Expand the Frontiers of Urban Sustainability." *Nature News* 536, no. 7617 (2016): 391.

Wade, Matt. "Hyper-Planning Jakarta: The Great Garuda and Planning the Global Spectacle." *Singapore Journal of Tropical Geography* 40, no. 1 (2019): 158–172.

Waldheim, Charles. "Landscape as Urbanism." In *The Landscape Urbanism Reader*, edited by Charles Waldheim, 36–53. New York: Princeton Architectural Press, 2006.

Wall, Diana diZerega, Nan A. Rothschild, and Cynthia Copeland. "Seneca Village and Little Africa: Two African American Communities in Antebellum New York City." *Historical Archaeology* 41, no. 1 (2008): 97–107.

Warner, Sam Bass. *The Urban Wilderness: A History of the American City*. New York: Harper and Row, 1972.

Wasik, Bill. "#Riot: Self-Organized, Hyper-Networked Revolts—Coming to a City Near You." *Wired*, January 16, 2012. http://www.wired.com/magazine/2011/12/ff-riots/.

White House, Office of the Press Secretary. "Executive Order—Establishing the Hurricane Sandy Rebuilding Task Force." December 7, 2012. https://www.whitehouse.gov/the-press-office/2012/12/07/executive-order-establishing-hurricane-sandy-rebuilding-task-force.

White House, Office of the Press Secretary. "FACT SHEET: National Disaster Resilience Competition." June 14, 2014. http://www.whitehouse.gov/the-press-office/2014/06/14/fact-sheet-national-disaster-resilience-competition.

Wijsman, Katinka, and Mathieu Feagan. "Rethinking Knowledge Systems for Urban Resilience: Feminist and Decolonial Contributions to Just Transformations." *Environmental Science and Policy* 98 (2019): 70–76.

Williams, Raymond. *The Country and the City*. New York: Oxford University Press, 1975.

Williams, Raymond. *Problems in Materialism and Culture: Selected Essays*. London: Verso, 1980.

Wilson, Elizabeth, and Jake Piper. *Spatial Planning and Climate Change*. Abingdon, UK: Routledge, 2010.

Wirth, Louis. "Urbanism as a Way of Life." *American Journal of Sociology* 44 (1938): 1–24.

Wolsink, Maarten. "River Basin Approach and Integrated Water Management: Governance Pitfalls for the Dutch Space-Water-Adjustment Management Principle." *Geoforum* 37, no. 4 (2006): 473–487.

World Bank. *Turn down the Heat: Why a 4°C Wvarmer World Must Be Avoided*. Report for the World Bank by the Potsdam Institute for Climate Impact Research and Climate Analytics. Washington, DC: World Bank, 2012. http://issuu.com/world.bank.publications/docs/turn_down_the_heat.

Zim, Larry, Mel Lerner, and Herbert Rolfes. *The World of Tomorrow: The 1939 New York World's Fair*. New York: Harper and Row, 1988.

Zonneveld, Wil. "Governing a Complex Delta." In *Delta Urbanism: The Netherlands*, edited by Han Meyer, Inge Bobbink, and Steffen Nijhuis, 101–113. Chicago: American Planning Association, 2010.

Zukin, Sharon. *Loft Living: Culture and Capital in Urban Change*. Baltimore, MD: Johns Hopkins University Press, 1982.

Zukin, Sharon. "Memo from Manhattan: The High Line at Dusk." OUPblog, September 23, 2010. http://blog.oup.com/2010/09/high-line/.

Index

Note: Figures and tables are indicated by "f" and "t" respectively, following page numbers.

ABC No Rio, 58
Aboutaleb, Ahmed, 96
ACCCRN. *See* Asian Cities Climate Change Resilience Network
"Action Agenda for Architecture and Spatial Design 2013–2016," 222n15
Activism. *See also* Kampung design activism
  art and, 58
  climate justice and, 11
  counternetworks and, 162–164
  counterplans and, 164–166
  environmental justice and, 11
  kampungs and, 45, 70–75, 86, 124–130
  urban resistance and, 233n10
  West Village with queer struggles and, 211n13
Adaptation
  climate change and, 5, 47
  Jakarta, 46, 120
  more radical, 176–177
  New York City, 27
  resilience and, 5
  Rotterdam, 39, 41, 96
  sociospatial typology of, 168–171, 169f
Affirmations, methodological excursions and, 190–191

African Americans, 25, 55, 211n10
Aga Khan Award for Architecture, 67
Ahok. *See* Purnama, Basuki "Ahok" Tjahaja
Amazon, fires in, 7
American Institute for Architects, 204n26
Angola, 225n47
Anthropocene, 5
Antiglobalization activism, 205n39
Arab Spring, 162
ARCADIS, 100, 107, 109, 231n40
Architecture, 67
  economy influencing, 94
  International Architecture Biennale Rotterdam, 87, 96
  in Rotterdam, 40
Architecture for Humanity, 204n26
Architecture Sans Frontierès, 230n31
Arts
  activism and, 58
  Municipal Art Society, 37, 64
Arup, 116, 172, 228n3
Asian Cities Climate Change Resilience Network (ACCCRN), 104, 203n22, 228n3
Athens Charter of 1933, 209n68
Azwar, Sylvira, 70

Bakema, Jacob, 40
Bali Principles of Climate Justice, 205n39
Ban, Ki-moon, 151
Banda Aceh, 230n30
Bangladesh, 100, 102, 225n47, 225n52
Baruch Houses, 59
Basquiat, Jean-Michel, 58
Baswedan, Anies, 149–150, 184
BIG team, 61–62, 132, 132f, 135, 139, 143, 231n49
"BIG U" proposal, 61–62, 132, 231n41, 232n53
  as high profile, 231n49
  rendering of, 132f
Bijlmermeer development, 98
Bill and Melinda Gates Foundation, 151
Bloomberg, Michael, 26–27
Bloomberg Philanthropies, 224n38
Blusukan (walking around at grassroots level), 70, 158, 219n57
Boer, Florian, 98, 118, 226n64
Bons, Kees, 101, 123
Bouncing back, 8, 9, 10, 168, 204n27
Brasília, 233n3
Bratman, Eve, 234n15
Breezy Point, Queens, 50, 51f
Brenner, Neil, 7
Brinkman, JanJaap, 122
Brinkman, Johannes, 122
Brooklyn Bridge Park, 25
Brown, Anna, 118
Bryant Park Corporation, 25
Bukit Duri, 67f, 73, 74, 84
Bulkeley, Harriet, 17
Bullard, Robert, 11

C40 Cities, 6, 37, 224n38
Castells, Manuel, 112, 180
Cautions, methodological excursions and, 190–191
CDBG–DR. *See* Community Development Block Grants–Disaster Recovery

CDC. *See* Connecting Delta Cities
Central Park, NYC
  eminent domain in, 211n10
  environmental planning and, 25
  Seneca Village and, 25, 211n10
Central Park Conservancy, 25
Cha, Theresa Hak Kyung, 23
Chakrabarty, Dipesh, 5
Changing Course competition, New Orleans, 46
Chester, Amy, 65, 66, 117–118, 139, 141
China, 40, 225n47
CIAM. *See* Congrès Internationaux d'Architecture Moderne
Ciliwung Merdeka (Free Ciliwung), 36, 73, 73f, 75, 86, 126, 128f, 184, 188
Ciliwung River, 33, 35f, 74f, 150f
Cité Industrielle, 209n68
Citibank, 224n38
Cities. *See also* Jakarta; New York City; Rotterdam
  ACCCRN, 104, 203n22, 228n3
  C40 Cities, 6, 37, 224n38
  CDC, 39, 99–100, 102, 224n38
  climate change and future of, 2, 4–8
  climate proof, 7
  critical interrelationships, 46–48
  cyborg, 15
  The Death and Life of Great American Cities, 209n68
  dual, 52
  future proof, 7
  GHG emissions and, 7
  to globe, 99–103
  The Image of the City, 209n68
  kampungs and, 66–70
  nation states to, 103–106
  100 Resilient Cities, 6, 9, 204n25, 223n22, 228n3
  plans, counterplans and global networks, 42–46
  revanchist, 24
  Rotterdam Water City 2035 vision, 96

Index 263

sites and strategies, 23–42
urban regions and interconnections among primary plans, 43f
"City Resilience Framework," 172, 228n3
Clifton, Lucille, 149
Climate. *See* Climate change
Climate change
 ACCCRN, 104, 203n22, 228n3
 C40 Cities Climate Leadership group, 224n38
 cities influenced by, 2, 4–8
 climate proof, 3, 7
 Deltas in Times of Climate Change conference, 37, 47, 100, 102, 103f, 154f
 environmental planning and, 167
 IPCC, 5, 6
 Jakarta Climate Change Task Force, 70
 metropolitanization of, 7, 112
 NPCC, 27
 Planning for Climate Change, 227n1
 planning in NYC, 26–27
 poverty and, 9–10
 preparedness, 66, 96
 resiliency initiatives, 204n25
 social and spatial urban development and, 3, 152
 spatial planning and, 115–116
 Spatial Planning and Climate Change, 227n1
 UNFCCC, 6
 urban design and, 115–120
 urban futures, 168–177
 vulnerability to, 31, 213n29
 water management and, 94–96
Climate change, spatial politics of
 with contestation, nature of, 154–156
 with flows, nature of, 156–157
 plans and counterplans, 157–159
 political ecology of design and, 152–161
 reflection and synthesis, theoretical, 159–161

"Climate Change Adaptation in New York City" (NPCC), 27
Climate justice
 Bali Principles of Climate Justice, 205n39
 with climate change and future of cities, 4–8
 counternetworks and, 162–164
 counterplans and, 164–166
 EJ and, 12
 International Climate Justice Network, 13, 205n39
 resilience and, 8–11
 support for, 11–13
 urban futures and, 1–4
 urban movements for, 161–168
 with urban spatial climate politics, 13–14
 urban waves and, 166–168
Climate Justice Alliance, 13
Climate politics
 just urban spatial, 13–14
 weather and, 235n25
Clinton Climate Initiative, 224n38
Clinton Global Initiative, 204n26
Coalition building, 61, 70, 86–87, 125–126, 156
Coenen, Victor, 103f, 122
Cohen, Daniel Aldana, 235n25
Colombia, 225n47, 225n52
Colonialism, 32, 42, 104, 108, 153
 colonial city, 66, 75
Community, resiliency initiatives, 3, 56, 146
Community Development Block Grants–Disaster Recovery (CDBG–DR), 29, 46, 64, 232n53
Community groups, 2, 60, 85, 137, 138, 155
Con Edison, 28f, 59
Congrès Internationaux d'Architecture Moderne (CIAM), 209n68

Connecting Delta Cities (CDC), 39, 99–100, 102, 224n38
Contestation
 coalition building and, 86–87
 Hurricane Sandy and, 50–52
 Jakarta and nature of, 49, 66–81
 with knowledge, local, 85–86
 Lower East Side and, 58–62
 marginalization and urban environmental change, 81–84
 nature of, 154–156
 NYC and nature of, 49, 50–66
 Rebuild By Design and, 62–66
 Red Hook and, 52–58
 Rotterdam and nature of, 49
 with shared struggle and resilience, 84–85
 terrains of, 141–144
 urban marginalization and nature of, 14–16
COP15, 12
Copenhagen, 224n38
Costs
 design, 231n40, 231n41
 Hurricane Sandy and economic, 1, 51
Counternetworks
 climate justice and, 162–164
 diagram of, 165f
Counterplans
 as alternate narratives, 3, 43f, 44–45
 climate justice and, 164–166
 with spatial politics of climate change, 157–159
 synthesis of plans, connections and, 163t
Cousins, Fiona, 116
Crawford, Jenny, 227n1
Cronon, William, 15
Cuomo, Andrew, 28, 51
Cyborg cities, 15

Davis, Scott, 64
Davoudi, Simin, 227n1

Deaths
 Hurricane Sandy, 1, 50–51
 Jakarta flood, 1
 North Sea Flood, 92
The Death and Life of Great American Cities (Jacobs, Jane), 209n68
De Blasio, Bill, 52
"Declaiming Waters none may dread" (Dickinson), 89
Delta Commission, 39, 92, 94, 97
Deltares, 75, 90, 100–101
Deltas in Times of Climate Change conference, 37, 47, 100, 102, 103f, 154f
Delta Works, 38–39, 92, 93f, 103, 144, 222n9
Department of Housing and Urban Development (HUD), US, 27–28, 29, 37, 46, 62, 231n40
 Rebuild By Design and, 64–65, 91
 role of, 104
Desakota, 32
Design. *See also* Kampung design activism; Political ecology of design; Rebuild By Design
 activism, 124–130
 climate change and urban, 115–120
 costs, 231n40, 231n41
 explaining, 119–120
 imaginaries of urban spatial politics, 17–19
 Kampung design activism, 37, 188
 political ecology of, 20
 Resilient by Design Bay Area Challenge, 228n6
 worldview of, 116–119
Design with Nature (McHarg), 228n6
De Soto, Hernando, 129
Dickinson, Emily, 89
Dictee (Cha), 23
Disaster recovery
 CDBG–DR, 29, 46, 64, 232n53
 climate change preparedness and, 66

Index 265

with knowledge, local, 156
poverty and post-, 232n53
RHI and, 29–31, 55–58
Disaster Relief Appropriations Act of 2013, 64
DKI Jakarta, 31, 68–69, 77, 125, 218n48
Donovan, Shaun, 28, 62, 64–65, 89–90, 104, 108
Dual city, 52
Dubai, 122
Dumping in Dixie (Bullard), 11
Dutch. *See also* the Netherlands
  Delta Works, 38–39, 92, 93f, 103, 144, 222n9
  influence, 89–91
  monopoly and founding of Singapore, 225n49
  spatial planning, 29, 37, 39, 41, 47, 49, 89–92, 96, 105, 108–109, 130, 131, 143, 144, 156
  water management, 38–39, 92–99
Dutch environmental planning, 39, 95, 107

Earth Summit, 205n39
East River, FDR Drive along, 59, 60f
East Side Coastal Resiliency (ESCR) project, 140, 151, 233n4
East Village, NYC, 58, 59
Ecological debt, 12
Ecological enclaves, 6
Ecological security, 10, 172, 186
Economy
  costs, 1, 51, 231n40, 231n41
  financial crisis of 2008, global, 92, 94
  funding, 29, 46, 64–65, 91, 232n53
  global-urban networks and, 107
  Hurricane Sandy and damage to, 1, 51
Egypt, 102, 225n47, 225n52
Eisenhard, Jill, 31, 55, 56, 57, 62, 85, 147, 174–175
EJ. *See* Environmental justice

Elections, Indonesia, 70
Eminent domain, 211n10
Eng, Fook Chuan, 79
Engineering firms, economy and, 94
Environment, marginalization and change in urban, 81–84
Environmental justice (EJ)
  climate and, 12
  research and activism, 11
Environmental planning, 178, 189
  Central Park and, 25
  climate change and, 167
  Dutch, 39, 95, 107
  Jakarta, 105
  urban, 3, 156, 161
ESCR. *See* East Side Coastal Resiliency project
Estonia, 225n47
Ethiopia, 225n47
Ethnographic present, 20

Fainstein, Susan, 234n15
FDR Drive, along East River, 59, 60f
Federal Emergency Management Agency (FEMA), 52, 56, 85
Ferriss, Hugh, 24
Finch, Annie, 115
Fires, in Amazon, 7
Fleming, Billy, 229n7
Floating pavilion, Rijnhaven, 41, 42f, 97
Floods
  Ciliwung River during, 74f
  Great Garuda plan and, 75–81
  Hurricane Sandy, 51, 54f
  in Jakarta 2007, 31, 33, 75–81, 83, 90, 105
  in kampungs, 67–69, 68f
  in Lower East Side, 54f, 59
  in Red Hook, Brooklyn, 30, 53, 54f
  in the Netherlands, 91
  North Sea in 1953, 92
  politics of urban, 235n27

Flows
  with interconnections, multiscalar and multilevel, 91–106
  nature of, 89–91, 156–157
  network formation and, 110–113
  with networks, global-urban, 106–110
  Rebuild By Design and NCICD masterplan with, 90t
  space of, 112, 180
  urban socioecological change and, 16–17
Ford Foundation, 224n38
Free Ciliwung (Ciliwung Merdeka), 36, 73, 73f, 75, 86, 126, 184, 188
Funding
  CDBG–DR, 29, 46, 64, 232n53
  Giant Sea Wall, 90
  for Rebuild By Design, 46, 64–65, 91, 107
Future proof, cities, 7

Gandy, Matthew, 25
Garden City, 209n68
Gardner, Jean, 24–25
Garnier, Tony, 209n68
GeoDelft, 100
Georgia (country), 225n47
Georgieva, Kristalina, 151
Ghana, 225n47
GHG emissions. *See* Greenhouse gas emissions
Giant Sea Wall, Jakarta, 3, 34, 36f, 38, 44, 46, 76–81, 90t, 188. *See also* National Capital Integrated Coastal Development (NCICD), Great Garuda plan
  criticism of, 110
  Dutch influence on, 89–90
  funding, 90
  kampungs and, 71f
  plan, 77f
  role of, 36
  situational relationships and, 108

Gilmore, Ruth Wilson, 180
Global Climate Strike, 11
Global Commission on Adaptation, 151
Global Resilience Partnership, 46
Global South, 205n39
Global-urban networks
  diagram, 106f
  economic relationships, 107
  flows and, 106–110
  interface conditions and, 109–110
  situational relationships and, 107–109
Globe, city to, 99–103
Good Old Lower East Side (GOLES), 10, 86, 184
  disaster recovery and, 29
  location of, 54f
  role of, 59–60, 61, 62
Gotham, Kevin Fox, 232n53
Great Garuda plan. *See also* Giant Sea Wall
  flood of 2007 to, 75–81
  role of, 120–124
Greenberg, Miriam, 232n53
Green Heart (Groene Hart), 40
Greenhouse gas (GHG) emissions, 5, 7, 116, 224n38
Green New Deal, 6
Greenpoint, 25
Greenwashed, 9
Groene Hart (Green Heart), 40
Grontmij, 76

Haring, Keith, 58
Harvey, David, 14, 25
Hejinian, Lyn, 1
Herzog & de Meuron, 25
High Line, 25
Hill, Kristina, 228n7
Ho Chi Minh City, 89, 100, 190, 224n38
Holston, James, 20, 123, 179, 181
Hong Kong, 224n38

Housing, 60f, 209n68
  destroyed in Breezy Point, Queens, from Hurricane Sandy, 50, 51f
  Jakarta kampung, 70, 72–75
  Lower East Side, 59, 60f, 84
  NYCHA, 52–53, 56–57, 59, 60f, 217n21
  Red Hook, 30, 52, 55f, 85, 217n21
  rent gap, 24
Howard, Ebenezer, 209n68
HUD. *See* Department of Housing and Urban Development, US
Hudson River Park, 25, 26f
Hudson River Park Trust, 25
Humanitarian vertical kampung, design for, 128f
Hungary, 225n47
"Hunts Point Lifelines" proposal, 134, 136f
Hurricane Irene, 27, 50
Hurricane Sandy, 27–29, 50–52, 184
  with contestation, nature of, 50–52
  costs, 1, 51
  deaths, 1, 50–51
  houses destroyed in Breezy Point, Queens, 50, 51f
  Lower East Side and, 51, 59–62
  NYC and, 27, 50–52
  poverty and, 51–52
  Red Hook, Brooklyn, and, 52–55, 54f, 55f, 58
  RHI and, 30f
  RHI during recovery from, 146f
  surge impact map, 54f
  "tale of two Sandys," 51
Hurricane Sandy Rebuilding Task Force, 27–28, 29, 62–64, 89
Hyogo Framework for Action, 203n22

IAB. *See* International Advisory Board Rotterdam
ICLEI, 6, 224n38

IenM. *See* Ministry of Infrastructure and the Environment
IKEA, 53
The Image of the City (Lynch), 209n68
Imperial formations, 108
Income inequality, 52
India, 203n22, 225n47
Indonesia, 100, 102, 203n22. *See also* Jakarta, Indonesia
  elections, 70
  MOUs and, 225n52
  with NYC and New Orleans, 90–91
  Partners for Water and, 225n47
Inequality
  income, 52
  poverty and systemic, 29
Institute for Public Knowledge, NYU, 29, 64
Insurgent urban landscapes, 22, 177–181, 185
Interboro team, 132, 132f, 143
Interconnections, multiscalar and multilevel
  city to globe and, 99–103
  Deltas in Times of Climate Change conference, 103f
  Dutch Delta Works, map of, 93f
  with flows, nature of, 91–106
  Maeslant storm surge barrier, 94f
  nation states to cities, 103–106
  nation state to world and, 91–99
  "Room for the River" project, 95f
  timeline of relevant events in Rotterdam, 99t
Interface conditions, global-urban networks and, 109–110
Intergovernmental Panel on Climate Change (IPCC), 5, 6
International Advisory Board Rotterdam (IAB), 96–97
International Architecture Biennale Rotterdam, 87, 96

International Climate Justice Network, 13, 205n39
International Monetary Fund, 151
IPCC. *See* Intergovernmental Panel on Climate Change

Jacobs, Jane, 24, 138, 209n68
Jacobs, John, 96, 97, 223n23
Jakarta, Indonesia, 3. *See also* Giant Sea Wall, Jakarta
  in CDC network, 224n38
  climate change vulnerability and, 31, 213n29
  with contestation, nature of, 49, 66–81
  desakota and, 32
  DKI, 31, 68–69, 78, 125, 218n48
  flood of 2007, 31, 33, 75–81, 83, 90, 105
  Great Garuda plan and, 75–81, 120–124
  with kampung activism, 70–75
  kampung design activism, 124–130
  Kampung Pulo, 35f
  kampungs and/in city, 66–70
  Kota, 34f
  Medan Merdeka, 32, 33f
  NCICD, 36f
  NYC and, 1–2, 42, 44, 47, 87
  Pantai Mutiara and bay, 80f
  sea-level rise in, 31
  sites and strategies, 24f, 31–37
  urban development in, 32–33
  waterfront, 80f
Jakarta Climate Change Task Force, 70
Jakarta Coastal Defense Strategy (JCDS), 75–76, 76f
Jakarta environmental planning, 105
Jakarta Urgent Flood Mitigation Project / Jakarta Emergency Dredging Initiative (JUFMP/JEDI), 79
Japan, 108
Jasanoff, Sheila, 5, 86

JCDS. *See* Jakarta Coastal Defense Strategy
JICA, 33
Jogja, Arkom, 164
Jokowi. *See* Widodo, Joko
Jokowi, Taman, 125
Justice, 19–20. *See also* Climate justice; Environmental justice
Just urban spatial climate politics, 13–14

Kampung design activism, 37, 188
  humanitarian vertical kampung, Ciliwung Merdeka, 128f
  participatory design concept, UPC, 127f
  plan, 124–130
  Strenkali upgrading project, 129f
  Urban Poor Consortium and, 127f
  Waduk Pluit, 125f
Kampung Improvement Programme (KIP), 67
Kampung Pulo, 35f, 68f, 73, 74, 84
  Ciliwung River at, 35f
  evictions and demolitions in, 184
Kampungs. *See also* Bukit Duri; Kampung Pulo; Muara Baru
  activism and, 45, 70–75, 86
  city and, 66–70
  defined, 66
  demolition of, 230n31
  floods in, 67–69, 68f
  Giant Sea Wall and, 71f
  history, 66–68
  Jakarta Vertical Kampung exhibition, 75, 127f, 128f
  population, 66
Kathmandu, Nepal, 15
Kazakhstan, 225n47
Kenya, 225n47
Kete, Nancy, 64–65, 130–131, 173
KIP. *See* Kampung Improvement Programme
Klein, Naomi, 108

Klinenberg, Eric, 145
Knowledge
  contestation and local, 85–86
  disaster recovery and local, 156
  Institute for Public Knowledge, 29, 64
Knowledge for Climate, 37, 97, 100, 156
Koolhaas, Rem, 40
Kota, ruins in, 34f
Kota Kita, 126
Kuala Lumpur, 233n3
KuiperCompagnons, 76, 120–121
Kusumawijaya, Marco, 126, 230n28, 234n11
Kusworo, Yuli, 126

La Guardia Houses, 59, 60f
"Landing Under Water, I See Roots" (Finch), 115
Latinx youth, 55
Le Corbusier, 123, 209n68
Lefebvre, Henri, 8, 18–19, 124
Leitner, Helga, 233n10
Lembaga Bantuan Hukum, 164
LES Ready, 60, 62
Life (magazine), 53
"Living Breakwaters" proposal, 134, 137f, 144
"Living with the Bay" proposal, 132, 133f
Living with Water competition, 228n6
Loft living, 24
London, 224n38
Lower East Side, NYC, 44
  with contestation, nature of, 58–62
  FDR Drive along East River, 59, 60f
  GOLES, 10, 29, 54f, 59–60, 61, 62, 86, 184
  Hurricane Sandy and, 51, 59–62
  map of, 54f
  Peace Pentagon building, 58
  volunteers for Chinatown and, 61f
Lower East Side Long Term Recovery Group, 60–61

Lower Manhattan Development Corporation, 232n53
Lynch, Kevin, 209n68

Maeslant storm surge barrier, 38, 92, 94f
Malaysia, 225n47, 233n3
Mali, 225n47
Marginalization
  socioecological relationships of urban, 14–16
  urban environmental change and, 81–84
Maringanti, Anant, 233n10
Marrella, Michael, 118, 140
McFadden, Marion, 65
McGee, T. G., 32
McGregor, Alisdair, 116
McHarg, Ian, 228n6
Medan Merdeka, 32, 33f
Mehmood, Abid, 227n1
Melbourne, 224n38
Memorandums of understanding (MOUs), 103–104, 225n52
Methodological excursions
  cautions and affirmations, 190–191
  with relational urban research and reflexive sites, 188–190
  research worldview, 191–192
  sites and strategies, 187–188
Metropolitanization, of climate change, 7, 112
Mexico, 225n47, 225n52
Ministry of Infrastructure and the Environment (IenM), the Netherlands, 37, 103
MIT CAU+ZUS+URBANISTEN team, 133, 134f, 135, 143
Molenaar, Arnoud, 96, 97, 98, 223n23
MoMA. *See* Museum of Modern Art
Moral geography, 91–92
Moses, Robert, 24, 138
MOUs. *See* Memorandums of understanding

Mozambique, 102, 225n47
Muara Baru, 69, 70, 72f, 73, 84
Municipal Arts Society, 37, 64
Museum of Modern Art (MoMA), *Rising Currents* exhibit at, 27, 116, 130–131, 144, 228n5
Mutual aid, 82, 235n22
MVRDV, 40
Myanmar, 225n47
My Life (Hejinian), 1

Nandan, Gita, 56–57
National Capital Integrated Coastal Development (NCICD), 34, 36f, 38, 76–81, 90t. *See also* Giant Sea Wall
National Disaster Resilience Competition, 46
Nation building, spatial planning and, 92
Nation states
  to cities, 103–106
  to world, 91–99
NCICD. *See* National Capital Integrated Coastal Development
Neoliberalization of nature, 6
Netherlands
  city to globe, 99–103
  Dutch, 29, 37–39, 41, 47, 49, 89–92, 93f, 94, 96, 103, 105, 108–109, 130, 131, 143–144, 156, 222n9
  with financial crisis of 2008, 92, 94
  floods in, 91
  Giant Sea Wall and, 108
  global-urban network, 106–110
  influence of, 89–90
  Ministry of Infrastructure and the Environment, 37
  MOUs and, 225n52
  nation states to cities, 103–106
  as nation state to world, 91–99
  network formation and, 110–113
  population, 40
  Rotterdam, 2, 37–42, 38f, 42f, 47–49, 97, 99t, 223n22, 224n38

Netherlands Water Partnership (NWP), 37–38, 90–91, 101–102, 107–108, 157, 225n46
Network formation
  conceptual interfaces, relationships and, 111f
  flows and, 110–113
  role of, 91
  sample of, 188
Networks
  counter, 162–164, 165f
  global-urban, 106–110, 106f
  urban ecologies and global, 179f
"New Meadowlands" proposal, 133, 134f
New Orleans, 89
  in CDC network, 224n38
  Changing Course competition, 46
  Indonesia and, 90–91
New Waterway (Nieuwe Waterweg), 92, 94f
New York City (NYC). *See also* Central Park, NYC; Lower East Side, NYC; Rebuild By Design; Red Hook, Brooklyn
  Breezy Point, Queens, 50, 51f
  capital grants in, 232n53
  in CDC network, 224n38
  climate change planning in, 26–27
  with contestation, nature of, 49, 50–66
  East Village, 58, 59
  Hudson River Park, 26f
  Hurricane Sandy and, 27, 50–52
  Indonesia and, 90–91
  Jakarta and, 1–2, 42, 44, 47, 87
  Lower Manhattan, 28f
  Lower Manhattan in darkness after blackout, 59
  PlaNYC, 26–27
  population, 23
  process and participation, 137–141
  Rebuild By Design and, 130–137

Index   271

RHI and, 10, 30f, 183–184
Seneca Village, 25, 211n10
sites and strategies, 23–31, 24f
West Village, 211n13
Williamsburg, 25–26
New York City Climate Change Adaptation Task Force, 27
New York City Housing Authority (NYCHA), 52–53, 56–57, 59, 217n21
New York City Panel on Climate Change (NPCC), 27
New York Rising Community Reconstruction program (NYRCR), 56
New York University (NYU), Institute for Public Knowledge at, 29, 64
Nieuwe Waterweg (New Waterway), 92, 94f
9/11, 24
Nordensen, Guy, 116, 131
North Sea flood (1953), 92
NPCC. *See* New York City Panel on Climate Change
NWP. *See* Netherlands Water Partnership
NYC. *See* New York City
NYCHA. *See* New York City Housing Authority
NYRCR. *See* New York Rising Community Reconstruction program
NYU. *See* New York University

Obama, Barack, 27–28, 46, 62
Occupy Wall Street, 12, 162
Office for Metropolitan Architecture, 40. *See also* OMA team
OMA team, 133, 135, 135f, 143
100 Resilient Cities, 6, 9, 204n25, 223n22, 228n3
Ong, Aihwa, 16
On the Water | Palisade Bay (Nordenson, Seavitt and Yarinsky), 116, 131
Open Technology Institute (OTI), 58
"tunities for People, Science, Cities and Business" conference, 100

OTI. *See* Open Technology Institute
Oudkerk Pool, Chantal, 97, 99–100
Overseas Development Institute, 204n27
Ovink, Henk, 37, 38, 62, 89–90, 104, 108–110, 184
  at Deltas in Times of Climate Change II conference, 154f
  influence of, 153, 154f, 159
  Rebuild By Design and, 117, 118, 130, 131, 137, 141
  Water as Leverage and, 152
Oyster-tecture, SCAPE and, 144, 228n5

Palantir, 204n26
Pantai Mutiara, 80f
Partners for Water, 102, 225n47
Peace Pentagon building, Lower East Side, 58
Peck, Jamie, 17
PennDesign / OLIN team, 134, 135, 136f, 143
Piper, Jake, 227n1
Planning for Climate Change (Davoudi, Crawford and Mehmood), 227n1
PlaNYC, 26–27
Pluit City Park (Taman Jokowi, Taman Kota Waduk Pluit), 69, 69f, 125
Poland, 225n47
Political ecology of design, 20, 124
  in context, 149–152
  defined, 3
  insurgent urban landscapes and, 177–181
  just urban climate futures and, 168–177
  with spatial politics of climate change, 152–161
  with urban movements for climate justice, 161–168
Politics
  power and, 19, 107–108, 158
  of urban floods, 235n27

Pollution, poverty and, 11, 33
Populations
  growth, 27
  Jakarta, 31
  kampungs, 66
  the Netherlands, 40
  NYC, 23
  of residents in Red Hook Houses, 217n21
  Rotterdam, 39
Poverty
  climate change and, 9–10
  Hurricane Sandy and, 51–52
  pollution and, 11, 33
  with post-disaster recovery, 232n53
  spatial concentration and, 41
  spatial marginalization and, 165
  systemic, 185
  systemic inequality and, 29
  unemployment and, 52
  UPC, 36, 70, 72f, 75, 86, 127f, 125–126, 184, 230n31
Power, political, 19, 107–108, 158
Preparedness
  climate change, 66, 96
  disaster recovery and climate change, 66
Privilege, justice and, 19–20
The Production of Space (Lefebvre), 18
Pruitt-Igoe public housing complex, 209n68
Purnama, Basuki "Ahok" Tjahaja, 73, 82, 149, 219n62
Putrajaya, 233n3

Queer struggles, West Village with activism and, 211n13

Race, 25, 43, 180
Rademacher, Anne, 15, 188, 207n54
Raffles, Stamford, 225n49
Randstad, 40, 102

Ranganathan, Malini, 234n15
Rebuild By Design, 3, 44, 187, 203n22, 226n64, 231n40
  actors NCICD masterplan and, 90t
  "BIG U" proposal, 61–62, 132, 132f, 231n41, 231n49, 232n53
  with contestation, nature of, 62–66
  Dutch influence on, 89–90
  finalist teams and sites, 63, 63f
  funding for, 46, 64–65, 91, 107
  "Hunts Point Lifelines" proposal and, 134, 136f
  leadership, 38
  "Living Breakwaters" proposal and, 134, 137f, 144
  "Living with the Bay" proposal and, 132, 133f
  "New Meadowlands" proposal and, 133, 134f
  NYC and, 130–137
  Ovink and, 117, 118, 130, 131, 137, 141
  purpose of, 29, 31
  Red Hook and, 56
  "Resist, Delay, Store, Discharge" proposal and, 133, 135f
  Rising Currents exhibit and, 130–131, 228n5
  SCAPE, oyster-tecture and, 144, 228n5
Rebuilding
  in Banda Aceh, 230n30
  Hurricane Sandy Rebuilding Task Force, 27–28
Red Hook, Brooklyn, 44
  within Category 1 storm-surge zone, 216n13
  with contestation, nature of, 52–58
  Hurricane Sandy and, 53–55, 54f, 55f, 58
  map of, 54f
  Rebuild By Design and, 56
  waterfront, 53f

Index

Red Hook Houses, 30, 52, 85
  population of residents in, 217n21
  temporary boilers at, 55f
Red Hook Initiative (RHI), 10, 183–184
  alternative, 145–148
  designed by SUPER-INTERESTING!, 145, 145f
  disaster recovery and, 29–31, 55–58
  during Sandy recovery, 146f
  Hurricane Sandy and, 30f
  location of, 54f
  Red Hook WiFi project, 58, 59f, 86, 184
  role of, 30
  Smith, Rob, inspecting networking equipment, 59f
Red Hook WiFi project, 58, 59f, 86, 184
Reflection, theoretical synthesis and, 159–161
Reflexive sites, relational urban research and, 188–190
Regional Plan Association, 64
Relational geographies, 16, 91, 156, 188
Relational urban research, reflexive sites and, 188–190
Rent gap, 24
Renzo Piano Building Workshop, 25
Representational space, 19
Representations, of space, 18–19
Research
  EJ and, 11
  worldview and methodological excursions, 191–192
Resilience
  ACCCRN, 203n22, 228n3
  against, 8–11
  bouncing back and, 8, 9, 10, 168, 204n27
  climate change and, 5
  to climate justice, 8
  contestation with shared struggle and, 84–85
  criticism of, 8–11
  Global Resilience Partnership, 46
  Hyogo Framework for Action and, 203n22
  LES Ready and, 62
  National Disaster Resilience Competition, 46
  100 Resilient Cities, 6, 9
  Rebuild By Design and, 29, 62–63
  Red Hook residents and, 57
  reframing and a just, 171–176
  RHI and, 145
  Rotterdam Climate Proof and, 41
The Resilience Dividend (Rodin), 204n27
Resiliency initiatives
  climate, 204n25
  community, 3, 56, 146
"Resilient Bridgeport" proposal, 231n40
Resilient by Design Bay Area Challenge, 46, 228n6
"Resist, Delay, Store, Discharge" proposal, 133, 135f
Revanchist city, 24
Reyes, Damaris, 59–62, 84, 85, 86, 117, 138–139, 184
RHI. *See* Red Hook Initiative
Riis Houses, 59
Rijkswaterstaat, 101
Rijnhaven, Rotterdam, 41, 42f, 97
Rising Currents exhibit, at MoMA, 27, 116, 130–131, 144, 228n5
Roberts, Cole, 116
Rockefeller Foundation, 6, 9, 28, 104, 203n22, 204n25
  "City Resilience Framework" and, 172, 228n3
  Global Resilience Partnership and, 46
  NPCC and, 27
  100 Resilient Cities, 6, 9, 151, 223n22
  Rebuild By Design and, 29, 46, 64–65, 91
  Resilient by Design Bay Area Challenge and, 228n6

Rockefeller Foundation (cont.)
  with *Rising Currents* exhibit at MoMA, 27, 130–131, 144, 228n5
  role of, 130–131
Rodin, Judith, 28, 64–65, 130, 204n27
Romania, 225n47
"Room for the River," 39, 95, 95f, 110
Rosenzweig, Cynthia, 109
Rossi, Aldo, 209n68
Rotterdam, Netherlands, 2
  architecture in, 40
  in CDC network, 224n38
  with contestation, nature of, 49
  floating pavilion in Rijnhaven, 41, 42f, 97
  as modeling and outward-oriented, 47–48
  as part of 100 Resilient Cities, 223n22
  population, 39
  sites and strategies, 37–42
  as spatial planning model, 47, 49
  timeline of relevant events in, 99t
  Watersquare Benthemplein, 38f
Rotterdam Climate Initiative, 96
Rotterdam climate program, 37, 99, 100
Rotterdam Climate Proof, 3, 41, 96–98, 99, 157
Rotterdam Water City 2035 vision, 96
Rowe, Colin, 209n68
Roy, Ananya, 7, 16
Royal Haskoning, 102
Ruins, in Kota, 34f
Rujak, 86, 125, 164, 230n28
"Running Water" (Storni), 49
Russia, 225n47
Rutgers Houses, 59, 60f

Saidi, Edi, 70, 72–73, 125–126, 219n58
Sannen, Ad, 102, 103f
SCAPE team, 134–135, 137f, 143, 144, 228n5

Schama, Simon, 221n3
Schmid, Christian, 7
School strike, for climate actions, 11, 12
Schultz, Melanie, 34, 75, 103–104, 107–108, 153, 233n6
Sea-level rise
  in Jakarta, 31
  around Southeast Asian oceans, 213n30
Sea wall, 57. *See also* Giant Sea Wall
Seavitt, Catherine, 116, 131
Seneca Village, NYC, 25, 211n10
Shepherd, Ariel, 130
Sheppard, Eric, 233n10
Sianipar, Purba Robert, 103f
Siberia, 7
Sida. *See* Swedish International Development Cooperation Agency
Siemens, 224n38
Silver, Christopher, 66
Simone, AbdouMaliq, 234n11
Singapore, 100, 122, 225n49
Singapore-ETH Center, 34
Situational relationships, global-urban networks and, 107–109
Slovakia, 225n47
Smith, Neil, 14, 15
Smith, Rob, 59f
Smith Houses, 59
Social and spatial urban development, 3, 152
Socioecological change, 15, 16–17, 155, 166
Socioecological relationships, of urban marginalization, 14–16
Sociospatial
  typology of adaptation, 168–171
  typology of coastal urban adaptation strategies, 169f
  urban development, 3, 152
Soehodho, Sutanto, 103f
Soja, Edward, 19
South Africa, 225n47

Southeast Asia, 213n30
South Korea, 33, 108, 150
Space
 concepts of, 18–19
 design and, 119–120
 of flows, 112, 180
 representational, 19
 representations of, 18–19
 water management and, 98
Spatial concentration, poverty and, 41
Spatial marginalization, 14, 17, 36, 50, 83, 154–155, 165
Spatial planning
 climate change and, 115–116
 Dutch, 29, 37, 39, 41, 47, 49, 89–92, 96, 105, 108–109, 130, 131, 143, 144, 156
 nation building and, 92
Spatial Planning and Climate Change (Wilson and Piper), 227n1
Spatial politics, 3, 4, 16–17, 43, 137, 152–161
Spatial practice, 18
Spatial process, urbanization of, 7
Stoler, Ann, 108
Storm surges
 impact map, Hurricane Sandy, 54f
 Maeslant barrier, 38, 92, 94f
 zone, Category 1, 216n13
Storni, Alfonsina, 49
Strenkali upgrading project, 126, 129f, 230n31
Subianto, Prabowo, 70
Subsidence, land, 31, 75, 80–81, 221n81
Suharto, 32, 67
Sumardi, Sandyawan, 74, 75, 82, 130
Sunrise Movement, 12
Superfund sites, 52
SUPER-INTERESTING!, 145, 145f
Swedish International Development Cooperation Agency (Sida), 46
Swiss Re, 204n26

Synthesis
 of plans, counterplans and connections, 163t
 theoretical reflection and, 159–161
Sziarto, Kristin, 233n10

Taman Kota Waduk Pluit (Pluit City Park, Taman Jokowi), 69, 69f, 125
Taylor, John, 234n11
Thailand, 203n22, 225n47
Thunberg, Greta, 11, 12
TNO, 101
Tobing, Aisa, 70
Tokyo, 224n38
Transformative, 166, 234n12
Tri Irawaty, Dian, 234n11
Turkey, 225n47
Two Degrees (McGregor, Roberts and Cousins), 116

Ukraine, 225n47
UN Climate Action Summit, 11
Unemployment
 poverty and, 52
 systemic inequality and, 29
UN Framework Convention on Climate Change (UNFCCC), 6
United States (US), 100
 HUD, 27–28, 29, 37, 46, 62
 MOUs and, 225n52
 USAID, 6, 46
UN World Conference on Disaster Reduction, 203n22
UPC. *See* Urban Poor Consortium
Uplink, 230n30
UPROSE, 13
Urban, defined, 202n17. *See also* Urbanization
Urban development
 in Jakarta, 32–33, 82
 in New York City, 52
 in Rotterdam, 92
 social and spatial, 3, 152

Urban environment, 3, 156, 161. *See also* Environment
Urban fabric, 8
Urban futures
  climate justice and, 1–4
  with socioecological relationships of marginalization, 14–16
De Urbanisten, 38, 98, 107, 118, 133, 134f, 143–144
Urbanization, as spatial process, 7. *See also* Urban
Urban Poor Consortium (UPC), 36, 70, 72f, 75, 86, 125–126, 127f, 184, 230n31
Urban resistance, activism and, 233n10
Urban vulnerability, 6
US. *See* United States
US Agency for International Development (USAID), 6, 46

Vale, Lawrence, J., 19
Van Alen Institute, 64
Van den Boomen, Gijs, 120–121, 121f, 122–123
Van den Broek, Johannes, 40
Van der Vlugt, Leendert, 122
Van Koppen, Paul, 37–38, 102
Van Veenk Johan, 92
Van Zuid, Kop, 41
Vietnam, 100, 102, 203n22, 225n47
"Vision 2020," 27
Vladeck Houses, 59, 60f
Vulnerability, to climate change, 31, 213n29

Waal River, 95, 95f
Waduk Pluit, 70, 72, 125f
Waggonner and Ball Architects, 37. *See also* WB unabridged with Yale ARCADIS team
Wald Houses, 59
Walking around at grassroots level (*blusukan*), 70, 158, 219n57

Warner, Sam Bass, 52
Water
  "Declaiming Waters none may dread," 89
  floods, 1, 75–81, 90
  "Landing Under Water, I See Roots," 115
  "Living Breakwaters" proposal, 134, 137f, 144
  Living with Water competition, 228n6
  My Life, 1
  NWP, 37–38, 90–91, 101–102, 107–108, 157, 225n46
  On the Water | Palisade Bay, 116, 131
  Partners for Water, 102, 225n47
  "Room for the River," 39, 95, 95f, 110
  Rotterdam Water City 2035 vision, 96
  "Running water," 49
  "water sign woman," 149
Water as Leverage, 152
Waterfront
  design, 116, 118, 138
  development, 27, 32, 36, 53, 83
  Jakarta, 80f
  Red Hook, 53f
Water management
  climate change and, 94–96
  Dutch, 92, 94
  urban space and, 98
Water Plan 2 (2007), 96, 97
"water sign woman" (Clifton), 149
Watersquare Benthemplein, 38f, 98
WB unabridged with Yale ARCADIS team, 231n40. *See also* Waggonner and Ball Architects
Weather, climate politics and, 235n25
Westerhof, Edgar, 109
West Village, NYC, 211n13
Whitney Museum, 25
Widodo, Joko "Jokowi," 33, 68–69, 70, 73, 150, 219n62, 233n3
Williams, Raymond, 15
Williamsburg, Brooklyn, 25–26

Wilson, Elizabeth, 227n1
Witteveen+Bos, 76, 122
WL|Delft Hydraulics, 100
World
  cities, 16
  cities to globe and, 99–103
  financial crisis of 2008, 92, 94
  nation state to, 91–99
  "worlding," 16
World Bank, 6, 33, 79, 204n26, 204n27, 224n38
World Resources Institute, 224n38
World's Fair, 1939 and 1964, 24
World Trade Organization, 162
Worldview
  of design, 116–119
  research, 191–192

Yarinsky, Adam, 116, 131
Yeampierre, Elizabeth, 13

Urban and Industrial Environments

Series editor: Robert Gottlieb, Henry R. Luce Professor of Urban and Environmental Policy, Occidental College

Maureen Smith, *The U.S. Paper Industry and Sustainable Production: An Argument for Restructuring*

Keith Pezzoli, *Human Settlements and Planning for Ecological Sustainability: The Case of Mexico City*

Sarah Hammond Creighton, *Greening the Ivory Tower: Improving the Environmental Track Record of Universities, Colleges, and Other Institutions*

Jan Mazurek, *Making Microchips: Policy, Globalization, and Economic Restructuring in the Semiconductor Industry*

William A. Shutkin, *The Land That Could Be: Environmentalism and Democracy in the Twenty-First Century*

Richard Hofrichter, ed., *Reclaiming the Environmental Debate: The Politics of Health in a Toxic Culture*

Robert Gottlieb, *Environmentalism Unbound: Exploring New Pathways for Change*

Kenneth Geiser, *Materials Matter: Toward a Sustainable Materials Policy*

Thomas D. Beamish, *Silent Spill: The Organization of an Industrial Crisis*

Matthew Gandy, *Concrete and Clay: Reworking Nature in New York City*

David Naguib Pellow, *Garbage Wars: The Struggle for Environmental Justice in Chicago*

Julian Agyeman, Robert D. Bullard, and Bob Evans, eds., *Just Sustainabilities: Development in an Unequal World*

Barbara L. Allen, *Uneasy Alchemy: Citizens and Experts in Louisiana's Chemical Corridor Disputes*

Dara O'Rourke, *Community-Driven Regulation: Balancing Development and the Environment in Vietnam*

Brian K. Obach, *Labor and the Environmental Movement: The Quest for Common Ground*

Peggy F. Barlett and Geoffrey W. Chase, eds., *Sustainability on Campus: Stories and Strategies for Change*

Steve Lerner, *Diamond: A Struggle for Environmental Justice in Louisiana's Chemical Corridor*

Jason Corburn, *Street Science: Community Knowledge and Environmental Health Justice*

Peggy F. Barlett, ed., *Urban Place: Reconnecting with the Natural World*

David Naguib Pellow and Robert J. Brulle, eds., *Power, Justice, and the Environment: A Critical Appraisal of the Environmental Justice Movement*

Eran Ben-Joseph, *The Code of the City: Standards and the Hidden Language of Place Making*

Nancy J. Myers and Carolyn Raffensperger, eds., *Precautionary Tools for Reshaping Environmental Policy*

Kelly Sims Gallagher, *China Shifts Gears: Automakers, Oil, Pollution, and Development*

Kerry H. Whiteside, *Precautionary Politics: Principle and Practice in Confronting Environmental Risk*

Ronald Sandler and Phaedra C. Pezzullo, eds., *Environmental Justice and Environmentalism: The Social Justice Challenge to the Environmental Movement*

Julie Sze, *Noxious New York: The Racial Politics of Urban Health and Environmental Justice*

Robert D. Bullard, ed., *Growing Smarter: Achieving Livable Communities, Environmental Justice, and Regional Equity*

Ann Rappaport and Sarah Hammond Creighton, *Degrees That Matter: Climate Change and the University*

Michael Egan, *Barry Commoner and the Science of Survival: The Remaking of American Environmentalism*

David J. Hess, *Alternative Pathways in Science and Industry: Activism, Innovation, and the Environment in an Era of Globalization*

Peter F. Cannavò, *The Working Landscape: Founding, Preservation, and the Politics of Place*

Paul Stanton Kibel, ed., *Rivertown: Rethinking Urban Rivers*

Kevin P. Gallagher and Lyuba Zarsky, *The Enclave Economy: Foreign Investment and Sustainable Development in Mexico's Silicon Valley*

David N. Pellow, *Resisting Global Toxics: Transnational Movements for Environmental Justice*

Robert Gottlieb, *Reinventing Los Angeles: Nature and Community in the Global City*

David V. Carruthers, ed., *Environmental Justice in Latin America: Problems, Promise, and Practice*

Tom Angotti, *New York for Sale: Community Planning Confronts Global Real Estate*

Paloma Pavel, ed., *Breakthrough Communities: Sustainability and Justice in the Next American Metropolis*

Anastasia Loukaitou-Sideris and Renia Ehrenfeucht, *Sidewalks: Conflict and Negotiation over Public Space*

David J. Hess, *Localist Movements in a Global Economy: Sustainability, Justice, and Urban Development in the United States*

Julian Agyeman and Yelena Ogneva-Himmelberger, eds., *Environmental Justice and Sustainability in the Former Soviet Union*

Jason Corburn, *Toward the Healthy City: People, Places, and the Politics of Urban Planning*

JoAnn Carmin and Julian Agyeman, eds., *Environmental Inequalities Beyond Borders: Local Perspectives on Global Injustices*

Louise Mozingo, *Pastoral Capitalism: A History of Suburban Corporate Landscapes*

Gwen Ottinger and Benjamin Cohen, eds., *Technoscience and Environmental Justice: Expert Cultures in a Grassroots Movement*

Samantha MacBride, *Recycling Reconsidered: The Present Failure and Future Promise of Environmental Action in the United States*

Andrew Karvonen, *Politics of Urban Runoff: Nature, Technology, and the Sustainable City*

Daniel Schneider, *Hybrid Nature: Sewage Treatment and the Contradictions of the Industrial Ecosystem*

Catherine Tumber, *Small, Gritty, and Green: The Promise of America's Smaller Industrial Cities in a Low-Carbon World*

Sam Bass Warner and Andrew H. Whittemore, *American Urban Form: A Representative History*

John Pucher and Ralph Buehler, eds., *City Cycling*

Stephanie Foote and Elizabeth Mazzolini, eds., *Histories of the Dustheap: Waste, Material Cultures, Social Justice*

David J. Hess, *Good Green Jobs in a Global Economy: Making and Keeping New Industries in the United States*

Joseph F. C. DiMento and Clifford Ellis, *Changing Lanes: Visions and Histories of Urban Freeways*

Joanna Robinson, *Contested Water: The Struggle Against Water Privatization in the United States and Canada*

William B. Meyer, *The Environmental Advantages of Cities: Countering Commonsense Antiurbanism*

Rebecca L. Henn and Andrew J. Hoffman, eds., *Constructing Green: The Social Structures of Sustainability*

Peggy F. Barlett and Geoffrey W. Chase, eds., *Sustainability in Higher Education: Stories and Strategies for Transformation*

Isabelle Anguelovski, *Neighborhood as Refuge: Community Reconstruction, Place Remaking, and Environmental Justice in the City*

Kelly Sims Gallagher, *The Globalization of Clean Energy Technology: Lessons from China*

Vinit Mukhija and Anastasia Loukaitou-Sideris, eds., *The Informal American City: Beyond Taco Trucks and Day Labor*

Roxanne Warren, *Rail and the City: Shrinking Our Carbon Footprint While Reimagining Urban Space*

Marianne E. Krasny and Keith G. Tidball, *Civic Ecology: Adaptation and Transformation from the Ground Up*

Erik Swyngedouw, *Liquid Power: Contested Hydro-Modernities in Twentieth-Century Spain*

Ken Geiser, *Chemicals without Harm: Policies for a Sustainable World*

Duncan McLaren and Julian Agyeman, *Sharing Cities: A Case for Truly Smart and Sustainable Cities*

Jessica Smartt Gullion, *Fracking the Neighborhood: Reluctant Activists and Natural Gas Drilling*

Nicholas A. Phelps, *Sequel to Suburbia: Glimpses of America's Post-Suburban Future*

Shannon Elizabeth Bell, *Fighting King Coal: The Challenges to Micromobilization in Central Appalachia*

Theresa Enright, *The Making of Grand Paris: Metropolitan Urbanism in the Twenty-first Century*

Robert Gottlieb and Simon Ng, *Global Cities: Urban Environments in Los Angeles, Hong Kong, and China*

Anna Lora-Wainwright, *Resigned Activism: Living with Pollution in Rural China*

Scott L. Cummings, *Blue and Green: The Drive for Justice at America's Port*

David Bissell, *Transit Life: Cities, Commuting, and the Politics of Everyday Mobilities*

Javiera Barandiarán, *From Empire to Umpire: Science and Environmental Conflict in Neoliberal Chile*

Benjamin Pauli, *Flint Fights Back: Environmental Justice and Democracy in the Flint Water Crisis*

Karen Chapple and Anastasia Loukaitou-Sideris, *Transit-Oriented Displacement or Community Dividends? Understanding the Effects of Smarter Growth on Communities*

Henrik Ernstson and Sverker Sörlin, eds., *Grounding Urban Natures: Histories and Futures of Urban Ecologies*

Katrina Smith Korfmacher, *Bridging the Silos: Collaborating for Environment, Health, and Justice in Urban Communities*

Jill Lindsey Harrison, *From the Inside Out: The Fight for Environmental Justice within Government Agencies*

Anastasia Loukaitou-Sideris, Dana Cuff, Todd Presner, Maite Zubiaurre, and Jonathan Jae-an Crisman, *Urban Humanities: New Practices for Reimagining the City*

Govind Gopakumar, *Installing Automobility: Emerging Politics of Mobility and Streets in Indian Cities*

Amelia Thorpe, *Everyday Ownership: PARK(ing) Day and the Practice of Property*

Tridib Banerjee, *In the Images of Development: City Design in the Global South*

Ralph Buehler and John Pucher, eds., *Cycling for Sustainable Cities*

Casey J. Dawkins, *Just Housing: The Moral Foundations of American Housing Policy*

Kian Goh, *Form and Flow: The Spatial Politics of Urban Resilience and Climate Justice*